GREEKS AND ROMANS
A Social History

GREEKS AND ROMANS

A Social History

Michael Grant

Weidenfeld and Nicolson
London

Copyright © 1992 by Michael Grant Publications
Ltd
Maps drawn by Andras Bereznay
First published 1992 by
George Weidenfeld & Nicolson Ltd
Orion Publishing Group
Orion House
5, Upper St Martin's Lane,
London
WC2H 9EA

British Library Cataloguing in Publication Data
available upon request

Typeset at The Spartan Press Ltd,
Lymington, Hants
Printed in Great Britain by
Butler & Tanner Ltd
Frome, Somerset

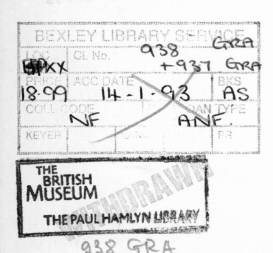

Contents

CONTENTS

vi

Maps

Acknowledgments

The author and publisher wish to thank the following for permission to quote extracts from the published works:

Penguin Books Ltd: Ammianus Marcellinus, *The Later Roman Empire*, edited by Walter Hamilton and A. Wallace-Hadrill; Hodder & Stoughton: *Jugurtha and Cataline: a translation of Sallust*, translated by I. Scott-Kilvert (New English Library series).

A substantial part of Appendix 2 has appeared in *Gallatin Review*, New York, to which the author and publisher owe a grateful acknowledgment.

Introduction

In my *A Short History of Classical Civilization* (1991; entitled *The Founders of the Western World* in the United States) I endeavoured to summarise the principal events in a wide variety of the principal walks of life during that epoch. Although the present book covers the same period – Greek and Roman antiquity – it is a different sort of volume, for it is intended to be a social history.

Social history, without which history as a whole is not understandable, was described by G. M. Trevelyan as history with the politics left out.[1] And that remains roughly true, although it is something of an oversimplification. Certainly it is history with the politics left out, except in so far as the politics affect ordinary, daily lives – in this case the lives of the Greeks and Romans. And the same applies to wars and other military events. They, also, are left out, with the same proviso. As for literature and philosophy, their treatment, too, has to be selective in a social history, for which they are, indeed, a principal source, although only parts of such writings, and not always very large parts of them, are relevant for this particular purpose. For even if our sources of information for the ancient world are voluminous and massive, they are also fragmentary and inadequate, and never more so than when an attempt is being made to reconstruct the social history of the times. In addition to the literary evidence, there are inscriptions, coins, works of art and archaeological remains, but they do not add up to anything like a complete picture. We have to do the best that we can, and that is what I have tried to do in this book.

If you leave out, as you must, such a lot of the politics and military events and so much else, you deprive the men of a great deal of the advantage that they would otherwise possess over the women as the subjects of a history. Indeed, I am not sure that, in a social history, they still preserve any priority over the women at all (except in so far as most of our material happens to be about men, and was created by them).

1

Social history means men and women: or does it mean women and men? Afflicted by doubts on this point, I have dealt with the women first, to see how it looks.

Scarcely more marked than the contrasted treatment accorded to women and men, in the ancient world, was the contrast between those who were included among fully-fledged human beings and those who were not. Citizens, of course, were included. And their women, too, were included, though in a different way and for different purposes and functions. But the unfree were excluded, and have to be treated as a separate theme altogether. Among them were categories of people which are no longer familiar to us at first hand, at least in some countries, notably serfs, however defined, and slaves. And another extremely important category was composed of those who escaped from the iron clamp of slavery, the freedmen and freedwomen, whose by no means infrequent emancipation or manumission, especially in Rome, provided a remarkable and unique example of upward social mobility.

So here are three main headings of the social history of the Greek and Roman worlds: women, men, and the unfree (who sometimes became freed). And I have added two appendices. The first is about foreigners, both the foreigners who lived in the same states and cities as the citizens, and those who lived elsewhere but whose impact on the Greek and Roman states played a significant part in their life. My second appendix is about Karl Marx and Marxist points of view, since they have exercised such an influence on social historians, although to a large extent, as I shall endeavour to suggest, these standpoints are outdated and misguided.

The principal events of Greek and Roman history are listed in a chronological table at the end of the book, and I hope that the bibliography which follows will to some extent make up for the deficiencies of my own account. I owe a great deal, as usual, to suggestions by my wife. And I am very grateful to Malcolm Gerratt and Charmian Hearne for editing the volume, and to Maria Ellis and Veronica Palmer for their assistance. I also want to convey my thanks to the translators whom I have quoted, and to their publishers. Finally, I am grateful to Andras Bereznay for drawing the maps.

MICHAEL GRANT

Part I

WOMEN

1

Greek Women

It must be repeated that ninety-nine per cent of what we learn about Greek and Roman women comes from men. So naturally the man defined their qualities in relation to himself. He did not, that is to say, in the normal course of events – from which exceptions and break-outs will be noted – concede them a political (or military) role. The clearly defined function of women was biological, to perpetuate the family by producing legitimate heirs. And it was social, in the sense that they looked after their households – the bases of society – and were required to do so with care and affection. Besides, their marriages linked families together; and the transmission of property was in their hands.

The corollary of all this was that they had to keep quiet. We learn from Sophocles of a saying: 'For women silence is a grace.'[1] The Athenian statesman Pericles, according to Thucydides, emphasised the point in what seem rather chilling words of consolation to the widows of those who had lost their lives in the first year of the Peloponnesian War.

> Perhaps I should say a word or two on the duties of women to those among you who are now widowed. I can say all I have to say in a short word of advice. Your greatest glory is not to be inferior to what God has made you, and the greatest glory of a woman is to be least talked about by men, whether they are praising you or criticising you.[2]

Sometimes, indeed – in Athenian households which could afford it – women were even physically segregated and secluded, so that they could get on with the jobs that were theirs, and avoid temptation. The orator Demosthenes has this to say against Simon, who was chasing a boy from Plataea named Theodotus:

5

Hearing that the boy was at my house, he came there at night in a drunken state, broke down the doors, and entered the women's rooms: within were my sister and my nieces, whose lives have been so well-ordered that they are ashamed to be seen even by their kinsmen.[3]

Most Greeks and Romans would have viewed the modern idea that women could do the same jobs as men, and do them equally well, with incomprehension. It is perfectly evident, in fact it goes without saying, that women played a vital and necessary part in the ancient world. But the Greeks and Romans carried this manifest fact to what they regarded as its logical conclusion – women had to get on with their own tasks, and men with theirs. The woman's task might not always look very interesting, but it was essential. In Aristophanes's play the *Lysistrata*, one of the women questions whether the rest of them will be able to get away from their homes in order to come to a meeting. Calonice replies that they will come – but it will not be easy.

> Oh my dear,
> They'll come. It's not easy for women to get away.
> We're always dancing attendance on our husbands,
> Or getting the maid moving, or putting
> The baby to bed, bathing it, feeding it.[4]

Let us leave out of account the theory that there had once been, in prehistoric societies, a matriarchal society. This hypothesis cannot be demonstrated or proved, and its too eager acceptance by Marxists such as Engels (Appendix 2) has damaged his credibility. At the most it can be said that there is some evidence for continuing matrilinear usages and successions; for primitive matriarchy there is less (matriarchal myths do not reflect past history, but are designed to display a world turned upside down). Certainly, it remains notable that Greek goddesses remained extremely prominent, but that is for the very good reason that women, even if excluded from politics and armies, kept life going.

They kept life going, but they generated constant, eternal anxiety and revulsion and fear of pollution and, indeed, opposition and hostility. One cannot entirely generalise from one community to another, but it did always seem a terribly dangerous possibility to the Greeks that their women might get out of hand and become a threat, endangering male order, life and sanity (and that is what myths like the story of the Amazons were meant to indicate). Yet at the same time, because of their vital role, women had to be protected. So although they were left out of public life (for which the alleged justification was their lesser intellectual and moral capacity to deal with such matters, diminished further by a patchy education), and although they were legally inferior (a Greek woman could not sign a contract of any importance, even a marriage agreement) and never formally came of age (they passed from father to husband), they were more carefully looked after, more closely guarded than women are today.

For even if they posed a threat to the community, yet they were, obviously, essential to its structure and survival. Their only civic role consisted of giving birth to citizens, but this made them citizens (*astoi*) of a kind themselves (though hardly in the modern sense): their status as wives and mothers could never be wholly degraded without degrading their husbands and sons. Women could only achieve anything through men. Yet men could not perpetuate their households, and could not even exist, without women. True, restricting women to their households, men indulged in homosexuality – or rather pederasty. This was an inevitable result of the restrictive nature of the heterosexual relationship, but did not weaken its biological essentiality.

The great outlet for women, outside the home, was provided by religious festivals, notably the Athenian Thesmophoria, the most widely attested festival in the Greek world, ensuring the fertility of women: a festival which was exclusively their sphere, and gave them a chance to leave their families, day and night, whatever their menfolk might think. Women were also very prominent in ritual, all their lives.

> I have been a sharer
> In all the lavish splendour
> Of the proud city.
> I bore the holy vessels
> At seven, then
> I pounded barley
> At the age of ten.
> And clad in yellow robes,
> Soon after this,
> I was Little Bear to
> Brauronian Artemis;
> Then neckleted with figs,
> Grown tall and pretty,
> I was a Basket Bearer.[5]

7

Athenian women acted as priestesses in more than forty cults. Although irrelevant to their lack of political status, such functions gave them an unchallenged field and acted as a psychological safety-valve, which compensated for their lack of access to other aspects of public life.

Homer is sometimes thought to belong to a freer, earlier time, before the limitations imposed on women had become so formidable, but their role is already limited in his poems. In a world presided over by warrior males, a woman is subordinate, and her place is inevitably the home. True, Hector and Andromache in the *Iliad* display a genuine, not unromantic, mutual affection. As Andromache declares, begging him not to go into battle:

> You, Hector, you are my father now, my noble mother,
> A brother too, and you are my husband, young and
> > warm and strong!
> Pity me please! Take your stand on the rampart here,
> Before you orphan your son and make your wife a
> > widow.[6]

And we hear also of Hector's reply.

> And tall Hector nodded, his helmet flashing:
> 'All this weighs on my mind, too, dear woman.
> But I would die of shame to face the men of Troy
> And the Trojan women trailing their long robes
> If I would shrink from battle now, a coward . . .
> In my heart and soul I know this well:
> The day will come when sacred Troy must die;
> Priam must die and all his people with him,
> Priam who hurls the strong ash spear. Even so,
> It is less the pain of the Trojans still to come
> That weighs me down . . .
> That is nothing, nothing beside *your* agony
> When some brazen Argive hales you off in tears,
> Wrenching away your day of light and freedom!
> Then far off in the land of Argos must you live,
> Labouring at a loom, at another woman's beck and call,
> Fetching water at some spring, Messeis or Hyperia,
> Resisting it all the way –

> The rough yoke of necessity at your neck.
> And a man may say, who sees you streaming tears,
> 'There is the wife of Hector, the bravest fighter
> They could field, those stallion-breaking Trojans,
> Long ago when the men fought for Troy.' So he will say
> And the fresh grief will swell your heart once more,
> Widowed, robbed of the one man strong enough
> To fight off your day of slavery.[7]

The whole Trojan War, indeed, had been fought for a woman, Helen – so that one man could get her back from another.

And Penelope, in the *Odyssey*, is in her way a heroic figure, who resists all comers until Odysseus can return to her, when they will be able to resume their happy married life.

> And weep he did, with his dear and loyal wife
> In his arms. And to her he was as welcome as sight
> Of land to swimmers whose sturdy ship Poseidon
> Has battered and shattered at sea where wind and big wave
> Beat hard upon it, and sweet indeed is the moment
> When the few survivors, having swum ashore and struggled
> Their way through the surf, set foot at last on dry land
> And escape the treacherous sea with their bodies all crusted
> With brine. Such was the gladness she felt to welcome
> Her husband again, as she feasted her eyes upon him
> And could not for a moment take her white arms from his neck.[8]

Yet Penelope is essentially a housewife. Certainly, she is a housewife of wisdom and skill: but the decisions do not rest with her. That is how Homeric women are. They are status-bound, exchanged, given as prizes, stolen and sold. When Agamemnon wants to reconcile himself with the sulking Achilles, this is what he says:

> Seven women I'll give him, flawless, skilled in
> > crafts,
> Women of Lesbos – the ones I chose, my privilege,
> That day he captured the Lesbian citadel himself:
> They outclassed the tribes of women in their beauty.
> These I will give, and along with them will go
> The one I took away at first, Briseus's daughter . . .[9]

9

There is a strict polarity between men's and women's roles, as Hector, in his tenderest mood, points out to Andromache.

> Andromache,
> Dear one, why so desperate? Why so much grief for me?
> No man will hurl me down to Death, against my Fate . . .
> So please go home and tend to your own tasks,
> The distaff and the loom, and keep the women
> Working hard as well. As for the fighting,
> Men will see to all that, all who were born in Troy:
> But I most of all.[10]

So working in wool was already a woman's typical occupation. She enjoys considerable social freedom, as well as economic security, but her position depends entirely on her husband's success.

It was Hesiod, writing on the other side of the Aegean – whether before or after Homer is uncertain – who really launched Greek mythology. His story of Pandora sees women as a beautiful evil bestowed on males as punishment, because Prometheus had stolen fire from Zeus, and given it to humankind. Zeus upbraids him, and declares

> 'They'll pay for fire! I'll give another gift
> To men, an evil thing for their delight,
> And all will love this ruin in their hearts.'
> So spoke the father of men and gods, and laughed.

That gift is the woman Pandora, whom he next told Hephaestus to create. She was to be a lovely virgin, but that was not all.

> Zeus ordered, then,
> The killer of Argus, Hermes, to put in
> Sly manners, and the morals of a bitch . . .
> Hermes the Messenger put in her breast
> Lies and persuasive words and cunning ways:
> The herald of the gods then named the girl
> Pandora, for the gifts which all the gods
> Had given her, this ruin of mankind.
> The deep and total trap was now complete.

Zeus sent Hermes to take a casket to Epimetheus, Prometheus's brother. Prometheus advised him to send it back, but too late. For Pandora opened it.

The woman opened up the cask,
And scattered pains and evils among men.
Inside the cask's hard walls remained one thing,
Hope, only, which did not fly through the door.
The lid stopped her, but all the others flew,
Thousands of troubles, wandering the earth.[11]

Here is a malevolent invective which presented the progress of civilisation as the triumph of male over female forces, and transmitted for ever the tradition of an anti-feminist bias. The theme was taken up with enthusiasm by Semonides of Amorgos.

In the beginning the god made the female mind separately. One he made from a long-bristled sow. In her house everything lies in disorder . . . Another he made from a wicked vixen: a woman who knows everything . . . Another he made from a bitch, vicious, own daughter of her mother, who wants to hear everything and know everything . . . Another the Olympians moulded out of the earth, a stunted creature; you see, a woman like her knows nothing, bad or good . . . Another he made from the sea: she has two characters – like the ocean, she has a changeable nature. Another he made from an ash-grey ass that has suffered many blows . . . When she comes to the act of love, she accepts any partner. Another he made from a ferret . . . she is mad for the bed of love, but she makes any man she has with her sick . . . Another was the offspring of a proud mare with a long mane . . . Another is from a monkey . . . Hard luck on the poor man who holds such a misery in his arms! She knows every trick and twist, just like a monkey . . . Another is from a bee; the man who gets her is fortunate, for on her alone blame does not settle . . .

Yes, this is the worst plague Zeus has made, women . . . He has bound them to us with a fetter that cannot be broken.[12]

What Semonides has done, as part of a bourgeois polemic against luxury, is to compare different sorts of women with various types of animals – ferret women, donkey women, monkey women and so on – in a crassly unchivalrous vein reminiscent of the mutual sex-vituperation familiar from the folktales of peasants of many countries. His 'bee woman', certainly, is praised (though her primary achievement is to maintain the value of her husband's property). But other sorts of women come off badly; criticism of them has been established as a stock

11

theme of Greek poetry. Another poet, Phocylides, takes up the same theme, as an antidote to the current aristocratic romanticism which sought to idealise an earlier age.

Certainly Sappho gives a very different and unique picture of the good times and poignant feelings of women and girls living together, and she does so in a totally feminine context.

> Yesterday you
> Came to my house
> And sang to me.
> Now I
> Come to you.
> Talk to me. Do.
> Lavish on me
> Your own beauty.
> For we walk to a wedding,
> As well you know.
> Please send away
> Your maids. O may
> Heaven then present me
> With all that heaven ever meant to me![13]

> I have not heard one word from her.
> Frankly I wish I were dead.
> When she left, she wept
> A great deal; she said to
> Me, 'This parting must be
> Endured, Sappho. I go unwillingly.'
> I said, 'Go, and be happy.
> But remember (you know
> Well) whom you have shackled by love.'[14]

But the very reason why these women have worked up this intense, all-female society is because of their total exclusion from the politico-military world of men. Nor did they set themselves apart from a woman's household functions: Sappho's friends, as we saw from the first poem, got married, and she herself, even if she had had a Lesbian past, and retained such inclinations, became a wife and mother. Unfortunately, we cannot tell whether the extraordinary community she had gathered around her was peculiar to Lesbos, and might have been paralleled elsewhere if we had the necessary information. But at all events here is an intriguing, rare glimpse of how women managed to get on with their lives on their own despite the limitations imposed on them by their men – from whom we usually hear about them.

The Athenian statesman Solon saw women as a perpetual source of friction among men, and took steps to minimise this friction by regulations. That is to say, he gave brotherless daughters an enforceable right to inherit their father's property. This benefited women, because it gave official recognition to their right to inherit. And at the same time it enhanced the status of the household, which was their sphere, by asserting the primacy of the father's family over the husband's, to which she was only 'loaned out'; the ménage no longer had to be returned to the clan in the absence of male heirs. Solon may not have been fond of women, but he defined and legalised their role.

As for the historians, Herodotus was genuinely interested in women and enlightened about them, and he knew perfectly well, almost too well, that they had often precipitated or caused events, and acquired dominance: thus they moved outside their homes, especially in foreign lands, though in his own country, too, he saw them as full partners. Predictably he felt a special interest in women who had acted or suffered bizarrely, but there is no denying that he felt a fascination for the sex, not unmingled with a somewhat shocked respect.

But it was in Athenian tragic drama that women really came into their own and received careful study, although despite the powerful females who appear in these plays, and the unmistakable evidence that they dominated the male imagination, the underlying tone is hardly one calculated to please modern feminists. For, in the first place, no woman in Greek tragedy succeeds without male assistance, upon which she depends for her way of life, with little recognition for her own accomplishments. Her roles in tragic plays are very varied, but it is difficult to ignore the old suspicion and subjugation that emerges from them. Women as a whole are disparaged, and there is fear of their negative power. For people believed that they were more liable to extremes of emotion and sexuality and consequent violent actions.

So these women in drama, based upon similar dissonances in myth, are the ones who refuse to stay in line, and who disturb the norm by their deviations. They are essential – nurturing and lifegiving – but they are uncomfortable, because they blur the firm line between masculine and feminine, intruding on the former sphere as they were

13

supposed not to do. It is scarcely surprising, in view of this ambival-
ence, that people nowadays want to examine the strange dichotomy
which enabled women to dominate Athenian drama, while at the same
time they were being severely repressed in real life.

The unforgettable Clytemnestra of Aeschylus's triad the *Oresteia* is
typical of this discord. She has murdered her husband Agamemnon
because he had offered up their daughter as a human sacrifice – and by
this act she rose up against the male authority in patriarchal society,
and shattered the social pattern. But because she had done what she
did she was killed by her own son Orestes. And in the *Eumenides* the god
Apollo justifies this killing by sexual biology. The mother, he affirms, is
only the receptacle for her baby, who is the blood-relative of his father:
at Athens it was the father's status that determined the status of the
child.

> Here is the truth, I tell you – see how right I am.
> The woman you call the mother of the child
> Is not the parent, just a nurse to the seed,
> The new-sown seed that grows and swells inside her.
> The *man* is the source of life – the one who mounts.[15]

But Orestes has to be rescued from pursuit by the Furies (Erinyes,
Eumenides), female monsters that represent a regression to the deepest
fantasies of buried masculine terrors.

Sophocles's Antigone, who insists on doing honour to her dead
brother Polynices despite their father's veto, is a heroine, whereas
Clytemnestra had been a villain. Yet, to Greek eyes, Antigone is not a
heroine for the reasons that make us, today, believe she is. She is not
unconventional or independent (though her character is headstrong;
and it is a disaster that she had not married), but she is acting, she maintains, for her family, and doing what they might have expected of her.

'What?' says her sister Ismene. 'You'd bury him – when a law forbids
the city [i.e. forbids the citizens to do so]?' 'Yes!' replies Antigone. 'He
is my brother and – deny it as you will – your brother too. No one will
ever convict me as a traitor!'[16] Yet this means that she is forced out of
the proper behaviour pattern for women – because of a situation that
has been imposed on her by a man, the king. Sophocles displays an
acute and complex insight into the predicaments of women.

But it was Euripides, above all, who was famous for this – so much so
that he has variously been assailed as a misogynist and, contrariwise,

14

has been hailed as the founder, or at least the publiciser, of feminism. In fact, he holds no brief for or against women's rights; he is examining their situation clinically, and his depiction of Phaedra, in the face of the virulent misogyny of Hippolytus in the play named after him, does not mean that he himself hated women. Nor can this be deduced from his attribution to Heracles's daughter Macaria, in the *Children of Heracles*, of an apology for the limitations of women.

> Strangers, before all else, I hope you won't
> Think it was brazen of me to come out.
> I know a woman should be quiet and
> Discreet, and that her place is in the home.
> Yet I came out because I heard your cries.
> Although I'm not the family head,
> I have a right to be concerned about the fate
> Of my own brothers . . .

But it is significant that Heracles's old friend Iolaus replies:

> I've always thought your family contains
> No cooler head than yours, Macaria.[17]

Euripides is not a woman-hater, but he is taking the original step of making a close understanding of women into one of his central themes. Take his Medea, who after betraying her family for a stranger has been jilted by Jason, on whose behalf she had performed that betrayal.

> We women are the most unfortunate creatures.
> Firstly, with an excess of wealth it is required
> For us to buy a husband and take for our bodies
> A master: for not to take one is even worse.
> And now the question is serious whether we take
> A good or bad one: for there is no easy escape
> For a woman, nor can she say no to her marriage . . .
> What they say of us is that we have a peaceful time
> Living at home, while they do the fighting in war.
> How wrong they are! I would much rather stand
> Three times in the front of battle than bear one child . . .
>   In other ways a woman
> Is full of fear, defenceless, dreads the sight of cold
> Steel; but, when once she is wronged in the matter of love,
> No other soul can hold so many thoughts of blood.[18]

Medea is speaking in the name of ill-treated women for the first time in Greek literature, and rebelling against the sufferings of the female condition. But although Euripides, or his characters through him, question masculine ideals, something goes wrong when women try to operate outside the domestic world, and attempt to fight against the inevitable: especially when they have cut themselves off, as Medea has, from the family which is their natural protection, so that then they become victims of traditional society.

All this fascinated the comic dramatist Aristophanes, who specialised in displaying women in roles that they could not attain in real life. Three of his eleven comedies present gender role inversions, in which women are on top. In the *Lysistrata* they deny their husbands their sexual favours in order to stop the Peloponnesian War. Comedy was an exorcist of fears, and behind the fusillade of sexual jokes in the *Lysistrata* one can detect a mood of paranoiac anxiety and suspicion. The *Ecclesiazusae* – and what an absurd idea, that women should sneak into the *ecclesia* (Assembly) in disguise – is deeply conscious of the disparity between the ideal of human freedom and the reality of women's inferior status and men's neuroses. Aristophanes was not more pro-feminist than the average Athenian. Indeed he laughs at Euripides for supposedly being just that. But he sees very well how women's peculiar position can be made the subject of comedy – and his jokes are funny precisely because the situations they envisage are so ludicrously unlikely at Athens.

It was true, however, that in the late fifth century BC, when Aristophanes was composing his comedies, a new interest in women's rights and personalities had become apparent. This is particularly clear from the visual arts. Of course, draped women had long been sculpted – the *korai* of Athens were famous. Yet the Parthenon, and particularly the Nike (Victory) of Paeonius (425), and the sculptors of the balustrade of her Athenian temple, exploited, by means of their new drills, the novel, wind-blown, clinging, revealing possibilities of such clothing, in such a way as to emphasise the female form. But more notable still was the interest in women's bodies shown by statues that were naked. This, again, was not entirely new. The Aphrodite (?) of the Ludovisi throne, with her diaphanous, revealing drapery, dated from *c.*475–470 – a time when vases, too, greatly increased the depiction of women. But it was the painter Zeuxis who carried this tendency furthest, his best known picture being a representation of Helen, ideal,

16

ethical and physical, derived from various human models. This was painted at the end of the century, when curiosity about women was markedly on the increase.

Yet for many decades before that the favourite subjects of gems had no longer been mythical heroes but the daily lives of women. As for vases, they make quite a sharp distinction between two types of women, respectable wives and mothers on the one hand, and *hetairai*, concubines and companions, on the other. The *hetairai*, who wanted to establish long-term relationships with wealthy and agreeable men, were much freer, and frequently better educated, than the wives. But they were often non-Athenians, without citizen status. The most famous of them was the Milesian Aspasia, the mistress of the city's leader Pericles, who formed a lasting union with her after divorcing his wife. Aspasia supposedly talked with Socrates, and taught rhetoric, and held broad-minded views about women. The comic dramatist Hermippus attacked her (for impiety and procuring), in order to get at Pericles. But citizenship was conferred on her, as a special favour.

Xenophon's attitude to women seems to us pretty exasperating, or at least smug and patronising, although in terms of contemporary thought his attitude was not illiberal. He saw a divided world, of men separated from women, who were equal in intelligence and moral capacity, but different. For their sphere was different, being the domestic sphere; in this – and Xenophon was interested in this part of life, which was unusual – they could govern. But it was also their duty to stay fixed in that sphere, and to remain obedient.

> Your business will be to stay indoors and help to despatch the servants who work outside, while supervising those who work indoors. You will receive incoming revenue and allocate it to any necessary expenditure, you will be responsible for any surplus and see that the allocation for the year's expenses is not spent in a month. When wool is delivered to you you will see that garments are made for those that need them, and take care that the dried grain is kept free for consumption. And there is another of your duties which I'm afraid may seem to you rather thankless – you will have to see that any of the servants who is ill gets proper treatment.[19]

Xenophon appreciated women, knew they were useful, and wanted to keep them just the way they were.

Plato, on the other hand, whose *Symposium* was coyly sympathetic to a homosexual society, does not seem to have cared for women very much. He gave thanks, we are told, that he was not a woman or a foreigner.[20] Moreover, a passage in the *Timaeus* suggests a not entirely sympathetic attitude to the activities in which they were involved.

> The men of the first generation who lived cowardly or immoral lives were, it is reasonable to suppose, reborn in the second generation as women; and it was therefore at that point of time that the gods produced sexual love . . . A man's genitals are naturally disobedient and self-willed, like a creature that will not listen to reason, and will do anything in their mad lust for possession. Much the same is true of the matrix or womb in women . . . If it is left unfertilised long beyond the normal time, it causes extreme unrest, strays about the body, blocks the channels of the breath, and causes in consequence acute distress and disorders of all kinds.[21]

Nevertheless, that is by no means all that Plato had to say about women, and some of his other observations are a good deal more positive. In particular, he said, women could be Guardians – the rulers of his ideal state – because, although there was an obvious contrast between the male, who begets, and the female, who bears, women were capable of possessing the same virtues and capacities – as another philosopher, Antisthenes (*c.*445–360), considered the founder of the Cynic school, also emphasised.[22] Yet not very many women, Plato reflected, were able to achieve this high level, since, on average, they were inferior to men, and weaker. True, superior females were better than low-grade men – the philosophical Diotima, perhaps imaginary, whom he admired, represented one such high-powered woman – but for the most part they were less valuable, 'imperfect men', of less strength. That is to say, they were not, in fact, equal, though they had, and should have, equality of opportunity. And so, despite all these reservations, Plato emerges as one of the most sympathetic ancient authorities to women, the nearest approach to a systematic feminist produced by the Greco-Roman world.

Aristotle, too, believed that women were capable of virtue and understanding, and knew that their relationship with men was the most natural form of association. Yet after that, proceeding as often from popular beliefs, he was less liberal than Plato. Women, he said, are physically, morally and socially inferior; their virtue and understanding do not, cannot, equal men's – it is as though they are mutilated males (and that, he felt, was a universal feature of the animal kingdom). Men are spirit, and women are matter. Even marriages are friendships between unequals. Men rule, and women are ruled. When the opposite occurs, as at Sparta – where the power and licence of women were notorious – disaster follows, and tyranny is on the way.

The orator Demosthenes, in *Against Neaera*, pressed the point home, taking a coldly functional view of women, whom he divided into three categories, housewives, companions and sex mates.[23] But orators, of course, employed misogyny to further their cases, seeing women as docile home-bodies if they were on one's own side, and as nasty harridans if they were one's opponents.

All the same, whatever the philosophers and orators might say, Athenian public attitudes to women were changing, and becoming more sympathetic. The visual arts provide evidence of this: and, most of all, Praxiteles's intense interest in the female body. He made statues of his model and mistress Phryne, a celebrated *hetaira*, who herself dedicated one of these sculptures to Apollo at Delphi. And Praxiteles's Aphrodite of Cnidus (364–0 BC), which Pliny the elder regarded as the finest statue ever made,[24] devised a new formula for the female body. Indeed, every sort of idea about the feminine nude was put into effect by Praxiteles. And then Apelles's Aphrodite rising from the waves was hailed as a masterpiece of fidelity. People were obviously coming to think of women as persons, with bodies of their own that deserved curious and careful attention.

But meanwhile a novel sort of thinking about women had reached the public consciousness. That is to say, they were invading the traditional male sphere, and becoming political leaders, of great potency. This was not just a question of their being bandied about for political reasons by polygamous tyrants such as Dionysius I of Syracuse, though some of the tyrants' wives had achieved considerable power, notably Demarete the wife of Gelon who helped Carthage to secure a better peace after the battle of Himera (480 BC). Nor was it just a question of non-Greek foreigners, of whose regnant queens Herodotus was fascinatedly aware, notably Artemisia I, a widow standing in for her late husband, who ruled Halicarnassus and Caria for Xerxes I of Persia. But in Greek lands, too, an occasional woman had ruled, notably Pheretime and Eryxo at Cyrene. That was in a distant part of the Greek lands, but nearer home, too, Thargelia had reigned in Thessaly for thirty years, resisting Darius I in 490.

Yet even that was only on the fringe of the Greek sphere, and it was from the same northern fringe, though a little farther away, that the influence arrived which really changed the attitude of the Greeks towards women. It came from Macedonia. It is not certain that Philip II's mother Eurydice I had been quite as powerful as she was made out to be, but there is little doubt that such queens were ambitious, shrewd and ruthless – controlling, for example, their own extensive personal properties, without guardians – and that they influenced their sons, in a relationship that was stronger and more significant than the bond between husband and wife. The Macedonians, unlike the Greeks, were pastoralists, which meant that women were freer, and this was, of course, most evident at the top. Philip II indulged in the old-fashioned monarchical practice of polygamy, for the purpose of alliances and conquests. But at least one of his wives came from a Black Sea people whose women rode horses and hunted and fought – people such as the Sauromatians, who may have helped to inspire the Amazon myths (one of the tombs at Aegae [Vergina], of a woman equipped with war weapons,[25] may have been of one of these queens).

But the wife of Philip who played a decisive part was the passionate, mystical and murderous Olympias, the daughter of Neoptolemus of Molossia (Epirus) – descended (she claimed) from the man of the same name who had been the son of Achilles, and on her mother's side from Helenus, son of Priam of Troy. It was she more than anyone else who changed the Greeks' ideas about womanhood. After the murder of Philip II, their son Alexander III (the Great) left her at home when he went to Asia, and her indestructible, demonic, quasi-regal power was a thorn in the flesh of his viceroy or regent Antipater. She virtually ruled in Epirus – 'the Molossian land is mine'[26] – but failed, finally, to secure Macedonia, being killed by Cassander. 'The Macedonians would never submit to be ruled by a woman,' Alexander had said:[27] which showed that the idea crossed his mind, as it might well, owing to her unique position.

The way was now open, after the death of Alexander, for the queens of the Ptolemies of Egypt – themselves of Macedonian origin – to exercise a political power that was alien to anything the Greek tradition had known before. Berenice I, wife of Ptolemy I Soter, was portrayed on the coinage, and the pair were proclaimed Saviour Gods by their son Ptolemy II Philadelphus (c.316–270 BC). This was the first of the

20

Ptolemaic family's brother-sister marriages, which raised them above ordinary mortals. Arsinoe II was only queen of Egypt for a few years (dying long before her husband), but it was the time of the greatest Ptolemaic expansion overseas – for which she was mainly responsible – and of the greatest brilliance of the Alexandrian court. Her influence was as large as her husband's, or very probably larger, since she spurred him on. She was a patron of literature, and dedicated the biggest walled circular building in the Greek world (at Samothrace),[28] and she and her husband had already been deified, with pomp such as had never been seen on any previous occasion, at some date before 272 BC; moreover, she was also worshipped alone – thus showing the heights that a woman could attain. One of the most impressive female administrators who have ever lived, this woman of exceptional energy, versatility, foresight and unscrupulousness had created many precedents for women. All she had not done was to rule alone; but this was bound to come.

Later on, in 247, Berenice II married Ptolemy III Euergetes, and after his death personally led a rebellion against her mother and her mother's bridegroom, becoming joint ruler with her son Ptolemy IV Epiphanes, who then murdered her. Papyri called her the female pharaoh, and her portrait appeared alone on coins. So did the head of her daughter Arsinoe III Philopator, wife of Ptolemy IV – the first Ptolemaic queen to appear unveiled in the visual arts. Cleopatra I, the wife of Ptolemy V Epiphanes (193), ruled for four years as regent for her young son Ptolemy VI Philometor, whose name is preceded by hers on several papyri. She was the mother of Cleopatra II, who had a long and complicated career of co-regencies, and some papyri record her alone. Her daughter Cleopatra III (like her grandmother) often took precedence over the kings her sons in dating formulae. The extraordinary career of Cleopatra VII, who, under the successive protection of Caesar and Antony, ruled an Egyptian empire on her own account – with young brothers or sons as her titular colleagues – is well known.

In other Hellenistic countries, too, there were female monarchs. One was Cleopatra Thea, daughter of Ptolemy VI Philometor, who married three Seleucid kings, and was the mother of another two – between whose reigns (she had the elder one murdered) she appeared on Seleucid coinage in her own name and in her own right. And elsewhere there were other Hellenistic queens, whose male consorts were insignificant or, at times, non-existent.

Rulers of the vast Hellenistic states, under threat, needed the participation of their wives and mothers. And these female monarchs, especially in Egypt, surpassed even the Roman empresses to come, because they had access to the national treasury. Furthermore, their power and freedom, infinitely far removed from the restrictions imposed on earlier classical Greeks of their sex, percolated down the social scale, so that ordinary Hellenistic women, too, became much freer. This is clear enough from the writers of the time, and so, too, is a much wider, less blinkered approach to femininity as a general phenomenon. The women in Menander's New Comedy are no longer just the objects of mishaps and misfortunes but, like men, have good and bad qualities of their own, and cause suffering and suffer themselves (often through misunderstandings) – and their sexuality gives them power, although male characters can still make offensive remarks about them.

As for the Greek literature of Hellenistic Alexandria, it displays a woman's viewpoint in an unfamiliar fashion – and often stresses intimacy rather than hostility between the sexes. The poetry of Theocritus, for example, is a revelation. It delineates the possibilities of a female world capable of running itself – and operating on various, emancipated, levels. True, his housewives Gorgo and Praxinoa, exchanging back-chat at the festival of Adonis, although they are quite well-off, remain trivial and vulgar.[29] Yet Simaetha, in another poem, displays heartfelt erotic agony, and authentic female consciousness.

> The sea is still, still are the winds.
> Yet the fire in my heart is never stilled.
> My whole being is aflame for the man,
> The man who has made me a slave,
> Not a wife, and – to my shame – no virgin now . . .
> One look, and I totally lost my mind.
> My heart was on fire; great pain already;
> The colour quickly drained from my cheeks.
> I thought no more about my processions,
> Nor do I know how I came to get home.
> But a fever parched me, my whole frame shivered,
> And I lay on my bed ten days and nights . . .
> My skin had turned a deathly yellow,
> The hair was all dropping out of my scalp;
> There was nothing left of me but skin and bone.[30]

Meanwhile Apollonius Rhodius was the first poet to make romantic love the central theme for an epic poem.

> At his desire
> She would have plucked the very life from her breast
> And given it him, such bright and beautiful fire
> On Jason's yellow hair, love's influence, played.
> The flashings of her eyes he captive made,
> And all her heart its secret warmth discloses.
> Melting like morning dew upon the roses
> That warm day melts: and now
> Shyly they to the ground their eyes abase,
> And now gaze at each other face to face,
> Each smiling love under a shining brow.[31]

And Meleager of Gadara, too, is one of the great poets of heterosexual love.

> Soul counsels flight
> From Heliodora's affections,
> 'Those pangs, those tears.'
> Soul warns, but warns
> Sans will to flight:
> Incontinent and
> Warning still, soul
> Turns and loves her.
>
> Love's night and a lamp
> Judged our vows:
> That she would love me ever
> And I should never leave her.
> Love's night and you, lamp,
> Witnessed the pact.
> Today the vow runs:
> 'Oaths such as these, waterwords!'
> Tonight, lamp,
> Witness her lying
>   – in other arms.[32]

This new tendency to understand women was also displayed by Hellenistic sculptors. Eutychides's Tyche (Fortune) – a mighty patron

23

goddess – became the most famous female statue of the age. And then there were the Victory of Samothrace, the Bathing Aphrodite of Doidalsas, and the Venus of Milo. At the same time, too, the novel concepts of the woman's personality and form that these statues embodied were encouraged by members of the medical profession such as Herophilus, who was the first to employ Greek terms describing the female anatomy in a technical context.

And women were now embarking on literary and artistic careers themselves. They had helped philosophers before, and continued to do so, but Hipparchia also went round giving lectures herself, with her Cynic friend Crates, and living the same life as he did,[33] and sharing his taste for ultra-individualism. Other women professed to be Pythagoreans. Others again were wives or mistresses of the friends of Epicurus, men who supported the pro-feminist line (even if they had little impact on official attitudes); while Stoicism, although denying the moral and intellectual inferiority of women, sought to divert their energies to marriage and motherhood. As for woman poets, there had been others beside Sappho from time to time, but Erinna of Telos and Nossis of Locri Epizephyrii, at the end of the fourth century, and Corinna of Tanagra who probably lived in the third, achieved particular note, and Aristodama, a poet of Smyrna, was made an honorary citizen by the Aetolians (218).

Yet some of these literary women evidently laboured under something of an inferiority complex. For Corinna reproached a female friend, Myrtis, for competing with Pindar: and these women did mostly write about men's subjects and men's occasions, although Nossis consciously saw herself as an heir of Sappho,[34] and Erinna chose her own girlhood, and the domestic life of girls, and the death of a woman-friend, as her themes. Male chauvinism denied that she had the capacity to write the poems attributed to her, but without justification. Yet it must be confessed that these women's contribution to literature did not amount to a great deal, or, at least, its potential was never fully realised. But there were also Alexandrian woman painters and sculptors, and Phile of Priene constructed a reservoir and an aqueduct. Menophila of Sardis was honoured by her city for being clever (she is sculptured holding a book) and as a leader, and in the second century BC a woman became an archon at Istros. However, these manifestations, too, were rare and fragmentary.

Yet, women's education had improved by now, and so had their

24

status, in a world where the conquests of Alexander had weakened the traditional city-state. Women had a broader social life, and their equality was increasingly respected, and their legal capacities, too, obtained new recognition, so that they gained more and more control over their inheritances and properties. Although the exposure of infant girls continued, Greco-Egyptian usage recognised woman guardians, in a country where the vast prominence of queens could not fail to have an effect. Marriages by consent, for love, had become commoner, and Egyptian marriage contracts – from which a great deal of valuable information is obtained – enforced monogamy, and sometimes forbade men to take concubines or boy-lovers.

> Apollonia shall remain with Philiscus, obeying him as a wife should obey her husband, owning their property jointly with him. Philiscus, whether he is at home or away from home, shall furnish Apollonia with everything necessary and clothing and whatsoever is proper to a wedded wife, in proportion to their means. It shall not be lawful for Philiscus to bring home another wife in addition to Apollonia or to have a concubine or boy-lover, nor to beget children by another woman while Apollonia is alive nor to maintain another house of which Apollonia is not mistress, nor to eject or insult or ill-treat her nor to alienate any of their property with injustice to Apollonia . . . In the same way it shall not be lawful for Apollonia to spend night or day away from the house of Philiscus without Philiscus's knowledge, or to have intercourse with another man or to ruin the common household or to bring shame upon Philiscus in whatever causes a husband shame.[35]

Divorces became more numerous, and in the Lake Moeris area (the Fayum) a wife had the right to leave her husband of her own free will. Moreover, Hellenistic women were prominent as manumitters of slaves (Chapter 7), and many more women worked away from home.

Sparta was even more famous than before for the independence and wealth of its women, who obstructed King Agis IV (244–241 BC) when he wanted to introduce land reforms.

> At this time the greater part of the wealth of Sparta was in the hands of women, and this made the task of Agis laborious and difficult. For the women offered resistance when they saw that not only were they being deprived of the luxurious standard of living which their lack of

taste made them believe constituted real happiness, but that they would also forfeit the honour and power they derived from their wealth.[36]

Such spectacles of powerful women, of course, increased misogyny among the men who saw what was happening. Indeed, it was perhaps more sharply expressed than ever, as the male sex saw its old certainties wavering, and brought out old prejudices as popular wisdom.

But religion was the women's great strength. It had always been so, but now priestesses were abundant and honoured on a scale that had not been seen hitherto. And never previously had there been a goddess like Isis, Egyptian but widely exported elsewhere, who was the immensely important patron of the whole female sex, passionately worshipped by women, praised for giving them equal strength to men, and even for encouraging wives to feel superior and give orders to their husbands, who promised them obedience.[37] Once again the powerful Ptolemaic queens had a lot to do with this. Not only were they deified themselves, but they were intimately associated and even identified with Isis, whose example and instruction encouraged their consciousness of their power.

2

Roman Women

Etruscan women enjoyed considerably greater freedom than those of classical Greece. Possibly this was inherited from pre-urban Italy, but we cannot be sure. We must not exaggerate, as the scandalised attention of contemporaries inclines us to do. But there is ample evidence, for example, from paintings and reliefs which show the women of Etruria eating with men; and an Etruscan woman presided over games for the dead at Clusium. There was also a notoriously masterful Etruscan queen, Tanaquil, about whom the evidence cannot be altogether discounted.

Some of this, obviously, percolated through to the Romans – if early Roman women had inheritance rights, they probably came from the Etruscans – although such advantages were counterbalanced by a powerful series of restrictions. 'Our ancestors', observed Cicero, 'established the rule that all women, because of their weakness of intellect, should be under the power of guardians'[1] – men, always, whose guardianship for life effectively nullified the legal capacities of Roman women. True, a woman's property was separate from her husband's, but he or another man controlled it. So these women possessed no legal personality on their own account: they had no vote or role in government, needless to say, and they could not plead.

The fact was that from the earliest visible time the Roman family was rigorously patriarchal, and the *paterfamilias* possessed remarkable power. The Twelve Tables (451–450 BC) somewhat limited this, but only to transfer a measure of the power to a Roman woman's husband (with whom her marriage was the central moment of her life). But there were, in fact, three forms of early Roman marriage, which were replaced – in the course of lengthy legislation – by a 'freer' kind; so in

27

one way and another the wife was not entirely tied down, and in fact, considering that this was a traditional agrarian society, she possessed an unfamiliar degree of latitude. The Roman matron, in particular, secured a dignity and respect that were unknown elsewhere, guaranteeing her not only protection but mutual trust. Certainly, however, her home life was stressed, because the family was a potent economic, social and religious unit, and there was – as in Greek lands – a deep-rooted tradition that the woman's sphere was in the house, and the man's outside it.

The popular Roman picture of the chaste, domesticated, faithful mother was provided by a number of epigraphic eulogies and models. Here is the inscription on the tombstone of an unknown Claudia.

> Friend, I have not much to say; stop and read it. This tomb, which is not fair, is for a fair woman. Her parents gave her the name of Claudia. She loved her husband in her heart. She bore two sons, one of whom she left on earth, the other beneath it. She was pleasant to talk with, and she walked in grace. She kept the house and worked in wool. That is all. You may go.[2]

But the prototype of ideal Roman womanhood – evidently more enterprising than Claudia – was Cornelia, the mother of the Gracchi. As Plutarch describes her:

> After her husband died, leaving Cornelia twelve children by him, she took charge both of the children and of her husband's property, and proved herself a woman of discretion and noble ideals and a devoted mother . . . Her boys she brought up with such care and such ambitious hopes that, although by common consent no Romans have ever been more naturally gifted, they were considered to owe their virtues even more to their education than to their heredity . . . [After their deaths] she went to the promontory called Misenum and made no change in her normal mode of life.[3]

And Plutarch goes on to stress again Cornelia's noble nature, honourable ancestry and virtuous upbringing. In particular, as he records, she was respected as the parent of adult sons – and that role was interpreted in a more serious sense than the Greeks had ever known. Upper-class Romans, observed Cornelius Nepos, believed that their women enjoyed greater social freedom than those of the Greeks,[4] and despite restrictions and exclusion from politics, this opinion was

28

right. Within limits, they were less segregated than Greek women. They were expected, as the account of Cornelia showed, to educate their sons for citizenship; and more importance was attached to the part played by their daughters.

The role of Roman women was enhanced by the worship of the great goddesses, especially Juno whose chief function was to supervise female lives; and further solemnity was added by the grandeur of the Vestal Virgins. Roman matrons played an important part in Roman religious cults. There were a few rebellious women, of course – but their notoriety only stressed the need for the others to behave properly, and to be repressed if they did not. How they themselves felt about the whole business we scarcely know – as was also the case in Greece. But the Etruscan Tanaquil was not wholly forgotten; nor was the power of Hellenistic queens. That is to say, there had long been Roman women who exercised political power behind the scenes – they possessed contacts, and used them. Livy was aware of this, and cites the legendary Veturia and Volumnia to suggest that it was a phenomenon that had long been in existence.[5]

One of the restrictions imposed, originally, on Roman women was that patricians could not marry plebeians. But this veto was lifted by the Lex Canuleia of the tribune Gaius Canuleius which, in *c*.445 BC, authorised such intermarriages, by recognising the legitimacy of the children of plebeian mothers and admitting them to patrician clans (*gentes*). During the Second Punic War the Lex Oppia of the tribune Gaius Oppius (215) was a wartime measure forbidding women to indulge in luxuries, but it was repealed in 195, after vigorous demonstrations, despite the fierce opposition of the traditionalist Cato the elder, who was alleged to have said: 'all people rule their wives: we rule all peoples: our wives rule us'.[6]

The female characters depicted by the comic dramatist Plautus, in the same period, are merely stock stereotypes, yet this was a period when Roman regard for women was increasing, partly because after Hannibal had killed their fathers and brothers their portions of wealth had increased. One of the reasons why the Bacchanalian rites were suppressed by the Roman senate in 186 was because the emotionalism of these 'orgies' was said to encourage sexuality in women.[7]

Nevertheless, whatever the law might say, Roman women were playing a larger and freer part in the second century BC. The principle of permanent guardianship had become eroded into a mere formality, and soon afterwards was legally abandoned. Moreover, issues were raised about whom women might decide to meet, and to marry, which they could do with increasing freedom of choice. Certainly, Roman men in the first century – especially in the wealthier families – divorced their wives for adultery, whereas there is little evidence for the reverse, and there were still declarations that a woman's place was *not* to do men's jobs. Yet, all the same, the convulsions of the late Republic gave wives a greatly increased share in the decisions their husbands had to make. True, their new liberties were largely derived from the prominence of their men, who used them to serve their own political ambitions; and great stress was still laid, a little nostalgically, on feminine domestic virtues. But none the less the Roman women of the late Republic possessed a freedom and independence almost unparalleled until the present century. These advances were signalised by the first public funeral oration for a woman, Popilia, in 102 BC, and by Caesar's encomia on his aunt and his young wife (69, 68).

This new formidable emancipation of Roman women drove some men into the arms of more pliable freedwomen (Chapter 7). Cicero, in his speech *For Caelius*, assails the character of Clodia as an example of the type of woman who lived a life of pleasure, in contrast with the traditional *matrona*.

> Gentlemen, the whole of the case revolves round Clodia. She is a woman of noble birth; but she also has a notorious reputation . . . As for you, woman, for now I am speaking to you directly and not through some stage personage, if you will condescend to justify your goings on, your declarations, your fabrications, your intrigues, your allegations, it is also your responsibility to explain and account in full for this intimacy [with Caelius], this familiarity, this whole relationship. The prosecutors are making play with orgies, cohabitations, adulteries, trips to Baiae, beach parties, dinner parties, drinking parties, musical parties, concert parties, boating parties . . .[8]

Such women, it was insisted, were a danger to men. And Sallust singled out a certain Sempronia as the object of his attack:

> Catiline is said to have won over many supporters from all classes, including even a number of women. These had been accustomed earlier in life to indulge their expensive tastes by prostituting themselves, but the time came when advancing years reduced their

trade, though not their extravagance, and in consequence they had contracted enormous debts . . . Among these supporters was Sempronia, a woman who had committed many crimes which were audacious enough to be the work of a man. Fortune had been generous to her, not only in her noble birth and exceptional beauty, but also in the character of her husband and children. She was well read in the literature of Greece and Rome, could sing, dance and play the lyre with more talent than an honest woman needs, and possessed many of the other accomplishments which enhance a life of luxury. Modesty and chastity, on the other hand, were qualities for which she had little use, and it would have been hard to say whether she was more careless of her money or her reputation; indeed so little could she control her passions that she was most often the suitor in her love affairs. Even before the time of the conspiracy, her extravagance and lack of money had launched her on the downward path, so that she had often broken her word, forsworn money placed in her charge, and acted as an accomplice to murder. Yet in spite of this she was a woman of exceptional gifts; she could write verses and hold her own in repartee, while her talk could be modest, tender or wanton as she chose, and to sum up her personality combined wit and charm to a remarkable degree.[9]

That, then, was the woman whom Sallust chose to denounce, as the typical political adventuress and intriguer, energetic and audacious: a woman who displayed the qualities of men, and in consequence threatened them directly.

But it was during the tormented years that followed Julius Caesar's death that powerful women really came into their own, to help their fathers and husbands – or at their expense. There was Servilia, for example, whose character and family connections made her the most important woman in late Republican politics; she was the woman who arranged meetings with leading men and women (described by Cicero), in order to decide what her son Brutus should do.[10] And there was Turia, who saved her husband from the Triumvirs' proscriptions.

Marriages as long as ours are rare, marriages that are ended by death and not broken by divorce. For we were fortunate enough to see our marriage last without disharmony for fully forty years . . . Why should I now hold up to view our intimate and secret plans and private conversations: how I was saved by your good advice when I

31

was roused by startling reports to meet sudden and imminent dangers; how you did not allow me imprudently to tempt providence by an overbold step but prepared a safe hiding place for me? . . . There would be no end, if I tried to go into all this. It is enough for me and for you that I was hidden and my life was secured.[11]

Moreover, at dramatic risk and hardship to herself, Turia induced Octavian, despite Lepidus's opposition, to reinstate her outlawed husband. 'In gratitude', the husband continues, 'for your great services towards me let me display before the eyes of all men my public acknowledgment that you saved my life.'

As for Antony's wife Fulvia, she wanted to rule a male ruler, and command a commander. The first dominant wife in Roman history (as Shakespeare appreciated), she schooled Antony to obey a woman (as he later obeyed Cleopatra VII), and was subjected to merciless hostile propaganda from Octavian. The Second Triumvirate, moreover, had to cope with agitation from 1,400 matrons, complaining of a tax on rich women. When Hortensia spoke, 'you would hardly have guessed', remarked Appian, 'that it was a woman speaking'.[12]

Augustus tried to put a stop to all this by a whole series of laws restricting the freedoms of women; he wanted less adultery (a criminal offence for women, but not for men), less extravagance, less inter-marriage between classes, continued guardianship for orphaned daughters (only giving birth to three children – four for a freedwoman – could release them),[13] and larger families; and he rejected the principle that marriage was a family matter largely outside the scope of the law. To press the point home, police espionage was needed. And he had his granddaughters taught the traditional household skills. But the whole enterprise proved useless; Augustus was brilliant in many other spheres, but not in this.

Some Roman women studied politics and law, and tombstones mention a doctor, and a few secretaries and clerks. Women represented on the friezes of the Ara Pacis chat without veiling their heads. And Sulpicia is a poet who avows her love with directness and warmth. Men, too, such as Propertius, show insight into a woman's feelings,[14] artfully comparing men's public triumphs with women's private ones, and adding a hint that woman is the enslaver and man the slave. He admires that figure of the past, Cornelia, for adhering to the traditional behaviour code, but prefers the living Cynthia, who does not, but is more exciting. As for Ovid, he has an enormous amount to write about women, by no means all of it to Augustus's taste, since what the poet says is psychologically, clinically, sympathetically observant and frank, if not cynical. More Augustan was the lesson to be derived from Virgil's ambitious, domineering, sexy Dido, which was that Romans must not abandon their country for a woman, especially a foreign woman (like Cleopatra), and must not allow their feelings for her to interfere with the task of running the state, which was their job and not hers.

A complication was Augustus's wife Livia. The historian Tacitus venomously accused her of every possible vice, as Robert Graves's book *I Claudius* has let us know. She was surely not as bad as all that, and may even have humanised Augustus. All the same, the interferences of this 'Ulysses (Odysseus) in petticoats' (as Caligula called her)[15] were evidently far-reaching and devious: though domestically she remained a modest paragon, seldom to be seen in public, and Augustus, just before he died, fitted her into the traditional, subordinate picture by declaring: 'always remember whose wife you have been'.[16]

Yet Livia's unprecedented position, underlined by the privileges she received in his will, launched the list of extraordinary Roman empresses. In fact, what they were doing was to repeat and reconstitute the power of the Hellenistic queens: but on a much wider canvas, and in the glare of wider publicity, since they had Tacitus and Suetonius to write about them. That is how we have such terrifying pictures of Claudius's wives Messalina and the younger Agrippina, powerful, cruel, salacious and flamboyant. What Tacitus found particularly abhorrent about Agrippina was her 'almost masculine despotism'.[17]

Some of this power, of course, percolated down the social scale – and not only at Rome. Eumachia, at Pompeii, was priestess of Venus, and president of the corporation of fullers and dyers – that is to say, leader of the wool industry – and an important woman, as this inscription shows:

> Eumachia, daughter of Lucius, public priestess, in her own name and that of her son Marcus Numistrius Fronto, built with her own funds the porch, covered passage and colonnade, and dedicated them to Concordia Augusta and to Pietas.[18]

Inevitably, too, the writers have various things to say about women, other than empresses. Valerius Maximus does not like female speech-making, and Petronius's *Satyricon* depicts Trimalchio's freed-

woman wife Fortunata as a dreadful vulgarian. But the younger Seneca
has a relatively generous opinion of some women's capabilities. Or at
least he tells his mother Helvia that she lacks a woman's weaknesses,
and is more like a man; that is the way he chooses to console her
bereavement.

> The best course is the mean between affection and reason – both to
> have a sense of loss and crush it . . . The excuse of being a woman can
> be of no avail to one who has always lacked all the weaknesses of a
> woman . . . You cannot, therefore, allege your womanhood as an
> excuse for persistent grief, for your very virtues set you apart. You
> must be as far removed from woman's tears as from her vices.[19]

Musonius Rufus went so far as to deplore the legal and educational
inequalities from which women still suffered. Pliny the younger set
aside a large sum of money for the maintenance of free girls (who had to
be educated nowadays, up to a point) as well as boys. And he also
struck a welcome, human, personal note in his letters. He was very
distressed by the death of a friend's twelve-year-old daughter. And he
greatly missed his wife, when they were apart.

> You cannot believe how much I miss you. I love you so much, and we
> are not used to separation. So I stay awake most of the night thinking
> of you, and by day I find my feet carrying me (a true word, carrying)
> to your room at the times I usually visited you. Then, finding it
> empty, I depart, as sick and sorrowful as a lover locked out.[20]

Plutarch thought that, as in ancient Greek days, official religion was
a suitable occupation for a woman.

> A wife ought not to make friends of her own, but to enjoy her
> husband's friends together with him. And the first and best friends
> are the gods in whom her husband believes, and to shut her door to
> all magic ceremonies and foreign superstitions. For no god can be
> pleased by stealthy and surreptitious rites performed by a woman.[21]

Nevertheless, in his *Great Deeds by Women* Plutarch recognises that
upper-class Roman women shared in their husbands' achievements
more than their Athenian counterparts, and that joint decisions are
made.[22] But the husband leads, and the 'Great Deeds' are limited to
crises, with no real social or political role for the women.

Meanwhile the Greek middle-brow romantic novel had come very much into its own, and women, naturally, fill its pages. For the novel focused on a love relationship in which due attention is devoted to the femal partner, rather gutless though she is inclined to be. The central figures are, almost invariably, a young man and his fiancée or wife, whose reciprocal faithfulness, rectitude and courage are tested by one tribulation after another: finally, all these hazards are overcome, and they live happily ever after.

By way of extreme contrast, the sixth satire of Juvenal is a huge, ruthless, cynical denunciation of immoral, pretentious and vicious wives – all equally bad, from the empresses to the lowest.

> Postumus, are you *really*
> Taking a wife? You used to be sane enough – what
> Fury's got into you, what snake has stung you up?
> Why endure such bitch-tyranny when rope's available
> By the fathom, when all those dizzying top-floor windows
> Are open for you, when there are bridges handy
> To jump from? . . . Really, if *you* take a wife, I'll
> Credit anything, friend. You were once the randiest
> Hot-rod-about-town, you hid in more bedroom cupboards
> Than a comedy juvenile lead. Can this be the man now
> Sticking his silly neck out for the matrimonial halter?
> And as for your insistence on a wife with old-fashioned
> Moral virtues – man, you need your blood-pressure checked! . . .
> Tell me, will Hiberina
> Think one man enough? You'll find it much less trouble
> To make her agree to being blinded in one eye.[23]

No wonder, if any of Juvenal's assumptions were correct, that concubinage had become socially acceptable, however much it weakened the traditional marriage bond.

Greek poets of Roman imperial times likewise had some disagreeable things to say about women.

> Philistion's a hard bitch:
> In her book 'penniless lover'
> Is a mere contradiction in terms.
> She seems more bearable now? She
> Mellows? One may die from the bite
> Of a less than totally hostile snake.[24]

You bought hair, rouge, cream, teeth and paste.
It'd cost the same to buy a face.[25]

The novelist Apuleius eloquently glorified the goddess Isis as
sovereign and saviour. A prayer to Isis, in the second century AD,
declared: 'you gave women equal power with men'.[26] And for a short
time they had even greater power. Only custom, observed the lawyer
Ulpian in his *Digest*, excluded women from public life, but that custom
was abruptly broken by a family of women who came from Emesa
(Homs) in Syria, where they belonged to a royal, priestly house. No
Roman woman had ever received so much power, privilege and honour
as Julia Domna, the wife of the north African Septimius Severus (193–
211). Yet, even so, Severus remained in charge, and so did his son
Caracalla (211–217), although Julia Domna was still alive. But he
allowed her a considerable amount of authority.

> Caracalla's mother gave him much excellent advice. He had
> appointed her to receive petitions and to have charge of his
> correspondence in both languages, except in very important cases,
> and used to include her name, in terms of high praise, together with
> his own and that of the legions, in his letters to the senate, stating that
> she was well. Need I add that she held public receptions for all the
> most prominent men, precisely as did the emperor? She devoted
> herself more and more to the study of philosophy with these men.[27]

Then, after Julia Domna was dead, her sister Julia Maesa completely
dominated her juvenile, homosexual grandson Elagabalus (218–222),
and when she decided to drop Elagabalus in favour of his cousin
Severus Alexander (222–235) and then died, it was her daughter Julia
Mamaea who controlled the empire for the rest of his reign.

> After he succeeded to the imperial power, while still a boy, he used to
> do everything in conjunction with his mother, so that she seemed to
> have an equal share in the rule, a woman greatly revered, but
> covetous and greedy for gold and silver.[28]

This period was an unparalleled phenomenon in the ancient world,
though it has not always been recognised as such, since the third
century AD is not extensively studied. Ancient women never attained
such pinnacles of power again, with the possible exception of Galla
Placidia, who married Constantius III (417) and then, in the face of

numerous obstacles, elevated their son Valentinian III to the throne of the western empire (425), and largely controlled his policy for the next quarter of a century.

Taking the empire as a whole, it has been calculated that, up to the time of Constantine I the Great (306–337), twenty-four emperors had been betrayed or killed by nearly thirty women.

The late Latin historian Ammianus Marcellinus did not think much of the women he saw around him in Rome. He, a foreigner, had been ejected from the city, but many disreputable females were not.

> The ultimate disgrace, not long ago, when foreigners were banished in headlong haste from the city because a famine was expected, [was that] the hangers-on of actresses and those who posed as such for the occasion, together with three thousand dancers with their choruses and the same number of dancing instructors, were allowed to remain without even being questioned. Wherever you turn your eyes you can see any number of women with curled ringlets, old enough, if they were married, to be mothers of three, skimming the floor with their feet to the point of exhaustion and launching themselves into the bird-like evolutions by which they represent the countless scenes which form the imaginary content of theatrical pieces . . . The women scream from cock-crow like a flock of starving peacocks.[29]

In the Christian world – in which the New Testament had sent out various complex signals about women, that cannot be discussed here – St Jerome, who suffered from sexual anxiety, marshalled the evidence against marriage and women, and Augustine, afflicted with deep sadness on the same subject, was the son of the dominating Monica. Melania the elder (c.340–before 410) and her granddaughter of the same name were enormously wealthy women. The learned pagan Hypatia was torn to pieces by a Christian mob, instigated by bishop (later Saint) Cyril of Alexandria (415).

Part II
MEN

3

The Rich

So, with a number of terrific exceptions and breakouts, the place for ancient women was the home, and the place for men was the world outside, political and military. These men fell sharply into classes, the rich (or, in the first place, noble) and the poor, the rulers and the ruled. There were changes and shifts in the compositions of these two classes as time went on, but the modern idea that we should elect or reelect our ruling class every few years would have seemed ludicrous, or incomprehensible, to the ancients.

The rich, upper class produced almost the whole of Greek civilisation, exploiting the labour of others in order to do so, since that was the only possible way to proceed. As Karl Marx observed – right in this respect, though not always (Appendix 2) – 'the ideas of the ruling class are, in every age, the ruling ideas'.[1] That was abundantly true of the Greeks and Romans, so that our literature has a leisure-class bias. Hierarchical values were built into the education of people at all levels and those values were obsessively concerned with wealth, as a determinant of status.

How marked the distinction between the two classes already is in Homer! The leaders, the *basileis*, are the big men. Their most notable skill is the capacity to fight.

> So now the heart of Sarpedon stalwart as a god
> Impelled him to charge the wall and break it down.
> He quickly called Hippolochus' son: 'Glaucus,
> Why do they hold us both in honour, first by far
> With pride of place, choice meats and brimming cups,
> In Lycia where all our people look on us like gods ? . .

So that now the duty's ours –
We are the ones to head our Lycian front,
Brace and fling ourselves in the blaze of war.[2]

And how illuminating is the story of Thersites, the lower-grade person in the *Iliad* who had the nerve to get up and question the big leaders' decisions.

Achilles despised him most. Odysseus too –
He was always abusing both chiefs, but now
He went for majestic Agamemnon, hollering out,
Taunting the king with strings of cutting insults.

But the result was that Odysseus answered him back, in equally abusive terms, and then, humiliatingly, struck him.

He cracked his sceptre across his back and shoulders.
The rascal doubled over, tears streaking his face,
And a bloody welt bulged up between his blades,
Under the stroke of the golden sceptre's studs.
He squatted low, cringing, stunned with pain,
Blinking like some idiot . . .
Rubbing his tears off dumbly with a fist.
Their morale was low but the men laughed now.[3]

Some protest was evidently in the air – an uncomfortable presage of others that were to come. But it was abruptly and definitively squashed.

As for the *Odyssey*, when a Phaeacian suggested to Odysseus (reluctant to join an archery competition) that he was perhaps a merchant, this went down very badly.

Now Seareach [Euryalus] put his word in, and contentiously . . .
'The reason being, as I see it, friend,
You never learnt a sport, and have no skill
In any of the contests of fighting men.
You must have been the skipper of some tramp
That crawled from one port to the next, jam full
Of chaffering hands: a tallier of cargoes,
Itching for gold – not, by your looks, an athlete.'
Odysseus frowned, and eyed him coldly, saying,
'That was uncalled for, friend, you talk like a you talk fool.'[4]

42

Odysseus, in fact, was deeply insulted. He was, of course, a great prince and landowner, whose life, when he was at home, centred round his household (*oikos*). The basic institution in the Homeric world is this aristocratic household, and the big men of the *oikoi* associated with each other through an elaborate system of gift-giving. Thus when Achilles is angry with Agamemnon, Agamemnon offers him a rich gift, and Phoenix advises Achilles (his ward) to accept it, since this will enhance his prestige.

> Now – while the gifts still wait – go out and fight!
> Go – the Achaeans all will honour you like a god!
> But enter this man-killing war without gifts –
> Your fame will flag, no longer the same honour,
> Even though you hurl the Trojans home![5]

In Hesiod, the heroic ideal is reversed. He looked at the privileged world from outside the charmed circle, and without much favour, unimpressed by its sanctions. He lived at a time of transition. Rulership in the recently established city-states was being transferred from monarchs to groups of aristocrats. Not that this helped the excluded class, for the new rulers were just as exclusive, or more so, maintaining, from the eighth century BC, a life-style compounded of clubs (*hetaireiai*) and dinner parties (*symposia*) that has characterised upper-class societies ever since. Archilochus makes this aristocratic ethos clearly visible.

Another important shift occurred when the rulers became not so much noblemen as men of wealth – a change deplored by the conservative poet Theognis.

> It is property that they prize: a good
> man has married the child of a bad one,
> a bad man the child of a good one.
> Wealth has thrown lineage into confusion.
> So do not be surprised, son of Polypaus [Cyrnus],
> that the lineage of the citizens is being
> dimmed: good things are being intermingled with bad.[6]

This redistribution of power in the topmost class again did nothing for the class which was neither noble nor rich. An intervening stage, however, in some cities, brought tyrants to the top, and they, on occasion, *did* sometimes call in the poor to prop up their cause (Pittacus

43

did this on the island of Lesbos, much to the resentment of the diehard
poet Alcaeus), though once more without doing anything lasting to
help them. Certainly, the new sets of rulers did engage, themselves, in
economic activities, in order to keep wealthy: though it is a Marxist
illusion that any separate 'commercial' class existed (Appendix 2).

For the basis of the wealth of the ruling class was, to a very great
extent, not commerce but agriculture, as it always had been and always
would be in the ancient world. Most people lived off the land, and the
aristocratic city-governments were founded on landownership,
reinforced, no doubt, by profitable commerce when possible, but
fundamentally agricultural all the same. When Plutarch suggested that
the Athenian reformer Solon (chief archon 594–593 or 592–591)
deliberately aimed to turn Athens to trade,[7] he was misleading. Solon
was perfectly clear that landed property (with its income) was the basic
principle, and he ensured that this, rather than birth, should be
regularised as such (when, himself a noble [Medontid], he classed
himself with the poor, he was only making a political point).

One cannot, of course, generalise about ancient Greece. Sparta, for
example, had a system entirely of its own, in which, however, the
labour force suffered worst of all. And eloquent praises of the old system
based on aristocratic birth continued, notably in the poetry of the
Boeotian Pindar. To him, innate and inherited qualities (*phua*) are
decisive. 'It is a vain struggle, if one seeks to hide one's inborn
character.'[8] The Olympic victor needs a trainer, certainly, but the
trainer's job is only to 'sharpen' the inborn abilities of 'one born to
prowess'.[9]

> A man has much weight if glory belongs to his breed,
> But whoso needs to be taught,
> His spirit blows here and there in the dark,
> Nor ever enters he the lists with sure foot,
> Though countless the glories his futile fancy savours.[10]

Yet almost everywhere, by that epoch, the timocratic sort of ruling
class, based on wealth, prevailed. Athens, for example, continued to be
controlled by upper-class leaders of this type, although, it is true,
wealth was often coincidental with noble origins, and the nobles
(Eupatrids) maintained a near-monopoly of Attica's landed estates, so
that for a long time only the families that had always ruled could have
the leisure and experience needed for leadership.

The sixth-century Athenian tyrant Pisistratus was himself, like most earlier tyrants, a nobleman, yet he saw great dangers, all the same, in the historic opposition between the various factions of noble and rich men, and took measures to bring this to an end. Nevertheless, even in the middle of the next century, most Athenian politicians were still relatively well-to-do, walking a knife-edge path between a popular stance and excessive élitism. Lip-service could be devoted to poverty, but poor statesmen remained exceptional. Cimon and Pericles were noble; Cimon was extremely rich, and Pericles was not poor.

But then, in the critical Peloponnesian War against Sparta (431–404 BC), there came a change. After the death of Pericles, power fell into the hands of the 'demagogues', of whom Cleon, Hyperbolus and Cleophon were the most famous. They set a new model of prominence without the backing of consistent military achievement, and supported by a more popular and opportunistic oratorical style than had been witnessed hitherto. They were attacked for their breaches of tradition with extraordinary savagery, and charged with low birth among much else, and assailed for being 'in trade'. Yet they were not tradesmen, but men of inherited wealth which had, admittedly, come in the first place no longer from land, but from successful commerce.

These demagogues also relied more than their predecessors on the support of the masses of the people. During the emergencies of the Peloponnesian War, however, specialist ability was also needed, and the capacity to win popular favour was no longer enough (nor did the two best Athenian generals in the war, Lamachus and Demosthenes, have any interest in politics). Whether the 'demagogues' who, to Thucydides's distaste, took control of Athens during the war were really any better than the earlier sort of Athenian leader is another matter. Certainly they were clever, but certainly, also, they had to think more about protecting their own positions; and they encouraged the Assembly (which relied on leadership to make up its mind) to reach disastrous decisions which brought about the loss of the war. The traditional upper classes, more than once, reacted to this removal of power from their hands by terrorist acts.

In fourth-century Athens the development of fortunes other than in land continued; and the well-rounded amateur leader was increasingly replaced by the trained, professional expert (still, for the most part, with financial resources of his own). The philosophers did not want

45

anything more democratic to appear. True, Socrates, Plato and Aristotle fully recognised and condemned aristocratic degeneration, but they were intellectuals who were not keen on allowing the uneducated any power; indeed the concept of an upper class which rightly disdained physical labour and economic rivalry, and left such matters to its inferiors, was largely their creation. According to Aristotle, 'a well-ordered state needed breeding, training and reasoning'.[11] Breeding, in his day, had to be dispensed with, but not the others – which you were not going to get from the poor. So, just as Aristophanes had attacked the allegedly low-class origins of Cleon, so the orator Demosthenes sneered at those of his rival Aeschines – and caused his client Euxitheus to apologise about his mother, who was in trade.[12]

Then, in Hellenistic times, one important thing changed: the greater part of the Greek world was once again ruled by monarchs. But, as far as social history was concerned, the change was not so great. For although the monarchs themselves owned a lot of the land – according to Macedonian tradition – their upper-class supporters owned most of the rest, and continued therefore to hold power. About their varied land tenures, for example, under the Ptolemies, we have a good deal of evidence.

We have spoken so far as if there were only two main classes in Greece, the rich and the poor. But something must also be said about those who stood between – though they never truly constituted a middle class, because they gravitated towards one extremity or the other.

Hesiod, in a way, could be described as middle-class, because he became so critical of the nobles. As already mentioned, the Marxist emergence of a separate 'merchant class' is a myth; commerce was *not* the master factor. But what about the hoplites, the bourgeois infantry armies of the cities that supplied their own weapons, and won the battles of Marathon (490) and Plataea (479) against the Persians? They were, for the most part, not noble, but they were not proletarian either: the sailors who fought in the Peloponnesian War were closer to that. The hoplites were mostly middling peasants with some resources of their own. Yet they never took political control; they were not homogeneous enough to do so. They aped the rich, and allowed themselves to be controlled by the politicians.

Aristotle, devoted to the Mean, felt that a stable middle element in Athenian society was essential:

46

Surely the ideal of the state is to consist as much as possible of persons that are equal and alike, and this similarity is most found in the middle classes; therefore the middle-class state will necessarily be best constituted in respect of those elements of which we say that the state is by nature composed. And also this class of citizens have the greatest security in states . . . It is clear therefore also that the political community administered by the middle class is the best . . . Hence it is the greatest good fortune if the men that have political power possess a moderate and sufficient substance . . .[13]

And this middle class existed as a disunited, conservative lot of people. They existed, that is to say, socially, though scarcely politically. Certainly, a strong middle-class bias occurs frequently in Greek moralising, which condemned both rich and poor alike. Yet, despite Aristotle, we can scarcely speak of a Greek middle class. There were basically two classes, not three.

One of the chief reasons why the rich, the governing class, need special attention is because it was *individuals* from that class who created Greek civilisation. This has become a slightly unfashionable view, thought to owe too much to the ancient writers who, out of their desire to illustrate a moral or a 'type', or tell a picturesque story, exalted individuals at the expense of their environments and of the general, underlying impersonal movements and tendencies of their age.

Moreover, this demotion of the individual has been accelerated by various developments in times nearer to our own. The first was a misleading observation by Friedrich Engels (Appendix 2) to the effect that, if Napoleon had not existed, someone else would have arisen, and would have done much the same. This view does not begin to do justice to the positive part that individuals play – which is, indeed, recognised by some Marxists. And the second reason why people have found it uncomfortable to talk about individuals is because there have been such horrible individual leaders in this twentieth century. Besides, somehow, it does not seem very 'democratic', or as people now say 'politically correct', to exalt individuals; which is no doubt why, in many schools and universities, they are accorded insufficient justice in relation to the ancient world, with the result that its history, including its social history, becomes blurred or distorted.

As for ancient Greece, 'leading persons in the city-states', I wrote in

The Classical Greeks, 'were by no means just labels and cogs, since decisive events and developments were put in motion by a minute proportion of the population, the tip of an invisible iceberg. True, whatever influences of environment and inheritance and borrowing their communities underwent affected them as much as their fellow-citizens, so that in that sense they are reflections of the society to which they belonged. But it was the few individuals themselves who delivered the creative responses which this society prompted, and it was they, individually, who understood and shaped and transformed the world around them according to their personal wills.'[14]

Indeed, despite the levelling tendencies (such as the city-state and democracy and sociability) which operated in the opposite direction, what has just been said was more true of the Greeks than of any other people before or since, because they were uniquely competitive individual persons, intensely concerned with gaining the approval of their peers. This emerges emphatically and repeatedly from their entire history and literature, from Homer onwards.

> The old horseman Peleus urged his son Achilles,
> 'Now always be the best, my boy, the bravest,
> And hold your head up high above the others.'[15]

As for Hesiod, he was an aggressive individualist, though he realised that men need the supportive paternalism of their social unit. In the time of Archilochus and Sappho, individuals flourished as they never had before. Archilochus was the first surviving personality of the western world – operating, again, within a collective context – and Sappho's expression is individualistic to the highest degree. Then the individualism proclaimed by the sophists fascinated the young, and the main theme of drama was the difficult choices a man or woman, on his or her own account, has to make.

One of the most typical principles of the Athenian constitution is the initiative of the individual – despite the widespread recognition of the dangers of licence. 'Even if you are superior to the ordinary run of men,' the orator Demosthenes advised a client, 'do not give up the effort to excel everyone else: let it be your ambition to be first in everything. To aim at this target brings more credit than respectable mediocrity.'[16] The thing that interests Plato most is what the latent personality of a human being is capable of becoming; and, like him, Aristotle sees the state as a rational scheme for realising man's nature. Menander goes further, abandoning Aristotle's social and political overtones in favour of wholehearted individual psychology. And in the Hellenistic world the impersonal vastness of the states meant that individualism had every reason to develop; as it did in the philosophy of Epicurus, the most thoroughgoing individualistic doctrine yet seen, in which society and the state had become secondary, and private life was more important than its public counterpart.

As G. M. Trevelyan observed in 1922, it is not safe, 'in pursuit of generalised truth, to overlook the personality and influence of great men, who are often in large measure the cause of some "tendency" which only they rendered "inevitable"'.[17]

Rome was always a hierarchic community. The praise of the current régime by Velleius Paterculus, an officer of Tiberius, could have been uttered at any time, as a hoped-for ideal:

> The humble man respects the great but does not fear him, the great has precedence over the lowly but does not despise him.[18]

For Rome was a society with strong legal distinctions of status, dependent on property-holding; and social congruence was expected. In early days, the relationship and difference between rich and poor, rulers and ruled, were highly distinct and formalised and snobbish. There were patricians, and there were plebeians. When the kings were ejected towards the end of the sixth century BC, it was the patricians who ejected them, and from then onwards it was the patricians who ruled. The richer plebeians constantly sought to equal and join them, and get their share of public land, and after a long time, despite the ruthless reactions that threats to privilege inevitably triggered off, they partially succeeded, replacing the patrician oligarchy by an oligarchy that was patricio-plebeian.

'In all ages,' remarked Ronald Syme, 'an oligarchy lies behind the façade . . . Roman history is the history of the governing class.'[19] That will, of course, not quite do for the social historian. But he will have to bear in mind that the famous Roman Law was biased in favour of the privileged classes, and that their words and persons carried an ill-defined but very real authority (auctoritas), based on the social estimation of his honour, and the prestige his position and career evoked in those around him. Nobilitas may not have been a legal term, but it carried immense social and honorific weight. Besides, the ruling groups controlled the means of production, and exploited the labour which extracted the surplus assets they needed in order to enforce their power. True, patricians and rich men were not necessarily the same persons, but for a long initial period, by and large, they were.

In the last resort, it was wealth that gave honour at Rome. Landed wealth was the only truly respectable asset – and the best thing of all was to have inherited it. Public office was unpaid, and demanded economic independence; a senator must be able to live on his unearned income. This would, naturally, come from his estates, because trade was not quite reputable, and too time-consuming (and risky) to leave room for the pursuits proper to a gentleman. So the senate was dominated by a few noble families – in the course of 300 years only 14 new men occupied 24 consulships. The greater the wealth, the greater the senator's rights and duties. And he asserted his political and social position through armies of dependants: the very root of Roman society was the institution of a relatively few rich patrons inextricably linked with their more numerous poor clients, who backed them in return for their patrons' support.

The ruling class also used religion as an aspect of government, to reinforce its superiority, as Cicero understood very clearly, when in the second book of his work *On Laws* he provided a long analysis of the religious regulations needed in his ideal state. The divine law (*ius divinum, pax deorum*) was a contractual, patriotic conception, which meant that it was designed to support the interests of the ruling class, who alone, the people were persuaded, could perform the state's religious rituals. The chief priest Quintus Mucius Scaevola even went so far as to say that it was expedient for the populace to be deceived in matters of religion.[20]

Most 'new men' assimilated themselves with the aristocracy, but Gaius Flaminius (tribune 232, consul 223 BC) did not. The greatest popular leader who had so far challenged noble rule, he put forward measures favouring the peasantry. Then the Second Punic War meant that some men of humble origin had to be given jobs: Gaius Terentius Varro (consul 216) was said by his enemies to be the son of a butcher – and they blamed him, not quite fairly, for the disaster at Cannae. But the Punic Wars, and influx of funds from eastern conquests, gave rich men their chance. They increased the size of their estates, and a law against their engaging in trade caused them to invest more and more in land. Cato the elder, himself a new man – one of the few people in this category who founded an enduring, powerful house – was constantly preoccupied with the abuse of wealth (although he was keen enough to make some for himself). But meanwhile the oligarchy, enriched, closed its ranks. Between 199 and 58 BC only about 50 new men managed to get the consulship, and even they were mostly descended from holders of other prominent offices, or were members of local Italian aristocracies.

But then matters began to break up. Although Sallust nostalgically over-idealises the 'balance' of the older order, his moralistic analysis is a valuable contribution to social as well as political history.

Party strife, the clashes of factions and all their attendant evils, had become a regular feature of Roman life, and this was the direct result of a long peace and the abundance of all the things which men prize most highly. Down to the time of the destruction of Carthage [146 BC], the senate and the Roman people shared the government of the state in a spirit of harmony and moderation. There was no rivalry between the citizens either for prestige or for power, for the ever-present fear of the enemy ensured that men's best qualities were kept in constant employment.

But once this fear had been lifted from men's minds, it was not long before pride and wantonness took its place, for those are the vices which prosperity always attracts. Thus the state of ease and security for which the Romans had yearned in time of crisis proved, as soon as they had won it, to be harsher and more bitter than adversity itself. The aristocrats now began to exploit their rank and the people their freedom, each for their own selfish ends, and each man proceeded to seize, plunder and rob on his own account. In this way the Romans became divided into two parties, and the state which had hitherto united their interests was torn asunder.

The aristocrats were the stronger of the parties because of their superior organisation: the people's strength could not make itself felt so effectively, because it was dispersed among a multitude. Political action both in war and in domestic affairs was determined by the will of a small clique, which also controlled the treasury, the provinces, the disposal of public offices, and the award of honours and triumphs. The generals seized the spoils of war and divided them with a few associates: the people's share consisted of grinding poverty and military service, while the parents or children of the soldiers might find themselves thrust out of house and home by some more powerful neighbour.

In this way greed, unbounded in its appetite, unchecked by any scruple, and now allied with power, spread throughout the life of the community, corrupting or devouring everything in its path: it respected nothing and held nothing sacred, until finally it worked its own destruction. As soon as members of the nobility were found who preferred true glory to power unjustly exercised, then the foundations of the state were shaken, and civil strife made itself felt like some convulsion of the earth.[21]

The upheaval was launched by the brothers Tiberius and Gaius Sempronius Gracchus: they challenged and attempted to reform the conservative system, and were both killed (133, 121 BC). Sallust observed:

> As events turned out, the nobles abused their victory so as to indulge their desire for revenge. They resorted to the sword or exile to remove many of their opponents from their path, and for the future they inspired a dread of their vindictiveness rather than any respect for their power.

But although the two brothers met violent deaths, they had dented the system, and the 'new man' Gaius Marius (c.157–86 BC) dented it further, by encouraging the soldiers – who were not noble, but were needed, as the hoplites had been in the Greek city-states (though, in order to appease the nobility, too, he appealed to its military origins).

This was also the time when the knights (*equites*) first began to become conspicuous. But it is wrong to consider them a 'middle class', between the landowners and the poor. They were mostly landowners of high birth and wealth, and there was no 'class struggle' between them and the senators, although there were quarrels about which should serve on the juries, and in what proportions; and one section of the knights (for they were considerably diversified) specialised in finance (the *publicani*). There was also much talk about *optimates* ('best people') and *populares*, already adumbrated in Sallust's reference to 'two parties'. But they were not political parties – they were much too fragmented for that, and concerned with individual and family programmes – and once again no 'class struggle' was involved. True, the *populares* appealed deliberately to the lower orders, by showing

52

willingness to pass their measures directly through the Assembly, without consulting the senate first. But the dominant figures among the *populares* were always senators themselves, though at odds with the traditional oligarchic leaders.

A good many knights got into the senate in the first century BC, so that – although, as we saw, the two classes had never been far removed from one another – there was a measure of social mobility. The aristocracy needed new blood, because its own birthrate was low, and some families had come to an end, while others had flagged; and objections to the new entries were muted by the wealth and good provincial families of most of the entrants – even if there were, of course, complaints that many of them came from very low-class origins, and those at the very top, by way of reaction, tried to redefine *nobilitas* more exclusively, limiting it to families which had gained a consulship in the past.

But what counted was money. In the last century BC, great riches could be quickly amassed; as usual, it went into landowning, which caused a diminution of the landowners' cash flow that could only be remedied by acquiring even greater tracts of land. In this free-for-all situation, hereditary alliances between one family and another, if they had ever amounted to much, were discarded in favour of aggressive individual ambitions; and it was also, nowadays, possible to rise to influence through oratory, as Cicero did, 'new man' though he was (and quite often reminded of the fact). However, the main point was that pedigrees were no longer necessary to acquire fortunes – or political power.

Yet none of this was particularly democratic, and snobbery was still intense. True, there were means of penetrating upwards into the governing class. But, changed though it was, its separation from the rest of the populace remained absolute. Cicero himself, though one of those who had got in, was particularly explicit about the overriding importance of property-rights: indeed the protection of private property, he felt, was the prime function of a state. Certainly, he was well aware of the dangers of unbridled individualism, and deplored its excesses. But his solution (which did not work) was to harness and assimilate it to the interests of the state.

After disruption had reached its peak in the Second Triumvirate, amid the gloomy comments of Sallust, the whole social situation (like everything else) was taken in hand by Augustus (31 BC–AD 14). One of his solutions, whatever the old *nobiles* might think of it (and he reckoned they would not object, because they liked the Pax Augusta), was to let a lot of 'new men' into the senate – men, frequently, whom he needed to reward for having backed his cause. (Agrippa was a conspicuous example of a 'new man' whom, although unpopular, he regarded as indispensable.) Having done that, however, he bolstered the senate up, paid tribute to heredity, ancestry and pedigree, and recognised and supported the claims of the senatorial, governing class to rule the empire. To rule it, that is to say, under himself. For his position as emperor completely transformed the traditional relations of Roman society. Now, he himself was patron of every citizen; every citizen was his client. Yet, under him, it must be repeated, the old conservative dichotomy of ruler and ruled, rich and poor, was fully maintained, for Augustus saw that the upper class could be kept content by enhancing its self-respect despite its loss of power. Although the dividing line between classes had been shifted, it firmly remained in existence, even more sharply defined than before. To each class was assigned its own functions, and Augustan society exhibited a highly developed system of formal stratification by orders and estates. It was a very status-conscious community.

There was much talk of *libertas*, freedom, but the *libertas* of the Roman aristocrats, as now defined, meant the preeminence of their own class (under the emperor) – even if the senate itself now had many more functions than powers – and the perpetuation of their privileges, involving the massive exploitation of others who did not enjoy them. The historians like to tell of frictions between emperors and senate, but they were trivial, since basically the emperor guaranteed the power of the upper class. The checks and balances of the régime worked wholeheartedly in its favour. And what really counted was money, as one could see by looking at some of the people who did well: 'a man is what he is worth'. Wealth became increasingly concentrated in fewer, bigger holdings – and this applied in other parts of the empire, too, as well as Italy; in Asia Minor, for example, the leading families became richer than ever. Moreover, Augustus had fully learnt the lesson handed down from earlier epochs of Roman history, that religion could serve governmental control. Countless measures were taken to revive religion and its shrines, which the ruling class duly served.

Yet this ruling class was far from static in composition. Reference has been made to Augustus's infusion of 'new men', and under subsequent emperors this form of social mobility continued. The élites, first of Italy, and then of the provinces as well, found themselves becoming Roman senators. Public careers in the service of the régime, and military service in particular, constituted powerful means of admission first to the knighthood (the *ordo equestris*, on which Augustus's successors increasingly relied) and then to the senate, though it might take two or three generations of work to achieve the breakthrough: which was facilitated by the continued decay or extinction of some of the most ancient houses. Certainly, Augustus, as we saw, encountered opposition – when he promoted Agrippa – and so did Tiberius when he elevated another 'new man' (by Roman standards), Sejanus: but that opposition could be ignored or overruled. Tacitus has preserved, or recast, a remarkable speech made by Claudius (41–54) in favour of admitting Gauls to the senate. Then came an emperor, Otho (69), whose nobility was quite recent: he came of a noble Etruscan house, it was true (like Augustus's adviser Maecenas; and Tiberius's minister Sejanus was also Etruscan), but his father had been made a patrician by Claudius. As for Vespasian (69–79), he was of Italian municipal origin, which encouraged him to promote people like his own fairly humble self. Pliny, Tacitus and Agricola were all senators of Italian or provincial origin (which made them all the more hostile to those who had risen from lower still).

The rich senators of the imperial epoch strayed somewhat beyond the traditionally respectable field of landowning, into other profitable activities. True, the prospects of alternative investment were limited, and an epitaph remarks that 'whoever hopes he may grow rich by trade will be fooled in his hopes', but, if that proved not to be the case, and if he made enough to retire to a country estate, a large-scale merchant need not fear about his reputation. Besides, there was also money-lending to be considered, as writers remind us, and that was less risky. And in the second century AD there were new fortunes to be made, by business men and imperial agents (procurators).

Senators tended to become somewhat less important than in earlier days, as foreign threats from the time of Marcus Aurelius onwards called for men of ability from outside their ranks; and the third century, in consequence, was the heyday of the knights, who became a second nobility and produced an even greater number of procurators than before. Moreover, they even produced an emperor (Macrinus, 217–218). Under a later emperor, Maximinus I (235–238), foreign, violent and disliked, it was said that one could meet a poor man who had been rich the day before. That is to say, in those troubled times, there was social mobility downwards as well as upwards.

But then subsequently, in the later empire, the senators made a conspicuous recovery. It was not that the senate regained any of its independence; indeed it was little more than a rubber stamp. But senators possessed both wealth and prestige, and, under the emperor's protection, unlimited economic and political power were in the hands of the property class. Constantine I the Great (306–337) engaged aristocrats in high positions. And later, after the division of the empire between east and west (364), we hear a lot more about their immense status, especially in the west where they owned enormous lands (unlike the east, where they were often craftsmen). Symmachus declared that the aristocracy was 'the better part of the human race', and 'the flower of the whole world'.[22] Synesius complained that every wealthy home was crammed with Gothic or Scythian slaves.[23] Ammianus Marcellinus attacked the nobles for their arrogance:

> When such people, each attended by a train of some fifty, enter the public baths, they shout in a peremptory voice: 'What has become of our girls?' If they hear of the sudden appearance of some obscure strumpet, some old street-walker who has earned her living by selling herself to the townsfolk, they vie in courting and caressing the newcomer, and praise her in outrageously flattering terms . . .
>
> If one tries to greet these people with an embrace they turn their head to one side like a bad-tempered bull, though that is the natural place for a kiss, and offer their knee or their hand instead, as if that should be enough to make anyone happy for life . . . Though they are so solemn and think themselves so cultured, the news that someone has announced the arrival of horses or drivers, no matter from where, causes them to pester him with knowing questions, and to show him much respect . . .
>
> Their houses are the resort of idle gossips, who greet every word uttered by the great man with various expressions of hypocritical applause . . . Some of them hate learning like poison, but read Juvenal and Marius Maximus with avidity. These are the only volumes that they turn over in their idle moments, but why this should be so is not for a man like me to say. Considering their claims to distinction and long descent, they ought to read a variety of books.[24]

And Christian writers, too, resented the various abuses the members of this governing class inflicted.

Unimpressed by their emperors at Mediolanum and Ravenna, they slipped away to their estates, which were self-sufficient economic units. The writings of Sidonius Apollinaris show what it was like to lead this sort of life in Gaul. When the poor were ground down by imperial taxation and conscription, the rich let them into their estates as tenants, provided that they worked: until one day the great landowners came to an understanding with the imperial government, thus depriving these migrants of escape.

The lesser aristocracy, however, or those just below the aristocracy, had a less fortunate destiny. These were the local town-councillors, or *curiales*. Theoretically, these carefully chosen members of the local councils were rather important, more than a middle class and with potentialities of social mobility that gave them a good chance of even becoming senators. Their eminence, indeed, was honoured by Salvian's description of them as 'local tyrants'.[25] But their functions were ominously two-faced. For not only did they, prestigiously, run their own local communities, but it was also their more painful duty to collect the imperial revenues – indeed, by the time of Constantine, it was almost the only duty that remained to them. And the increasing difficulty of doing this caused them to be seriously oppressed by the imperial government, to the point of destruction and collapse, unless they had resources of their own to protect them. They tried to take refuge with the army or the clergy, but Constantine I the Great issued enactments attempting to stop such evasions:

> Since some men desert the municipal councils and flee for refuge to the protection of the military service, we command that all persons who are found to be not yet under the authority of the chief centurion shall be discharged from the military service and shall be returned to the municipal council.

> An enactment was issued which directs that henceforth no decurion or descendant of a decurion, or even any person provided with adequate resources and suitable for undertaking compulsory public services, shall take refuge in the name and service of the clergy.[26]

So the decurions or *curiales* form a kind of footnote to the history of the

Greek and Roman governing class. They started by being among its members, but failed to hold their place. They became detached, that is to say, from the rich and powerful, who, for their part, continued to maintain their position.

4

The Poor

This, above all, is the chapter that makes the difference between a social history and a history. For the poor do not figure very much in most histories, except to illustrate a point relating to the policy-makers, who were not poor themselves. Yet voiceless toilers formed the huge majority of the population of the ancient world, very much as they still do today (except in the west). They did not speak up much on their own account, any more than they figure in the histories written by others, so that it is the duty of the social historian to try and find out something about this huge number of inarticulate people. Our information about them is very deficient.

In early Greece, and indeed at most times in Greek history, the rich were not extremely rich, but the contrast between them and the poor – which was the contrast, people felt, between those who could live without working and those who could not – was sufficiently stark for the two categories to be justifiably polarised as the two main elements in society. In spite of the comforting bulwark of Athenian or other citizenship, to be poor, as Theognis observed, was a disaster.

> Poverty, Cyrnus, breaks a gallant man
> More than white hairs or shivering fevers can.
> To flee it, Cyrnus, in the deep sea drown,
> Or from a towering precipice leap down.
> Broken by poverty, a man's denied
> All power of speech and act: his tongue is tied.[1]

True, a law at Athens forbade reproaches for poverty and humble birth, but the poor were sneered at all the same, with an openness that would be avoided today. Thus it was a stock form of abuse to mock

59

people's low origins. Comic playwrights, as we saw in the last chapter, mocked the demagogues because they were ill-born (which they were not). They also mocked Isocrates because his father was an oboe-maker (he was a prosperous knight). They mocked the orator Aeschines, who was said to have boasted of wealth he did not possess.

For the Greeks chose to believe that the poor man was tempted to robbery and fraud, and Aristotle called poverty the parent of revolution and crime. It is a 'grievous and resistless ill', declares Alcaeus.[2] Money brings a man friends and positions, confirmed the dramatists, but nobody wants a poor friend. The vast majority of Greek citizens were comparatively poor, and many of them very poor indeed. 'Land alone', observed Amphis, 'knows how to cover up poverty.'[3] Ownership of property, mainly land, was the chief dividing line, and obviously a large number of those who did not possess it felt antagonistic to those who did.

This polarisation conflicts sharply with the spirit and system of community get-together and mutual service represented by the *polis*. But the *polis* did not iron the contrast out, or iron out the inequalities and injustices that resulted from it. To what extent, then, can it be said that there was a 'class struggle' in the ancient world? Certainly, there were periodical outbursts of faction fighting (*stasis*) within the Greek city-states, and these meant that the social misery of poverty had spread into the political field, for the 'have-nots' were adult male citizens whipped up against the 'haves' – led, not by their own class, but by ambitious 'haves' – and mobilised in attempts to have more 'democratic' instead of oligarchic governments. Yet, despite Marxist arguments to the contrary (Appendix 2), to describe the history of the Greek (or Roman) world as a continual class-struggle is misguided, since *stasis*, for all its severity, only occurred from time to time, and the poor were not sufficiently united or organised to produce any more regular or continuous phenomenon.

As early as the society depicted by Homer, although there is no 'class struggle' rhetoric, a deep social cleavage is apparent. Beggars and suppliants are protected by Zeus, but the poor are further away from the gods than the rich, because they cannot provide gifts and sacrifices. We saw, in the last chapter, how sharply Odysseus, in the *Iliad*, dealt with Thersites, the man of inferior standing who tried to challenge the recognised leaders; he is the first vicious class caricature.

Here was the ugliest man who ever came to Troy.
Bandy-legged he was, with one foot clubbed,
Both shoulders humped together, curving over
His caved-in chest, and bobbing above them
His skull warped to a point,
Sprouting clumps of scraggly, woolly hair.[4]

That is the sort of manner in which the Homeric poems define the poor man. He 'sits in silence' at meetings. When Odysseus, in the *Odyssey*, meets the ghost of Achilles in the other world, the best way in which Achilles can express the horror of being dead is to say that it is even worse than being a *thes*, a poor man. Odysseus has urged him not to be so upset because he is dead, but Achilles replies:

O shining Odysseus, never try to console me for dying.
I would rather follow the plough as thrall to another
Man, one with no land allotted him and not much to live on,
Than be a king over all the perished dead.[5]

That farm-hand or *thes*, the lowest creature on earth of whom Achilles can think, was not a slave, but a 'free' man who has to work for someone else, who has contracted away his control over his own labour, that is to say, so that his true freedom is lost – and he is less secure than a slave. Hesiod, neither rich nor really poor (though his maxims are those of someone badly off), reminds us slightly of Thersites; he sees how precarious the life of a man without resources can be, if he has no backing.

Archilochus, however, saw that it was a world of change and opportunity, in which beggars could aspire to become monarchs; and later on the fifth-century wars gave poor Greeks a new chance, because it was realised that as rowers they had won the battle of Salamis, and that as rowers, again, they were indispensable in the Peloponnesian War. In politics, too, they sat in the democratic Assembly, though opinions differ whether they did more good than harm. Certainly, some of their decisions, prompted by persuasive speakers, caused the Peloponnesian War to be lost – the Syracusan expedition (415–413), for example, and the executions of the generals after the battle of Arginusae (406), were disastrous. It was for such reasons, among others, that philosophers such as Plato and Aristotle did not believe in democracy. Later, in Hellenistic times, the poor had little say, and so did not contribute to mistaken policies.

But now we have got onto politics, which, although in practice inextricable from other matters, is beyond the bounds of what truly constitutes social history. What we must do, then, is to consider the poor, instead, as an element in society. Primarily, in the Greek world, they were an agricultural phenomenon. For that world was overwhelmingly agricultural. This is a point which it is all too easy to forget, when *polis* is mistranslated 'city-state'. The *polis* was not only the town, but the country around it, in which the vast bulk of the population worked, in hamlets, villages and farms. As at the present time – taking the world as a whole – so in the Greco-Roman past, the vast majority of the population were peasants.

Already in the epoch of Homer agriculture was the basis of civilisation, and centuries later Cicero emphatically agreed that this was still the case. In the meantime, Xenophon had expressed the view that agriculture was the only work suitable for an Athenian citizen – because it promoted the qualities needed by the state. The dramatist Amphis, who, as we have seen, declared that land alone knew how to cover up poverty, added that 'agricultural land is the father of life to man', and it is on land that ancient discussions of property ownership centre. The importance of the 'peasant' citizen was recognised, and he was variously honoured or mocked.

This predominance of agriculture is derived from the nature of the Mediterranean lands. It is upon agriculture that those who own these lands necessarily depended, and, except for a switch from pasturage to arable farming in 750–650 BC, this picture was scarcely modified throughout ancient history. At first, after that switch, there was a large growth in food production, but thereafter productivity was relatively small. Nor did land ownership very often change hands. Ten people were needed on a property to enable one person to live away from it; but, in general, the surpluses needed and extracted were fairly small. Indeed, Athens would have benefited greatly if they had been larger, because it would not have had to import so much grain. But this benefit never arrived, partly because technology remained backward. There was no control over disease – and Attica had only half the rainfall of the western coast of Greece (which was itself not very fertile) and lay on the margin of cereal cultivation.

The Greeks ploughed and sowed in autumn, from October onwards, harvested their wheat and barley in May, and finally winnowed the grain in July. And then there was the olive, which liked the coastal semi-arid region. It was a subsistence crop; farmers were interested simply in conserving olive trees as a source of food. The vine was a cash crop. On the whole, people produced less for the market than for their own household.

Mediterranean agriculture, then, depended, as always, on seasonal labour, generally hired, and mainly free. Those who worked on the land, the vast majority of the population, did not earn very much, and were always poor, and had little to eat. Their lives were precarious. 'Poverty', as Herodotus remarked, 'is always the foster-sister of Greece.'[6] 'Freedom' did not help to guarantee a secure food supply. True, labourers on the land had a better chance to find food than a townsman, despite their inadequate exploitation of the soil, but all the same their task of sheer physical survival was daunting. The mentality of people faced with this ever-present subsistence hazard does not change greatly throughout the ages.

The *Odyssey* is well aware of the evil of hunger – which later became the commonest cause of all rioting. For, above all, there were shattering droughts and famines. They were far more frequent, both in Greece and in Rome, than historians have allowed for. Or, if 'famine' is too severe a word, at least subsistence crises, of dangerous magnitude, were endemic, and harvest failures and consequent total catastrophes were never far away: there is palaeopathological evidence of malnutrition and deficient diet. Hesiod was familiar enough with food emergencies, and knew that starvation was always close at hand, and could happen to anyone, and could only be avoided by unremitting toil.

The great dividing line between the two main social elements, rich and poor, was rarely crossed. The nearest to crossing it were the city states' infantrymen or hoplites, because although, as we saw in the last chapter, most of them came from the propertied section of the community, some, and perhaps a good many, did not, and were men who had to work for their living. So, despite their power in Councils and Assemblies, and their victories at Marathon (490) and Plataea (479), they were economically divided, and could not form a united pressure group, for or against the ruling class – which remained in charge, politically and socially. To become a hoplite, however, was at least one way of avoiding destitution. Another was to join one of the overseas colonies, which gave a living to many who would have otherwise starved – usually, in the first place, an agricultural rather than a commercial living, for that was the sort of work they were used to: and it could even make them into landowners in the colonial territories where they settled.

By the sixth century BC there seemed to be a hopeless deadlock, a widening gap between haves and have-nots, a gap all the wider because of the rising population and constant fragmentation of the already diminutive plots of fertile, alluvial land, in the absence of primogenital inheritance. At Athens, at the beginning of the next century (594–593 or 592–591), Solon tried to grapple with the problem. A sharp operator, but believing, apparently, that good social order is social justice, he modified his natural pessimism by an ability to see redemption in moderate policies. And so revolutionary pleas to redistribute the land among the poor met with no response from him. Yet he decisively checked the rich landowners' abuse of the peasants, by rescuing them from debt bondage (of which more will be said in the next chapter) and acting against the export of grain, by which large farmers had ruined the poor by driving up the price of grain at home. As was seen earlier, Solon chose to classify himself among the poor – but with his tongue in his cheek: for what he was aiming at, rather, was a middle-of-the-path balance. His solution helped his own class just below the high nobility, but it helped the poor as well, for Solon was the first Athenian to acknowledge that the humble worker, the *thes* – too impoverished to provide his own armour and arms – had any claim to be a full citizen, and to possess public rights. And so, although the underprivileged were not raised to power, a step was taken towards the erasure of aristocratic monopoly.

Then the Athenian tyrant Pisistratus (died 527) went a step further, because he needed the small farmers and the urban poor, on whom, indeed, dictators such as himself based their support; so although he kept them out of politics, he helped them, in order to eliminate agrarian discontent. And then, in *c*.508/7, Cleisthenes brought the poor truly into the picture, in the political field by creating the essentials of the most democratic form of government yet devised, and, socially, by establishing equal justice for all.

Then the Persian Wars churned up Greek society thoroughly, and after they were over the population of Attica increased at a prodigious rate; it may even have doubled between 480 and 431. This was the time when the famous democracy adumbrated earlier by Solon and Cleisthenes came into its own. Once again, it was political in substance, but it possessed marked social connotations as well. More than half the male population of Athens could read and write; and the people controlled the lawcourts. This was one of the very few ancient attempts at truly equalising the rich and the poor. Yet the conservative 'Old Oligarch' (Pseudo-Xenophon) condemned this democracy, because it favoured the interests of the poorer (inferior) sections of the community too much. Or rather, to be exact, he deplored it, but considered it inevitable because the poor manned the ships:

> About the political system of the Athenians, that they actually chose such a system – I don't congratulate them for it. For in so choosing they have chosen that people of no account do better than people of merit. I certainly don't congratulate them for that . . .
>
> [But] first I'll say this – it's fair enough that the poor and the general populace amount to more there than the well-born and rich, for this reason: because the general populace operates the ships and bestows power on the city . . . I forgive the populace their democracy! For it is pardonable for any man to help himself.[7]

Nevertheless the *demos*, as far as we can see, never attacked the fortunes or honours of the wealthy, and although it claimed equality, continued to leave the exercise of power to the few – whose competence and knowledge could gain them a hearing.

The Greeks, on the whole, did not believe that everyone has an inalienable right to life, liberty and happiness. But the Athenians went a long way in that direction. And if the poor still felt frustrated and left out, they had splendid religious festivals and Games to take their minds off their grievances. Indeed, the religion that lay behind these entertainments, like the later religion of the Romans, could be seen as a conscious and purposive lie, a safety-valve, a way of keeping them quiet and distracting them from social discontents.

But keeping this vastly increased population fed was a problem. As we saw, the population of Greece, and particularly Athens, had gone up immensely, and although the peasants played a huge part in keeping things going, the importation of grain on a large scale was essential. The whole of Athenian history could be rewritten round the grain-route from the Black Sea. And it was the poorer Athenians who benefited most from their empire, as settlers, and recipients of larger salaries. Although the rich benefited from the empire as well, the traditional Greek view that the common people were its main driving force and beneficiaries is correct.[8] Not that life was all that easy for them, all the same, since they had to cope with indirect taxation, military conscription, compulsory services and the extraordinary, unidentifiable epidemic that struck Athens at the outset of the Peloponnesian War, resulting from cramped and insanitary conditions among the countrymen who had overcrowded the city in order to escape successive Spartan invasions.

In general, as Thucydides observed, the Peloponnesian War everywhere exacerbated the antagonisms between the small rich minority and the masses of the poor.[9] And yet, to repeat the words of the Old Oligarch, the fact that they rowed in the fleet gave the poor the advantage. And quite right too, he concluded, conservative though he was, because the state had to depend on them, and so a levelling-down was essential. The poor thought they would make money out of the Sicilian expedition (415–413), but they proved wrong: and as vociferous members of the Assembly they made other mistakes too, as we have seen. At any rate, by the end of the war polarisation had not gone away. There was an upper- and middle-class Athenian army and a proletarian navy, and the contrast between rich and poor was starker than ever before. And the contrast had spread to other parts of the Greek world, because in order to win the war both sides exploited class tensions in many other cities as effectively as they could.

Whether the increased articulacy and volubility of the poor meant that they had unduly got above themselves – with lessons for future democracies – can still be argued. Certainly, the inequality of humankind remained a fundamental premise, never seriously challenged, except possibly by some democratic Athenian theorists. Attic drama shows some pity for the poor, but largely in order to put the presumptuous rich in their place. Plato, Isocrates and Aristotle deplore what they see as the democratic tyranny of the poor over the rich. Plato regards the idea of universally equal mental ability as absurd, and certainly does not believe that the uneducated poor come up to this standard. And to him, as to Aristotle, the distribution of property among persons of unequal merit should quite rightly be unequal, and there is nothing unjust about that.

Invention and technical progress continued to suffer from this point of view, because, if you could get a mass of poor men to do the job, why invent any labour-saving devices? So the technological level of the Greek world remained lower than it need have been. Yet social mobility was by no means non-existent. Owing to the Greek love of art, some of the principal beneficiaries in this respect were sculptors, painters, architects, potters, and metalworkers, who did well for themselves and, as producers of luxury goods for the rich, sometimes lived (even if on sufferance) around the fringes of polite society (emulating the legendary Daedalus). On the whole, they were considered inferior to producers of 'natural' wealth (agriculture), but superior to traders. Their work accepted current social values, and shows little or no trace of rebellion.

The agricultural labour force suffered worst and was most resentful where the aristocrats rode highest, as in Sparta. The revolt led by Cinadon in 397 BC was evidently very serious indeed, although we only hear little about it because of a literary tradition which insisted, inaccurately, that Sparta remained free of *stasis*.[10] But it appears that *all* the lower social categories joined Cinadon against the Peers, although nothing came of their uprising, because they were suppressed. In Athens, it seems likely that during the fourth century BC the rich were living more comfortably, and the poor more miserably, than before. Indeed, almost everywhere in Greece the gulf between rich and poor was widening. There were, as always, acts of individual generosity, it is true, but they were generally extended to the community, and not to the poor, who aroused little pity or sympathy. So there emerged egalitarian demands, and attempts at the redistribution of land and cancellation of debts, and outbreaks of *stasis*.

'The real difference between democracy and oligarchy is poverty and wealth,' observed Aristotle. 'Oligarchy is when the control of the government is in the hands of those that own the properties: democracy is when, on the contrary, it is in the hands of those that do not possess much property, but are poor.'[11]

Aristotle was simplifying, but not necessarily, as some say, oversimplifying, the basic Greek social and political problem, by his declaration that this gulf was fundamental to the history of the city-state, and the fundamental cause of its tensions. No wonder that Karl Marx was so interested in what Aristotle said, although he got some of it wrong (Appendix 2). Aristotle also commented that, in a democracy, the poor would despoil the rich as much as they could. And – although classical Athens was a society of peasant farmers – he ranked agricultural workers below leisured gentlemen citizens, sharing the widespread Greek notion that 'the condition of the free man is that he does not live for the benefit (or profit) of another'.[12] But his contemporary Philip II of Macedonia was one of the many leaders to employ numerous mercenary soldiers, who enrolled in his army to escape social and economic misery (the first extensive use of hired labour, said Marx). But they had to be watched, in case they got out of hand. And indeed in more general terms Philip – who had received a good deal of support from fifth columns in the cities – was aware of the danger from the poor, and arranged that his Hellenic League should brand and ban proposals for the redistribution of land and cancellation of debts as seditious.

'Redistribution of land and cancellation of debts', demands for a clean slate, were Utopian slogans, but they were always being heard. Aeneas Tacticus of Stymphalus, in the fourth century BC, had thought one ought to meet such demands halfway, although states did not generally do this:

> One must deal with those in the *polis* who wish to reverse the established order . . . It is very important to achieve harmony among the mass of the citizens for the time being, winning them over by a variety of means and relieving debtors by a reduction or abolition of interest, in particularly dangerous situations even remitting part of the capital – all of it, even, if necessary – since men of this kind who are waiting their opportunity are very dangerous; those who lack the necessities of life are to be well provided for.[13]

During the Hellenistic times that followed, when internal rebellions occurred, as frequently happened, it is often unclear if, and to what extent, a social protest was involved. Certainly, such uprisings were political, against the Hellenistic governments which, between them, had organised the total destruction and abolition of Greek democracy. Yet these movements did contain a social element as well. For the situation of the Hellenistic poor was bad. Mass starvation was an ever-present threat, and every Hellenistic state, or many of them, stood in fear of revolution: understandably, since we know of no fewer than sixty such uprisings, and there must have been others.

One way of dealing with this problem was for the leader of a state to ingratiate himself with its poor. That, for example, is what Agathocles, tyrant of Syracuse (316–289), did:

> There were many poor and indebted men who welcomed the change of régime. For Agathocles had promised in the assembly to carry out

68

a cancellation of debts and to distribute the poor . . . Undergoing a complete change, he showed himself considerate to the common people, conferring benefits on many, making encouraging promises to not a few; and by conversing in a friendly fashion with everyone he earned great favour.[14]

And the 'reforming' kings of Sparta, Agis IV, Cleomenes II and Nabis, likewise appealed to the lower classes, even if mainly in the interests of their own military, nationalistic aims.

From c.200 BC onwards the general impoverishment got worse. Several Greek cities were so greatly alarmed that in order to appease discontent they took the first steps towards municipal socialism, in regard to the grain supply, and medicine, and education. But the instability persisted, and polarisation became sharpened, owing to fluctuating prices, and shortages of food and work. Sometimes this friction took the form of conflicts between town and country – for example in Syria, Pergamum and Egypt. In Egypt, too, harsh measures were taken against convicted criminals, who were condemned to work in the Nubian mines:

Those who have been condemned – they form a great multitude and are all bound in chains – labour ceaselessly by day and throughout the whole night, without any respite, and they are carefully cut off from any chance of escape. They are watched over by guards of barbarian soldiers, who speak different languages, which makes it impossible for anyone to corrupt any of the guards by conversation or friendly contact.[15]

This terror was intended to keep the lower classes in order. For, throughout the Hellenistic world, the gulf between the classes, and the consequent mutual hostility, were immense. But the masses did not stand any chance of success, unless they received unifying leadership from some members of the governing class. But this they did not receive, or did not receive it sufficiently, and the established order prevailed. When the Romans intervened, the Greek populace very often identified itself with the struggle against them. But in vain, and the Romans won, and the poor remained poor.

Something has already been said, in the last chapter, about the struggle between the patricians and plebeians in early Rome. The plebeians involved in those struggles were the richer plebeians, who led the others. Those others were often very poor. Like Greece, it was an agricultural society, and the vast majority of the population were agricultural workers – whose only desire was for a fair share of public land. They had to work extremely hard to make enough to live on, existing at or near the lowest subsistence level, and were at the mercy of droughts and bad harvests and epidemics and consequent famines, causing acute malnutrition. And they had another trouble too. Under the Twelve Tables, debtors were liable to be sold into slavery by their creditors. So the status of the poor was extremely precarious. Debt bondage, it is true – which can be defined as a form of serfdom (Chapter 5) – was officially abolished in 326 or 321 BC. This apparent leniency was due to the régime's urgent need for soldiers, which thus proved the ordinary worker's protection. Yet the abolition did not wholly relieve the plight of the debtors, since this was still destined to become a major issue as late as the first century BC.

The stratification of Roman society was tight and stiff and minute. In a world obsessed with status and snobbery, and with their symbols and ethics and laws, everyone knew his place, and it was an offence (*contumacia*) not to show deference to those who were above you. In other words, there was class exploitation – but it met with little resistance (the plebeian protesters being, as has been said, men of some wealth) because, as in Greece only even more so, there was a lack of conscious, homogeneous, political organisation capable of fighting against the hierarchical system. Not that we should know much about it, if there had been, since Roman literature has an upper-class bias, but evidently this was the case.

Basically, despite nuances, there were, as in Greece, two classes, rich and poor. Some of the poor occasionally rioted (and resorted to crime), scenting chicanery behind serious food breakdowns, but one reason why they did not show more dangerous signs of discontent was the all-pervasive, double-edged Roman institution of *clientela*. The rich patron, as we saw, had his poor clients, who depended on him as he depended on them, and they were carefully organised and orchestrated to meet his needs. Another reason, as has likewise been mentioned, is that the poor got enrolled in the army, in which, even if life was dangerous, there was at least enough food to eat: although the conscription of the poor was a hardship (in the Second Punic War it eliminated many smallholders altogether), and their mobilisation meant that their plot of land back home got neglected. Through the army, and by other means, there was some upward social mobility, but not a great deal. And as for the influx of wealth through conquests abroad, it only exaggerated the differences between rich and poor.

The urban poor of Rome fared as miserably as the agricultural poor, or worse. They probably found it harder still to get enough to eat, since variations in quantities and prices of grain left them in constant danger of famine; and they lived in squalor. No wonder that successive governments were worried about what these people might do (and the worry persisted into imperial times). Yet although, as Sallust remarks, some of the impoverished population felt hostile to their government, their uprisings against it were never successful: they were never sufficiently unified to constitute a serious threat. The state did little enough for them, and gave them no political or even municipal rights. But it allowed them their safety-valves, or consolations. These included the *collegia*, trade guilds and district associations that provided an opportunity for social contacts. And there were also religious brotherhoods: for another comfort permitted to the poor was religion. It had to be watched, however. The ecstatic revivalist Bacchic cult was suppressed in 186 BC, because it was so popular among the lower classes (including slaves) – as well as women (Chapter 2), and seemed to have subversive overtones.

But it was in the countryside that the most serious difficulties were encountered. Devastations and confiscations in the Second Punic War eliminated many smallholders, and conscription erased others. Thereafter, things got worse. Expropriations continued, ex-soldiers fared badly, the lot of the peasants worsened further owing to the importation of cheap grain, and there was a continual drift from the land, partly to seek urban life – though this, as we have seen, would scarcely have benefited them, and in any case relations were unfriendly, because the city looked on the country merely as a provider of agricultural surplus – and partly to emigrate. Rapacious proprietors installing slave-staffed villas took over the emigrants' land, and indeed helped to get them out. The proportion of free Italian peasants to the total population declined by twenty or twenty-five per cent between 202 and 27 BC, from over four million to about three.

The reforming tribune Tiberius Gracchus (133) was well aware of this depopulation. As Plutarch records:

71

Tiberius's brother Gaius wrote in a political pamphlet that while Tiberius was travelling through Etruria on his way to Numantia, he saw for himself how the country had been deserted by its native inhabitants, and how those who tilled the soil or tended the flocks were barbarian slaves introduced from abroad; and that it was this experience which inspired the policy that later brought so many misfortunes upon the two brothers.

But it was above all the people themselves who did most to arouse Tiberius's energy and ambitions by inscribing slogans and appeals on porticoes, monuments and the walls of houses, calling upon him to recover the public land for the poor.[16]

Moreover, it has also been suggested that Tiberius Gracchus was motivated, in part, by the disastrous effect of this manpower shortage upon military recruitment.

Various alternative schemes, from his time onward, did something to retard the process, but their effects were only temporary. And the political convulsions of the last century BC did further damage, provoking, for example, crises in food distribution. True, some smallholders survived, since many poor men tilled their own fields with their own families; and the rich landowners sometimes needed free hired labour, finding it better than the labour of slaves. Yet the bulk of the *plebs rustica* were very badly off – and, despite flights from the land, they still formed, overwhelmingly, the bulk of the population. Nor were these troubles limited to Italy, since in Asia Minor landless rural poor flocked to the standard of Aristonicus, who led a revolt after the kingdom of Pergamum had been bequeathed to Rome (133).

Mention has been made of Tiberius Gracchus, and of his awareness of the bad effects that this situation must have upon military recruitment. But that was by no means necessarily his only motive. For there is good reason, also, to suppose that he was genuinely upset by the peasants' impoverishment – about which he spoke with deep emotion. At any rate, the Gracchi proposed a distribution of public land, which infuriated the landowners who were in occupation of much of it. In consequence, whatever the brothers' original intentions, it was inevitable that they should come to be regarded as the champions of the poor against the rich, of the ordinary man against the senate:

The wealthy classes and the landowners were bitterly opposed to these proceedings [by Tiberius Gracchus]. They hated the law out of sheer greed, and its originator out of personal resentment and party prejudice, and they did their utmost to turn the people against the reform by alleging that Tiberius's object in introducing redistribution of land was really to undermine the foundations of the state and stir up a general revolution. However, these tactics achieved nothing.[17]

And then, after the murder of Tiberius Gracchus:

All the most distinguished men in Rome without exception joined forces to oppose [his brother Gaius], but such an immense multitude poured into the city from various parts of Italy to support his candidature that many of them could find no lodging; and since the Campus Martius [Field of Mars] was too small to hold them, they climbed up to the attics and housetops to declare their support for Gaius.[18]

Thus, finally, something like a class struggle *did* emerge, although the underprivileged still had to depend on aristocratic leaders, who exploited them in their own interests.

We saw, in the last chapter, that Roman military leadership at the end of the second century BC took a new turn, because Marius's army inaugurated a novel trend of the army's dependence upon its general instead of upon the Roman government. Moreover, to a much larger extent than hitherto, he ignored the rules about property qualification and filled the army with unpropertied men – mostly volunteers, whose equipment was provided by the state. In other words, as Sallust expressed it, he sought the support of the very poor in his rise to power.[19]

And the army was an extremely important section of the poor community, since at least 13 per cent of the citizenry served in it, and sometimes as many as 35 per cent – at any one time, in the second century BC, over half the total of young adult males were serving as soldiers. Moreover, they had become a very self-contained body, divorced from civil life by their long service far away (and that is why they turned to their general), and ruinous, by their absence, to the peasant life from which most of them were drawn, and, besides, they constituted a further drain upon Rome's food supply owing to the priority their needs received.

The reforms of the Gracchi had only benefited relatively few people, and when Marcus Livius Drusus (tribune in 91 BC) wooed the poor by offering new distributions of grain and land, reckless of cost, his measures were cancelled and he himself was murdered, so that the flames were only fanned: and a period of endemic internal violence was under way. The dictator Sulla, who was not noted for a concern for the poor, failed to satisfy either the rural dispossessed or the city-mob or the soldiery. When Catiline stirred up discontent in the 60s, Sallust declared that many of his supporters were drawn from the poor and the plebs, of whom the historian took a gloomy view. He spoke of men who were harassed by disgrace or by poverty: and Catiline, he said,

> was encouraged in his enterprise by the enormous burdens of debt [see Chapter 5] which had been created in so many parts of the world, and by the fact that many of Sulla's veterans had squandered their gratuities or grants of land and were now longing for civil war . . .
>
> 'As for our life,' declared Catiline to his associates, 'all we have is poverty at home, creditors outside the door, a miserable present and an even more wretched future. In fact there is nothing left to us except the air we breathe. Well, then, is it not time to act? . . .'
>
> The men whom Catiline was addressing were sunk in misfortune of every kind, but possessed neither means of their own, nor any honest prospects of bettering themselves . . . It is not surprising that penniless men utterly lacking in principle should cherish grandiose hopes of gain, and should value their country as little as they did their own lives . . .
>
> And so, after many years of quiescence, the feud between the senatorial and the popular party now once more returned to threaten the state.[20]

It is certainly true that the displaced and bankrupt, including many ex-soldiers, were in a very volatile state of discontentment, and – lacking any organisation of their own – were willing to be orchestrated by the revolutionary designs to which, in order to confront violent opposition, Catiline turned: what the peasants and veterans wanted was decent land, and they thought, wrongly, that Catiline could get it for them.

Catiline was suppressed by the enterprise of the consul Cicero, but, thereafter, destitute people continued to flock to Rome, and violence became dominant and comprehensive. The city poor had given little encouragement to their fellow-victims from the countryside who favoured Catiline, but they did back the aristocratic agitator and gangster Clodius (tribune in 58 BC), who endeared himself to them by organising a free grain dole (which, as many were beginning to realise, had become a political necessity); and he hit on the idea of using the *collegia* (trade associations) as the focus of his activities. His patronage of the city *plebs* was the outstanding concept of his career, and sharpened conservative fears that he wanted a democracy of an extreme kind, such as Rome had never known (and would never get). Yet 58–56 were bad famine years, and hunger was the background and cause of constant violence, in which techniques communicated by Clodius were used. It was these scenes of violence, in the end, that destroyed the Republic, because its government was unable to cope with them.

Cicero, on the whole, is unsympathetic to the miseries of the lower classes, disbelieving in 'equality' and seeing how easily democracy (not that there was any danger of it) could degenerate into licence. But one trouble that simply had to be dealt with was the appalling indebtedness of the poor. Caesar the dictator did tackle this problem (Chapter 5), but before he could get his principal plans for the future of the Roman constitution into action (and we do not even know what they were), he was murdered.

The period after his death produced a number of serious famines, and grave discontents among the poor who had to give up their lands to ex-soldiers:

> The task of assigning the soldiers to their colonies and dividing the land was one of exceeding difficulty. For the soldiers demanded the cities which had been selected for them before the war as prizes for their valour, and the cities demanded that the whole of Italy should share the burden, or that lots should be cast with the other cities; they asked that the recipients pay the value of the land, and there was no money.
>
> They came to Rome in turns, young and old, women and children, to the Forum and the temples, uttering lamentations . . . The Romans mourned and wept with them . . . Octavian [the future Augustus] explained to the cities the necessities of the case, but he knew that it would not satisfy them – and it did not.[21]

Augustus, when he gained full power, remained well aware that it was largely the poor who had brought down the Republic. So although his régime, in effect, maintained the rule of the upper class, and the massive exploitations that this rule involved (ensuring, also, that all *collegia* must be approved by himself or the state), he also took steps to win the unprivileged to his side. It was 'for the protection of the common people' that he made the tribunician power (divorced from office) the pillar of his system.[22] And he let it be understood that the old institution of patrons and clients had been recast, so that henceforward *all* the people were his own, personal clients, including the poorest citizens. Meanwhile Virgil, too, had written the *Georgics*, exalting the life of the poor peasant and farmer as a moral ideal.

On the urban side, in practical terms, Juvenal's 'bread and circuses' was the somewhat cynical, but not altogether inaccurate, description of the policy that the emperors followed.[23] Food was the people's main need, and Augustus saw that they got it; 'his cheap food policy', as Tacitus recorded, 'was successful bait for civilians. Indeed, he attracted everyone's good will by the enjoyable gift of peace.'[24] For the Pax Augusta benefited the population enormously. And in addition, as Juvenal pointed out, in order to keep their minds off possible grievances he offered them a rich variety of entertainments, festivals and religious ceremonials – including Games at which the presence of the ruler himself was a conspicuous feature.

Although back-breaking poverty, of course, continued (however ill-recorded), and indeed most inhabitants of the empire remained illiterate and at bare subsistence level (with a life expectation of less than thirty), and although much residential accommodation at Rome was still sordid, the emperors' measures to ease unrest among the Roman and Italian poor produced a sufficient social equilibrium to last for centuries.

Yet it still remained a highly conservative society. As we saw earlier, Velleius Paterculus, a senior officer of Tiberius, wrote in its praise. 'The humble man', he said, 'respects the great, but does not fear him; the great has precedence over the lowly but does not despise him.'[25] And the younger Pliny echoes Cicero, repeating that nothing is more unfair than equality.[26] Yet the whole urban plebs received distribution of grain. Moreover, there were private endowments for poor children at least from the time of Augustus, and these endowments were nationally funded from the time of Nerva (AD 96–98) – whether the motive was care for the poor, or a desire to increase the birth-rate, or to improve agriculture can be disputed, but at least it was done. Nevertheless, the social adjustments under the emperors do not seem to have raised labour productivity. True, the volume of trade may have increased, but even with this possible upswing Rome remained an agrarian state.

However, despite all this poverty, and despite the perpetuation of the hierarchical tradition, there was some upward social mobility to be seen. The classic literary example is Trimalchio, the man in Petronius's *Satyricon* who has risen from the lowest level to become a millionaire, although Petronius makes him a very ludicrous one. And an inscription tells of a rural harvester from Mactaris in north Africa, who also rose to considerable heights.[27] But this was rare, indeed exceptional, however much, in theory, talent and integrity might be commended against birth. Obviously, the best way to get on was to belong to the emperor's own household, the *familia Caesaris* (Chapter 6). The watertight compartments of Roman society could be broken down, but their frontiers were bristling with barriers.

As in earlier Greece, literature and the arts could provide an upward channel. Most artists were Greeks or slaves, but some had pretensions to rise in the social scale. The Augustan artist Spurius Tadius signed his own work; and the fact that the emperors Nero and Hadrian were artists themselves must have had some effect. Internationally known Roman architects, too, were no longer a novelty. As for the medical profession, although it was in generally low repute, staffed by riff-raff and old slaves, some doctors achieved fame, such as Augustus's physician Antonius Musa and the Stertinii. From the time of Augustus, teachers of rhetoric were usually free-born Romans. A skill or qualification could enable the occasional poor man to rise to relative affluence.

And so the principate went on, pursuing its mainly peaceful but socially unprogressive course. In the Middle Empire, however, when military dangers first on the northern and then on the eastern frontier meant that the army became very much larger and more expensive, there was a severe increase in taxation: news of it seeps out to us, from the later third century onwards. The worst sufferers were the rural poor; for the peasants the tax-collector was the greatest dread. They came, before long, to regard the state as an enemy, and the local authorities did little to help them. Poor men's legal rights, too, were gradually whittled away.

Protests, in due course, became violent. The revolt of the deserter Maternus, in the time of Commodus (AD 186), was unparalleled in size and purpose. He recruited oppressed and expropriated men, among whom, it appears, army deserters took the lead. But he and they were

only objecting to their practical miseries; they had no social programme.
There were also further uprisings in Gaul, in which slaves and tenants
cooperated. When Bulla Felix rebelled under Septimius Severus
(205/208), he was joined not only by artisans of imperial establishments
but by young Italians whose impoverishment had compelled them to
become outlaws.

Yet, up to that time, the gulf between rich and poor had at least been
bridged by one thing: Roman citizenship. If you were an Italian, or a
member of the élite minority of provincials who became Roman citizens,
you at least had certain basic citizen rights – a certain degree of equality,
which other people did not share.

In the second century AD, however, and increasingly in the years
around and after 200, that equality became eroded, and the bridge
virtually destroyed. For what happened now was that these old civic
differences between Roman citizens and the rest were being replaced by
another distinction altogether. This perpetuated the division of the
community into two main groups, to which the law gave entirely
separate treatment. The superior class (*honestiores*) included senators,
knights, landowners, soldiers, civil servants and town councillors
(*decuriones*, *curiales*). Everyone else belonged to the lower category
(*humiliores*), who possessed inferior legal rights and incurred heavier
penalties in the courts.

Roman law, despite its famous concern for equity, had always
favoured the upper echelons of society, from which its great practitioners
came. And now such preferential treatment became crystallised in legal
forms. This development was ominous, for beneath the tranquil surface
of second-century life, which was soon to be sharply and increasingly
shattered by external threats, it confirmed, in explicit terms, the dep-
ressed condition of the underprivileged, and thus deepened the basic rift
between rich and poor: which would mean, in the end, that the empire
would become too disunited to confront its destroyers.

In this atmosphere the measure known as the *Constitutio Antoniniana* of
Caracalla (AD 212) was not as sensational as it looked. With the
exception of slaves, it bestowed the status of Roman citizenship upon
almost the entire population of the empire. Yet, as we have just seen, the
differentiation between citizen and non-citizen had become increasingly
blurred by the current distinction between *honestiores* and *humiliores*, so
that the enactment of Caracalla, although dramatic in its finality, was
not so much an epoch-making event in itself as a further step in a gradual

and already well-advanced process of dual standardisation. Its principal effect was to increase the numbers of those who had to pay the indirect dues on inheritance and the freeing of slaves – these being taxes which fell upon citizens of Rome. Those who had been liable to pay such taxes before could well have been classified as 'middle class', in so far as such a term is applicable to the ancient world, but under this new law many humbler people joined their ranks. More people, that is to say, had to pay these indirect taxes, and this rapidly made them poor.

This relation of Caracalla's measures to taxes formed part of a general picture. For the deepening frontier and succession crises of the third century AD, the army had to be made even larger and better equipped, and this meant that more taxes had to be paid – a burden which, since 'soak the rich' could not work in a society geared in their favour, fell with increasing ferocity upon the *humiliores*. This link of their new definition with the needs of the army is clearly perceptible. The miseries which this increased taxation caused were made worse by a high increase in the special, military police and informers and secret agents who proliferated in order to enforce these exactions. For to secure the money (or payments in kind) that it needed, the army, which itself ranked among the privileged *honestiores* and, according to Juvenal, enjoyed scandalously high privileges,[28] had to take a direct hand. To obtain their quota of supplies, or just out of sheer lawlessness, even ordinary soldiers became violent and menacing. Pertinax (193) ordered them to stop oppressing civilians, and we have a pathetic series of appeals, from various parts of the world, to successive third-century emperors, urging that these abuses should be stopped. 'Shall I be sold up?' one man asks an oracle. 'Am I to become a beggar? Shall I flee? Will my flight come to an end?'[29]

For flight was what it came to in the end. A panegyrist addressing Constantine I the Great (306–337) steps aside from his praises of the emperor to describe the sufferings of the contemporary poor:

I have told, O emperor, how much the Aeduans deserved the aid you brought them; it follows that I should tell how serious was their distress . . . Our community lay prostrate, not so much because of the destruction of our walls as from exhaustion of resources, ever since the severity of the new tax assessment had drained our very life . . . Anyone would deservedly forgive these tillers of the soil, who are grieved by labour that brings no return. Indeed a field which never meets expenses is of necessity deserted. Likewise the poor country

79

folk, staggering beneath debts, were not permitted to bring in water or cut down forests, so that whatever usable soil there was has been ruined by swamps and choked with briars.[30]

Libanius, in the same epoch has an equally sad story to tell.

While merchants can recoup themselves by speculations, those for whom the work of their hands scarcely furnishes a livelihood are crushed beneath the burden. The lowest cobbler cannot escape from it. I have seen some who, raising their hands to heaven and holding up their shoe-knife, swore that they would pay nothing more. But their protests did not abate the greed of their cruel oppressors, who pursued them with shouts and seemed quite ready to devour them.[31]

And things continued to get worse, as Salvian, presbyter of Massilia (*c*.400–480), records.

Taxation, however harsh and brutal, would still be less severe and brutal if all shared equally in the common lot. But the situation is made more shameful and disastrous by the fact that all do not bear the burden together. The tributes due from the rich are extorted from the poor, and the weaker bear the burdens of the stronger. The only reason why they do not bear the whole burden is that the exactions are greater than their resources ... They are outside the number when the remedies are being distributed.

Under such circumstances can we think ourselves undeserving of God's severe punishment when we ourselves continually so punish the poor?[32]

Racked by taxation and oppression, and forced into destitution, the poor fled and flocked into the estates of the rich, where they were protected from the government's oppressors at the cost of becoming virtually their protectors' serfs (for which reason the discussion of this phenomenon will be reserved for the next chapter). Amid an oppressive atmosphere in which the state tried to tie everyone down, on a hereditary basis, to their job and their place, the poor, the very poor, resisted by fleeing and going underground; but when they had ended up on a rich estate it meant that they had virtually ceased to be free men. Despite the efforts of Marxists to find one, there was no unified revolutionary ideology or movement – only despairing, uncoordinated efforts to resist personal oppression. There were numerous brigands (with whom, as with German invaders, the despairing population tended to side). And there were many hunger riots and mob attacks in Rome – three in the 350s alone – as well as in other cities. Ammianus Marcellinus (c.330–395) took a poor view of this Roman urban public:

> Of the multitude of lowest condition and greatest poverty some spend the entire night in wineshops, some lurk in the shade of the awnings of the theatres, which Catulus in his aedileship, imitating Campanian wantonness, was the first to spread, or they quarrel with one another in their games at dice, making a disgusting sound by drawing back the breath into their resounding nostrils. Or, which is the favourite among all amusements, from sunrise until evening, in sunshine and in rain, they stand open-mouthed, examining minutely the good points or the defects of charioteers and their horses . . .
>
> The idle and lazy proletariat . . . devote their whole life to drink, gambling, brothels, shows, and pleasure in general. Their temple, dwelling, meeting-place, in fact the centre of all their hopes and desires, is the Circus Maximus. You see them collected in groups about the squares, crossings, streets, and other public places, engaged in heated argument on one side or the other of some question . . . Most of these people are addicted to gluttony. Attracted by the smell of cooking and the shrill voices of the women . . . they stand about the courts on tip-toe, biting their fingers and waiting for the dishes to cool. Others keep their gaze fixed on some revolting mess of meat till it is ready.[33]

These people could easily be whipped up to make trouble. Deserters from the army, who played a large part in these agitations, were the targets of repealed, ineffective laws. The groups of violent men who abounded went under different names, according to their characteristics and regions. There were the Circumcelliones ('those who wander about from shrine to shrine') and Donatists in north Africa, and, above all, there were uprisings by people called Bagaudae in Gaul, which lasted for centuries.

Once again, however, none of these dispossessed, rejected malcontents were class strugglers or social revolutionaries. They were people who wanted to get enough to eat, and did not believe that the existing system could provide it for them. But their rebellions were never eventually successful, and the failure of agriculture (still basic), to which their flight contributed, has been blamed as one of the causes of the collapse of the western Roman empire. Nor did the urban poor, either, though badly off, fare any better when they tried to assert themselves, although individual cases of upward mobility can be traced.

Many of the Bagaudae were Christians, and the Circumcelliones and Donatists were Christian movements. The government of the empire, too, from the time of Constantine the Great, was Christian. Yet one of the most curious features of the age is that this religion, of which the founder had been so sympathetic to the poor and the original leaders had mostly been poor men themselves, did so extremely little, when it came to rule the Roman empire, to improve the lot of the impoverished. True, Valentinian I created Defenders of the Poor. Valentinian and his brother and colleague Valens wrote to Petronius Probus, Praetorian Prefect, in the following terms (364):

> We have decreed very beneficially that all the plebeians of Illyricum shall be defended by the offices of patrons against the outrages of the powerful. For each and every municipality of the aforesaid diocese Your Sincerity shall provide for the selection to this office of men of suitable character, whose past lives have been praiseworthy and who have either administered provinces or have practised as advocates, or who have completed their service among the imperial couriers or the palatines . . . Certainly, the appointments made in each town shall be referred to Our Wisdom.[34]

But the Defenders turned out a complete failure, because Theodosius I (379–395) allowed them to fall into the hands of the town councils, which, before becoming oppressed themselves, had been described as rapacious oppressors (Chapter 3).

Christian writers, too, support the poor, sometimes with passion, but the effect was once again, in practice, non-existent. The destitute had to be content with the assurance that their plight would stand them in good stead in the next life. Christianity, like so many other institutions, has been blamed for its contribution to the fall of the western Roman empire – because it perpetuated the internal social rifts. And there may be something in this, although the main contribution of the faith was to establish a focus of loyalty which was not the imperial court, and was not, in fact, of this world. But the fall of the empire was complex. External pressures played a major part. Internally, the main cause was not Christianity, but the gulf between the rich and the poor whom the rich exploited.

Part III

THE UNFREE AND THE FREED

5

Serfs

Karl Marx and others have been wrong to regard the people of the ancient world as divided into two categories, free and slaves (Appendix 2). There were also many people who were, as Pollux put it, between free men and slaves, possessing a status intermediate between slavery and complete freedom.[1] Let us call them serfs, although the validity of applying this essentially medieval term to the ancient world is disputed – and the ancient writers do not help, since they preferred to polarise their system into a dualistic world in which men and women were either free or unfree. But in between free and unfree were these very important and varied groups whose labour, though technically voluntary, was dependent on others, so that although they were not actually slaves, their 'freedom' had little or no meaning.

In the ancient Greek world, one such category (though comprising a variety of different types) consisted of whole communities that stood collectively in a dependent, serf-like relationship to other communities, and notably to city-states. By far the best known of these are the Helots controlled by the Spartans. The Helots of Laconia and Messenia were presumably the pre-Greek inhabitants subjected by the Spartan immigrants during the migrations and resettlements following the collapse of the Mycenaean civilisation, and the system was then extended to neighbouring Messenia by conquest. These Helots outnumbered the Spartans, and probably even outnumbered the total free populations of Laconia and Messenia. Unlike slaves, they were permitted to maintain family and even community relationships. They survived in Messenia until Thebes freed them in 369 BC, and in Laconia until nearly two centuries later.

Strabo indicates that they were the property of the Spartan state.[2]

Control and punishment, however, were shared between the state (through its secret police, the *krypteia*) and individual Spartans. The Helots' main responsibility to their individual Spartan masters was the provision of a fixed quota of supplies, amounting to one-half of their crop. Some domestic service was also required, including work as servants on military campaigns (in extreme emergencies, such as the Peloponnesian War, they also served as hoplites). In return, it was understood that they would not be sold away from their home.

Athenaeus quoted an assertion, probably quite accurate, that the Spartans treated the Helots very badly indeed. That the Spartans used the Helots cruelly is also related by the third(?)-century historian Myron of Priene in the second book of his *Messenian History*, where he writes as follows:

> They assign the Helots every shameful task leading to every disgrace. For they ordained that each one of them be required to wear a dogskin cap and to wrap himself in leather and to receive a stipulated number of blows every year apart from any wrongdoing, so that they would never forget they were slaves. In addition, if any exceeded the vigour proper to a slave's condition, they made death the penalty; and they assigned a punishment to their owners if they did not rebuke those who were growing fat. And on letting them have the land, they set them a portion of produce which they were constantly to hand over to them.[3]

Nor had Thucydides given a favourable picture of the way in which the Spartans treated the Helots. In 424, during the war, Sparta decided to attack some of Athens's allies:

> They were also glad to have a good excuse for sending some of their Helots out of the country, since in the present state of affairs, with Pylos in enemy hands, they feared a revolution. In fact they were so frightened of their unyielding character and of their numbers that they had had recourse to the following plan. (Spartan policy with regard to the Helots had always been based almost entirely on the idea of security.) They made a proclamation to the effect that the Helots should choose out of their own number those who claimed to have done the best service to Sparta on the battlefield, implying that they would be given their freedom. This was, however, a test conducted in the belief that the ones who showed most spirit and

86

came forward first to claim their freedom would be the most likely to turn against Sparta. So about 2,000 were selected, who put garlands on their heads and went round the temples under the impression that they were being made free men. Soon afterwards, however, the Spartans did away with them, and no one ever knew exactly how each one of them was killed.[4]

For, since the Helots' subjugation on their own land, which is what had happened, presented obvious perils, it was constantly feared that they would revolt – the Spartan government ceremonially declared war on them every year – and that, indeed, is what they did, particularly in Messenia, where nationalist feelings played a part, though a revolt in Laconia, too, in 396 BC, was particularly serious.

What is less generally realised, however, owing to an almost total lack of information, is that there were Helot-like populations attached to a considerable number of other Greek states besides Sparta. Their attachments took different forms, and the populations in question went by a variety of names. There were Penestai in Thessaly, again originally a conquered tribe, augmented by prisoners of war. There were Gymnetes ('Light-armed Men') round Argos. There were Korynephoroi ('Club-Carriers') or Katonakophoroi ('Weavers of Sheepskin Cloaks') belonging to Sicyon. There were the subjugated Mariandyni in the hinterland of Heraclea Pontica. There were Kyllyrioi in the territory of Syracuse. There were variously named groups in Crete (Klerotai, Mnoitai, Oikeis). And there were also other Helot-like peoples attached to Corinth, Epidaurus and Byzantium, in addition, probably, to a good many others elsewhere that we have not heard anything about.

And there was also another sort of what may loosely be described as serfdom, in which the victims depended on individuals and not on states. One such phenomenon, enormously important in the ancient world, was debt-bondage (the theme could have been allotted to my chapter on the free poor, but it seems better to describe it here, since it was virtually a condition of serfdom). Laws about debt were harsh in the ancient world. Debt-bondage was to be seen at its nastiest, or at any rate at its most conspicuous, in the seventh century BC at Athens, where creditors possessed absolute power over their debtors and could keep them, virtually though not legally, as chattels, under a permanent obligation. This meant that there was a continual state of ill-will between aristocratic creditors and peasants, who remained oppressed by the nightmarish debt laws, and were consequently ready enough to support any violent change of régime – such as tyranny – that might favour debt cancellation (or land distribution).

This became a particularly dangerous situation at Athens, where widespread debt-bondage meant that the state was on the brink of civil war. Landownership was concentrated in the hands of a small minority, while as population increased many farms were subdivided between sons until the allotments were no longer viable, so that the poor became destitute and had to borrow grain from their richer neighbours. By doing so, they became *hektemoroi*, sixth-part men – which probably means that, as a surety for their debts, they had to pay five-sixths of their produce to their creditors: this was the condition on which, as long as their debt remained unpaid, they were permitted to go on farming their soil at all. In other words they were in their creditors' power, and their position was not so much that of free men as debt-bondage and serfdom.

This was the problem that confronted Solon, when he became chief archon of Athens in 594/3 or 592/1. He used his powers boldly and cunningly. All debts for which land or personal freedom was the security were cancelled, and all borrowing on the security of the person was prohibited. Those deprived of their farms got them back, so that 'the fields were set free that had been enslaved before', and tenants' interest rates were restricted to an endurable level. It was an effortful and delicate compromise, and Solon was aware it caused offence;[5] for rich creditors had lost a lot – though he had resisted demands for wholesale land distribution. However, above all, he had eliminated debt-bondage. Or rather, he had eliminated it at Athens: because it continued elsewhere, and abounded in Hellenistic times, especially in the eastern regions of the now expanded Hellenism, but also within Greece itself.

Early Rome, too, experienced savage laws about debt, and knew the effect of debt-bondage. The oldest Roman legal system included an institution known as *nexum*, by which a man was reduced to bondage on account of what he owed. The exact nature of *nexum* is not clear, but it seems to have been a kind of self-sale or self-pledge by which the debtor assigned himself into the creditor's power to guarantee him the eventual repayment of the debt; that is to say, the poor had to work in bondage to the rich. *Nexum* is mentioned in the Twelve Tables, but it was partly invalidated in 326 BC when the Lex Poetelia Papiria of the consuls Gaius Poetelius Libo Visolus and Lucius Papirius, during the troubled period of the Second Samnite War, attempted social appeasement by prohibiting bondage and imprisonment for debt, enacting that loans should henceforward no longer be based on the debtor's personal freedom, but on the security of his property instead.

The law at least mitigated debt-bondage and made it dependent on legal decisions. However, the debt problem nagged on, and the form of virtual serfdom which it involved had not been abolished. The problem was at its worst in the mid-first century BC, when the state was racked by internal convulsions. Julius Caesar, as dictator, set out to tackle the crisis – and it was probably the greatest thing he ever did. At the beginning of the Civil War between him and Pompey (49 BC) a shortage of currency (hoarded, or amassed for the payment of the armies) had meant that debtors could only pay their debtors back by selling all they possessed, at miserable prices. In consequence many of them became destitute, and at the mercy of their creditors: they were no better than serfs. So something had to be done for them. Now, Caesar had been heavily in debt himself, and he had seen how the debtors flocked to the revolutionary Catiline's support. Yet would-be reformers had always been faced by a dilemma. For although the victims had to be helped, anything approaching a general cancellation of debts would destroy private property – and, in consequence, arouse violent opposition.

But one thing Caesar could do, and did, was to forbid hoarding. And he compelled creditors to accept whatever land or other property was offered to them as repayment of their loans, at pre-war prices. Both sides, however, were dissatisfied, and in Caesar's absence bloody violence ensued. On his return to Italy he concluded that it was the debtors who needed more benefits. He therefore decided to cancel all interest due on debts since the beginning of the Civil War. This, we are told, wiped out one quarter of all indebtedness at a single blow, which made Caesar popular with the masses (for whom he also provided largesses and colonisation), but it inflicted a serious loss on property-owning creditors. Yet they put up with it, since they were obliged to admit that they would never have seen much of the money anyway – so that Caesar was not the destroyer of private property that his political opponents had made him out to be. And his measures worked. Money began to be freely lent again, and the poor were relieved. Caesar had more or less broken the back of one of the Republic's most unmanageable problems, though, unsurprisingly, grave indebtedness did not altogether cease to exist.[6]

A new form of serfdom came into being after several more centuries had passed, in the later Roman empire. It was foreshadowed when some tenants found their landlords or masters so intolerable that they tried to change them. In AD 332 Constantine I the Great issued an edict which tried to put a stop to this practice:

> Any person in whose possession a tenant that belongs to another is found not only shall restore the aforesaid tenant to his place of origin but also shall assume the capitation tax for this man for the time that he was with him.
>
> Tenants who meditate flight may be bound with chains and reduced to a servile condition, so that by virtue of a servile condemnation they shall be compelled to fulfil the duties that befit free men.[7]

But the practice continued, and when small farmers and agricultural labourers were so overwhelmed by the burden of taxation that they found life intolerable, they sought protection – as we saw in the last chapter – in whatever quarter they could best find it.

Some whole villages formally declared army officers to be their 'patrons'. But many more, especially in the west, chose local landowners rather than soldiers to look after them. And not only corporate villages did this, but large numbers of individuals as well: small farmers for the most part, men reduced to abject poverty who abandoned their plots of land or labouring jobs and fled within the boundaries of the nearest large estate, where they remained for the rest of their lives as tenants (*coloni*). This had happened before, during the troubles of the third century AD, but in the late fourth and fifth the process repeated itself on a massive scale, and became one of the most important social developments of the age.

Now these landowners were pleased to have the displaced vagrants, since agricultural labour was difficult to come by. That was why, declared Salvian, the poor surrender unconditionally to the rich. 'The poor are being robbed, widows groan, orphans are trodden down – such is the case among almost all the lower classes.'[8] And so, indeed, it was, since the incoming families were virtually serfs – not exactly slaves, but foreshadowing the serfdom of the Middle Ages. Some of these men may already have been deeply in debt to the landowner before they arrived on his estate. From that time onwards, in any case, they had to make him a substantial payment, in case or kind, or more often contributed a huge proportion of the crop they were allowed to produce on his land, or sometimes served directly as part of his labour force. In return, they hoped to be able to rely on their new landlords to chase the government's tax collectors away.

And this worked for a time, in exchange for complete submission to the landowners, and only ceased to work during the last decades of the western empire, when the proprietors came to an understanding with its government (at Ravenna). Whereupon the refugees found themselves reinscribed on the official tax rolls in their new locations; so that serfdom to a local potentate would no longer save them, and all they could do to evade their hardships was to flee and go underground, joining the roaming gangs of bandits who infested the crumbling empire.

6

Greek Slaves

Slavery seems an appallingly inhumane institution, because its essential feature is that slaves have no independence or rights or legal personalities of their own, but are the property of their masters. Slavery was a feature of every advanced ancient civilization, not only those of the Greeks and Romans. And those Greeks and Romans who played a large part in public life or made important contributions to literature and art were enabled to do so by means of the spare time, or leisure, and financial surpluses, conferred upon them by their slaves (this was the only way in which such a surplus could be acquired).

There were various forms and nuances of ancient labour – something has been said about those who could be described as 'serfs' in the last chapter. But it was slavery, chattel slavery, that was the most significant kind of unfree labour at the highest periods of Greek and Roman history. Even if never ubiquitously predominant, it was extensive and general, and inherent in the very conception of the ancient state. Every action, belief or institution was in some way or other affected by the possibility that someone involved might be a slave. The contribution of slave labour was essential, so that it is justifiable to describe Greece and Rome as, to a large extent, slave societies, such as do not exist today, at least in the western world.

To insist on the history of the 'rights' of slaves is not very relevant. For, basically, they had none. Their total contrast with free men was a familiar rhetorical point. They were even regarded as kinless, and in Greece their marriages were unrecognised, and their owners could prevent them from taking place. The exploitation of slaves was based upon the direct use, or sanction, of force, not upon the 'free' play of economy, as in capitalist societies. This was the most extreme way in which one social group could use its power for economic advantage. Plato noted that the protection and defence of slave-holders was a crucial function of the government,[1] and Aristotle described the master-slave relationship as one of three most basic features of the household[2] – slaves being the best, most manageable, and most necessary property a man could possess.[3] A slave was not expected to display virtues, and the comic dramatist Menander gave his slaves special masks, displaying mental disharmony and moral deviance, to be expected from men who were mostly non-Greeks, and therefore natural barbarians and enemies. Their treatment, of course, varied. Relying on their lack of rights, a master might vilify or beat them with immunity. Or, remembering their indispensable services, he might choose to treat them decently – within the limits of their status. The result might be warm mutual affection.

> A Lydian, yes, a Lydian I;
> But though I was a slave,
> My master let his tutor lie
> In this, a free man's grave.
> Good years and happy be thy share!
> And when, with life's decline
> Thou comest, master, even there
> Timanthes will be thine.[4]

Or, alternatively, relations between master and slave might be deplorable.

What percentage of the total population of the Greek *poleis* the slaves constituted has been much debated and argued; and, in any case, each state was constituted differently. One recent estimate suggests that in the classical Athens of the fifth and fourth centuries there were between 80,000 and 100,000 slaves of both sexes, representing about one-third of the total population. But some say there were more, and some less. Anyway there were a lot, and there was always a sufficient supply of them. A very large number of these slaves were foreigners (Appendix 1) – there was a general opinion that one ought not to have Greek slaves – and they were obtained by capture in war, by sale in the huge slave-markets such as Delos (of which we know too little), and by birth to those who were already slavewomen.

How far all this slavery kept down the pay of free workers – who shared so many occupations with them – remains uncertain, but it must surely have done so (although we can detect no protests from the free poor) and must have caused some contempt for free labour. Numerous slaves worked in the basic field of agriculture, but many others in industry and public works. And another disputed question is the extent to which slavery impeded technological improvement, and so industrial advance. Once again, it must surely to some extent have done so – because when so much slave labour was at hand, even if not wholly efficient, why bother about better technology or rationalisation of production methods?

However, the slaves, although numerous, did not do *most* of Greek production. And the work they did was often in their master's household, to satisfy his needs and those of his family. Others could be hired out to a third party, or allowed to work independently, for instance as craftsmen. Others, again, had the state, not an individual, as their master. Some of these worked in mines, for instance Athens's notorious silver-mines in Laurium. That is to say they, and their functions, were varied and flexible, so that efforts to describe them as a single social 'class' must be rejected.

Slaves were at first not very numerous in Greece, but they always existed. Homeric slaves, being the products of wars and raids and piracy, were mostly women, but not all: Eumaeus, in the *Odyssey*, had been sold into slavery, and there were other male slaves as well. The households of Alcinous and Odysseus were said to possess fifty slaves each, but that is a conventional figure. In spite of the very low estimate accorded to impoverished free men, 'Zeus', remarks Eumaeus, 'takes away half a man's worth when the day of slavery comes upon him.'[5]

Yet Hesiod represented a widespread view when he saw slavery as essential to his slave-owning class. Another early writer, Aesop, was a slave himself, from Thrace, which was where so many slaves came from. He is a partly legendary figure, but seems to have written the earliest collection of fables. Whether he expressed views about the disadvantages of the slave status, or employed the slave situation to universalise the human experience, must remain conjectural.

In archaic Greece, slavery was still not very extensive. But then, in the sixth century, there was an astronomical increase. This was partly because Solon, at the beginning of the sixth century, abolished debt-bondage at Athens (though at other cities it remained in force). Something has been said about this elsewhere, when serfdom was discussed, but here one result of Solon's measure should be pointed out. It meant that Athens, deprived of the forced labour of its serfs, had to import many additional slaves from elsewhere to take the place of those who had thus been released from their serf-like obligations.

When wars broke out, slaves got new chances. For one thing, a city-state's mobilisation of free urban troops for war depended on the maintenance of production by the slaves who remained at home. And, furthermore, the slaves themselves were sometimes enrolled to fight. This occurred during internal convulsions (*staseis*), but it was also not unknown in external wars. Whether slaves fought against the Persians at Salamis is uncertain, but certainly they rowed in the Peloponnesian War, notably at Arginusae (406), though this was recognised as exceptional; and they occasionally served as soldiers as well.

They also made their mark in civilian capacities too. For example, some of the leading potters and vase-painters were almost certainly slaves. And in the labour force on the Acropolis slaves worked alongside free men. Increasing democracy at Athens, and emphasis on the rights of poor citizens, enhanced the general reliance on slavery. That is to say, individual freedom flourished when slavery was abundant as well. At Athens there were large private workshops manned by slaves, such as those of Lysias and his brother, and Pasion — both factories for making shields. But there were also other new, upwardly mobile, opportunities for slaves (still within their slave status), although always, of course, the iron distinction which kept them apart from, and under, free men was maintained.

Why, given this new degree of possible latitude, did the slaves in classical Athens not revolt? Partly because, being foreigners from all parts, they were polyglot and multi-ethnic, possessing no degree of unity. But what they did, instead, was to run away, and fugitive slaves were always a major problem; they could count on some degree of religious asylum. During the Peloponnesian War, after the Spartans fortified Deceleia in Attica, a very large number of the slaves employed by the Athenians at their Laurium silver-mines defected to the other side.[6]

In the following century, Athenian slave-owners displayed a tendency to replace enforced obedience by attempting to encourage spontaneous obedience, so that the legal personality of slaves began to emerge. True, people were still frightened of them, and were still eager enough to equate them with barbarians — enemies, against whose threat military training was necessary — and the 'free poor' struggled to maintain the citizen-slave distinction. Yet Athenian law came to protect slaves, in a limited way, and their killing was prohibited. Such sanctions, however, were religious or social rather than legal; and constraints on slave-masters were not so much motivated by a desire to protect the slaves as by the wish to protect the state against over-powerful slave-masters.

During the fifth and fourth centuries the writers all had their say on this theme. Herodotus, while denouncing the corporate enslavement of Greek states to the Persians, accepted *individual* slavery as the will of the gods. Euripides, as always, was more critical, observing that a good slave could have 'internal' freedom, and be a better person than a free man. He was echoing the sophists' (minority) view that slavery was *not* natural – so that it could not degrade anyone who was not 'really' a slave. A slave, that is to say, could be 'free in mind'. As Euripides causes a messenger, himself of slave status, to remark:

> It's low not to feel with your masters,
> Laugh with them, and sympathise in their sorrows.
> Born to service as I am, I would be
> Numbered among the noble
> Slaves, unfree in name,
> Free in mind. Better this than for one man
> To be doubly cursed – a slave in mind
> As well as slave in the words of his fellows.[7]

The comic dramatist Aristophanes, however, although he boasted of abandoning conventional jokes about slaves, did not really accept them as human beings. His conservative contemporary, known as the Old Oligarch, believed that in Athens they were too well treated!

Unrestraint on the part of slaves and resident aliens [Appendix 1] is very prevalent with the Athenians, and it isn't permitted to beat them there, nor will a slave stand aside for you.

I'll explain what's behind the local practice: if it were lawful for a free person to beat a slave, resident alien, or freedman [Chapter 8], lots of Athenians mistaken for slaves would get beaten. For the populace there is no better in its clothing than slaves and resident aliens, and its appearance is no better. If someone is amazed at this too, that they let slaves live it up and in some cases to lead lives of great splendour: this too they would seem to do on considered opinion. For where there is naval power it is necessary for slaves to work for money . . . And where there are rich slaves there is no longer any advantage in my slave's being afraid of you.[8]

Xenophon, aware of what the sophists had said, declared that the 'real' slave is the bad (free) man, in bondage to his own faults and lusts, whereas whether one is, or is not, an actual slave, is an accident of fortune – a convenient sop to the consciences of slave-owners: who, he also, more ominously, suggested, ought to avail themselves of unpaid bodyguards against the danger that slaves presented.[9] Antisthenes (*c.*445–360) wrote a work *On Liberty and Slavery*, giving a slant to the moralistic point of view by his comment that 'the man who fears others is a slave without knowing it'.[10]

Something has already been said about Plato's and Aristotle's views on the subject; but it may be added that Plato felt an aristocratic contempt for slaves, as well as for other manual workers, and barbarians. He saw no theoretical justification for the view that slavery was a mere convention, and his *Laws* are severer on slaves than the actual laws of his time.

Aristotle, however, provides the only surviving ancient attempt at a determined analysis of slavery. Like Plato, he considered it perfectly right and proper that some people are slaves. Aware of men who held the opposite view, he disagreed with them, maintaining that barbarians, for example, are slaves by nature, and that men conquered in war legitimately became the property of the ruler: the rule of the free man over the slave is a necessary institution:

The slave is not merely the slave of the master but wholly belongs to the master. These considerations therefore make clear the nature of the slave and his essential quality: one who is a human being belonging by nature not to himself but to another is by nature a slave . . .

The usefulness of slaves diverges little from that of animals; bodily service for the necessities of life is forthcoming from both, from slaves and from domestic animals alike . . .

There is also such a thing as a slave or a man that is in slavery by law, for the law is a sort of agreement under which the things conquered in war are said to belong to their conquerors.

Others however maintain that for one man to be another's master is contrary to nature, because it is only convention that makes the one a slave and the other a free man, and that there is no difference between them by nature, and that therefore it is unjust, because it is based on force.[11]

But after a prolonged and intricate argument Aristotle comes down firmly in favour of the principle of natural slavery: 'there exist certain persons who are essentially slaves everywhere, and certain others who are so nowhere . . . it is just and proper for the one party to be governed and the other to govern by the form of government for which they are by nature fitted'.[12]

The author of the *Oeconomica*, which was preserved under the name of Aristotle, reflected upon the character of a slave's existence:

> The slave who is best suited for his work is the kind that is neither too cowardly nor too courageous . . .
>
> Three things make up the life of a slave, work, punishment and food. To give them food but no punishment and no work makes them insolent. And that they should have work and punishment but no food is tyrannical and destroys their efficiency. It remains therefore to give them work and sufficient food; for it is impossible to rule over slaves without offering rewards, and a slave's reward is food . . . And since the drinking of wine makes even free men insolent . . . it is clear that wine ought never to be given to slaves, or at any rate very seldom.[13]

Meanwhile, however, the politician Hyperides proposed that slaves should be granted citizenship in order to fight against King Philip II of Macedonia. As for Menander (342/1–293/89 BC), he is aware of the literary and comic tradition, from the slave-owner's point of view, that slaves are lazy, sex-crazed or gluttonous, and need to be beaten. But some of his slaves (who figure extensively in his plays) are also clever and resourceful schemers – useful to free men, and helping them to see themselves as they are. As for the supply of slaves, he took it for granted that piracy would remain one of the principal sources.

> When the pirates
> Had all three in their power, they thought it not
> worth while
> To carry off the old woman; but they took the
> child
> And the slave to Mylasa, a Carian town, and
> offered them
> For sale in the market.[14]

Hellenistic Greece did not add a great deal. The slave-markets were active, because of wars and continued kidnapping by pirates, though slavery was also perpetuated by breeding. The Seleucid monarch Antiochus IV Epiphanes possessed a huge number of slaves of his own, and we hear (from a later age it is true) that they constituted one-third of the population of Pergamum. At Chios, in the third century BC, there was a slave rebellion under a certain Drimacus (this was another place where slaves were particularly abundant). In Ptolemaic Egypt the picture is mixed. There were not, it appears, a great many chattel slaves, since the free poor took their place. But we hear not only of debt-bondage but of various kinds of domestic slaves – and even of female slaves owned by women – and in the second century BC there was an Egyptian school for slaves.

In general, the idea of 'rights' for slaves began to take shape gradually, prompted by the growing individualism of the Hellenistic age. Attitudes varied, and the views of the Stoics were not altogether illiberal. True, they were somewhat contemptuous of slaves, but they did feel that the whole institution needed to be defined, and, in particular, that slaves ought to be properly treated. For slaves were allowed a capacity for virtue, seeing that moral status, the Stoics pointed out, depended on the soul, so that social status was irrelevant – and very often due to capricious fortune: the wise man alone is free, and the bad man is a slave.[15] The actual state of slavery, that is to say, as many people felt at the time, was 'an accident': unnatural perhaps, but indispensable and a fact of life.

99

7

Roman Slaves

In Rome, as in Greece, the slave was not a person but a property; the legal writer Gaius tells us so, adding that the distinction between free man and slave is fundamental. They had no status in the civil law, even though Ulpian pays lip service to the tradition that all men are equal in natural law – and adds that only custom excluded them from public life,[1] commenting, however, that 'the person of a freeman is beyond price'. Although Athenaeus (c.AD 200) devoted a lengthy discussion to slavery, the Romans did not write much about it, in depth. But the strong sense of property in Roman law is partly, or largely, derived from slave ownership.

In early Rome, slavery developed within the framework of the family. As in Greece, the existence and possession of slaves helped free Romans to engage in their various occupations, such as politics; and enabled them, too, to show off their wealth. People were afraid of slaves, and their treatment varied widely. They could be looked after decently – and form a respected part of the household – or they might be tortured, and thrown to wild beasts, and sexually abused, and have their families broken up by sale: in fact they could be treated very cruelly indeed. A slave was not allowed to dispose of his property as he wished, but he could own property, his *peculium* or private savings (to which he could add), and the legal recognition of this practice was something that had never existed in Greece. It gave slaves greater independence of action, and they carried on a lot of business at Rome, acting on their own account. Indeed, their prominence in these fields helped to degrade industry and trade in people's minds.

Rome can be called a society largely dependent on slaves from the third century BC onwards. During the Second Punic War (218–201) various developments occurred. First, military operations resulted in large-scale enslavements. Secondly, and exceptionally, slaves were called upon to fight, and were bought for the purpose. Thirdly, with so many free men away in the army, the role of slaves on the home front became more and more significant: they were employed in agricultural and industrial production on an unprecedented scale, without which the free recruits for the army could never have been raised and taken away. Conscious of their new powers, some slaves made trouble, especially in Campania. As a sop and a safety-valve, they were allowed religious activities, and, in particular, played a dramatic role in the annual Saturnalia (217), transformed into a Greek-style festival, in which slaves momentarily changed places with their masters – the compliment being intended to prompt future loyalty among the slaves, by showing gratitude for the work they were doing.

But free people were still really afraid of their slaves, as the plays of Plautus, despite comic exaggeration and irony, make clear. His slaves have much larger roles than those of Menander's Greek New Comedy on which he drew: male slaves are crafty and resourceful, and their female counterparts (on whose childbearing the future of the institution partly depended) are ubiquitous.

Cato the elder, in his *On Agriculture*, was probably more liberal than many of his contemporaries. But he regarded slaves as basically intractable, and went into somewhat chilling, pragmatic details about how they ought to be handled. It was only common sense, he said, that, like pieces of equipment, they should be cared for, but not as carefully as oxen, which could not look after themselves. Old and decrepit slaves might have their rations reduced and could be sold off, like worn-out tools or aged oxen or 'anything else that is superfluous'.[2] As for those who were still active, he established brothels (at a price) for their benefit:

> Being of the opinion that the greater cause of misbehaviour in slaves was their sexual passions, he arranged for the males to consort with the females at a fixed price, and permitted none to approach a woman outside the household . . .

And that was not all he did for them.

> He also lent money to those of his slaves who wished it. They would buy boys and, after training and teaching them at Cato's expense, would sell them again after a year . . .

101

When at home, a slave had to be either at work or asleep. Indeed, Cato greatly favoured the sleepy ones, accounting them more docile than those who were wakeful, and more fit for anything when refreshed with slumber than those who lacked it.[3]

Moreover, although Cato's slaves included a good teacher, Chilo, he did not have his own children taught by the man, but hired him out to other senators.

Cato's detailed comments, even if they sound damping, were timely, because from the end of the Second Punic War until the end of the Republic there was a dramatic increase of both urban and rural slavery in Italy. This was partly because of the influx of slaves during the eastern wars of conquest (augmented by piracy), which was facilitated by the vast slave-market at Delos and opened the way to the huge importation of slaves into Italian agriculture – including the large senatorial estates – and into manufacture and profitable state mines (at the expense, very often, of the free poor). The growth in the population of Rome itself, too, provided a large market for the new surplus provided by the slaves. As a result of all this, by the time of Caesar's death – although all statistics are dubious – it seems quite probable that one-third of Italy's total population of six or seven million were slaves, as against 10 per cent before the Second Punic War.

So the slaves, or some of them – not surprisingly – had begun to feel their strength, and express their discontents by forcible means. There were Italian slave risings in 198, 196 and 185 BC. Then there were three great revolts during periods of severe social strain, the first two in Sicily (c.139–132 and 104–100), and the third led by Spartacus in south Italy (73–71). Although their frequency and scale have been overemphasised, they were serious enough. But they were not, as Marxists have so often liked to argue, ideological manifestations of a 'class struggle', directed at the universal abolition of slavery (Appendix 2) – on the contrary, Eunus of Apamea, leader of the first revolt, had an imposing slave retinue himself – but responses to specific injustices, by specific groups of slaves in special circumstances, who objected, or whose leaders objected, to being ill-treated, and wanted to take revenge on their masters, or to get away.

Diodorus Siculus tells the story of this first revolt.

Never had there been such an uprising of slaves as now occurred in Sicily. In it many cities experienced terrible misfortunes, and untold numbers of women and children suffered most grievous calamities; and the whole island was on the point of falling into the power of the runaways, who set the complete destruction of their masters as the goal of their power . . .

The Slave War broke out from the following cause. The Sicilians, being grown very rich and elegant in their manner of living, bought up large numbers of slaves. They brought them in droves from the places where they were reared, and immediately branded them with marks on their bodies . . .

On account of the immense wealth of those exploiting this rich island, practically all the very wealthy revelled in luxury, arrogance and insolence . . . Oppressed by the grinding toil and beatings, maltreated for the most part beyond all reason, the slaves could endure it no longer . . . Consequently, as the slaves' hatred of their masters increased *pari passu* with the masters' cruelty towards their slaves, the hatred burst forth one day at an opportune moment. Then, without prearrangement, many thousands of slaves quickly gathered together to destroy their masters.[4]

Eunus's only programme was to seize Sicily for himself, and rule it as a sort of Hellenistic monarchy. As Diodorus goes on to explain, he appealed to religion and the divine world, and magic, for help. This insurrection evidently had some effect on the contemporary rising of Aristonicus in Asia Minor, although the extent of his slave following is not clear.

As for Spartacus, he has been overestimated by Marxists (see Appendix 2) – encouraged by the exaggerations of his contemporary Roman enemy Crassus, who wanted to build him up as a worthy foe. It was ludicrous to describe Spartacus as a 'precursor of social revolution' or 'the leader of a unified proletarian resistance front'. He started with 200 gladiators, of whom 78 made a successful break. The product of local conditions and scattered support (not including town slaves), he did not lead any lower-class unity movement, but tried to break out and return with a group of his own followers, in the hope of leading them back to Thrace, the land of his origin. What he wanted to do was not to lead a universal lower-class movement, but to fight in order to get his men back to their homelands.

All the slave revolts ended in failure, because the slaves were not powerful or unified enough to succeed. Republican society was cracking up for other reasons, but not because of the slave rebellions. More than a million slaves had been killed in the course of the fighting, and the slave-owners were not even dented. On the contrary, under the late Republic, the quantitative employment of slave labour reached its high-water mark in ancient history. Crassus possessed a vast number. A proposal that slaves should wear distinctive clothing was rejected, because it would have shown how numerous they were. Most were still obtained as prisoners of war. Although, on the whole, they were treated even worse than before, the potentialities of all these slaves as political supporters and pressure groups did not escape the notice of Roman public figures, so that slaves were now allowed to contract *contubernia* (nearly marriages) and their family life was, on occasion, encouraged, and they could attend *collegia* in which they met free members of the community. Politicians who wanted to defy the senate often called on slaves to help them (usually without success). Catiline stopped recruiting them, because he felt that mixing them with citizens would look so bad. But Clodius's gangs were composed not only of free men but of slaves, who included many gladiators; and his enemy Milo likewise had a slave bodyguard.

As Appian pointed out,[5] the Civil Wars after Caesar's death gave slaves not only, in the ex-slave Publilius Syrus's words, a share of their masters' power,[6] but even power over their masters, whom many of them saved during the proscription era (though others did not behave so well). It was therefore thought advisable to give some of them rewards and privileges. The question arose of arming them in the current conflicts. It was considered criminal to do so, and the worst offender, according to Octavian (Augustus), was his enemy Sextus Pompeius, who enlisted runaway slaves; Octavian described his war against Sextus as a 'slave war' (*bellum servorum*).[7] There followed a vast number of western enslavements after Octavian had won his civil wars, and became Augustus. Augustus also introduced a radical constitutional change, stressing state interference in slave-owners' rights over their slaves – who could now, even, inform against their masters. He also restricted the use of torture to extract evidence from them.

From then onwards the importation of slaves somewhat decreased, since wars of conquest, on the whole, diminished, and so did piracy. But slave-breeding largely filled the gap – with the assistance of disreputable professional slave-catchers – and there is no direct evidence for a decline in total slave numbers; probably the demand remained constant until the end of the second century AD. Some slave households were enormous. Gaius Caelius Isidorus, in Flavian times, left 4,116 slaves, and Petronius, too, in his *Satyricon*, gives the parvenu Trimalchio at least 400, in squads of ten, hardly any of whom were even known to their master. In the time of Augustus, it has been estimated, there were about 300,000 slaves at Rome, out of a total population of about one million. Many of them were small traders, among whom slaves were more numerous than free men.

There was a good deal of early imperial law-making to protect slaves, but it was not usually as humanitarian as it was made to look, since it was often a continuation of Augustus's policy of asserting state control. A senatorial decree under Claudius was directed against the marriages of free women to slaves – reducing the women to slave status themselves; a measure, incidentally, which reveals that such marital relationships existed on a not inconsiderable scale.

Yet, at the same time, a humane attitude to slaves was undeniably on the increase. For it was realised that they should not be too freely expendable – should, that is to say, receive better treatment – and the increasing number of home-bred slaves seemed to require more careful consideration, not least because it involved personal friendships with their masters and their masters' families. There were also two imperial training schools for slave boys which ensured many of them a proper education.

Besides, Stoic, cosmopolitan feelings were at work. They are particularly apparent in the writings of Seneca the younger, who offered our only detailed and thorough exposition of the relationship between masters and slaves, who ought, he declared to his correspondent, to be decently treated:

I am glad to learn, through those who come from you, that you live on friendly terms with your slaves. That befits a sensible and well-educated man like yourself. 'They are slaves,' people declare. No, rather, they are men. 'Slaves!' No, comrades. 'Slaves!' No, they are unpretentious friends [*humiles amici*]. 'Slaves!' No, they are our fellow-slaves, if one reflects that Fortune has equal rights over slaves and free men alike.

That is why I smile at those who think it is degrading for a man to dine with his slave. But why should they think it degrading? It is only because purse-proud etiquette surrounds a householder at his dinner with a mob of standing slaves . . . All night long they must stand about, hungry and dumb.

The result of all this is that these slaves, who may not talk in their master's presence, talk about their master . . . They are not enemies when we acquire them: we make them enemies . . . We maltreat them, not as if they were men, but as if they were beasts of burden . . . We Romans are excessively haughty, cruel and insulting to slaves. But this is the kernel of my advice. Treat your inferiors as you would be treated by your betters . . .

'He is a slave.' His soul, however, may be that of a free man. 'He is a slave.' But shall that stand in the way? Show me a man who is not a slave! One is a slave to lust, another to greed, another to ambition, and all men are slaves to fear. I will name you an ex-consul who is slave to an old hag, a millionaire who is slave to a serving maid. I will show you youths of the noblest birth in serfdom to pantomime players. No servitude is more disgraceful than that which is self-imposed.[8]

And Seneca went on to offer a catalogue of historic cases of loyalty on the part of slaves. It is possible to be a little cynical about his pronouncements, because he was not really abolitionist, and may not have been quoting his own personal beliefs, but merely giving voice to fashionable ideas – themes for rhetorical debate. Yet his contribution does show that liberal views were in the air – and he may well, to some extent, have shared them. In any case, he mirrored what was evidently a certain unease.

For certainly, in Seneca's time, there was an increasing recognition of the *moral* personality of slaves. Besides, in some ways a Roman domestic slave was better off than a poor freeman. This was most conspicuously the case in the astonishing phenomenon of the imperial household (*familia Caesaris*). Most of its leading members, as we shall see in the next chapter, were freedmen, but they also included unfreed slaves holding highly lucrative and influential posts at court, at Rome particularly – until Claudius replaced slave cabinet members by freedmen – but also in imperial offices elsewhere. Thus Musicus Scurranus, a mere cashier (*dispensator*) in one of the provincial treasuries of Tiberius (AD 14–37), was very rich, owning much silver plate, and had at least sixteen household slaves of his own, who dedicated a monument in his honour:

To Musicus Scurranus, slave of Tiberius Caesar Augustus, cashier of the Gallic treasury of the province of Lugdunum, by his slaves who were with him at Rome when he died, to their worthy master.

Venustus, agent; Decimianus, accountant; Decaeus, secretary; Mutatus, secretary; Creticus, secretary; Agathopus, doctor; Epaphra, butler; Primus, valet; Communis, chamberlain; Pothus, footman; Tiasus, cook; Facitis, footman; Anthus, butler; Hedylus, chamberlain; Firmus, cook; Secunda.[9]

If you had told Musicus Scurranus that, according to Marxist doctrine, he belonged to an 'oppressed' class (Appendix 2) he would have been very surprised and amused.

But a limit to this interpenetration of classes had to be drawn somewhere, to placate senatorial opinion; and that was probably why Claudius, as we have seen, restricted the marriages of these slaves with free women. For feeling against slaves, and fear of them, in leading circles was still strong. A classic case arose in AD 61 when the city prefect of Rome, Lucius Pedanius Secundus, was murdered by one of his 400 slaves. 'After the murder,' recounts Tacitus, 'ancient custom required that every slave residing under the same roof must be executed. But a crowd gathered, eager to save so many innocent lives; and rioting began. The senate house was besieged. Inside, there was feeling against excessive severity. But the majority opposed any change.'

And one of their number, Gaius Cassius Longinus, made a long and eloquent speech (not far removed, probably, from the version provided by Tacitus), urging that the mass executions should be carried out to the letter. 'Our ancestors', he is reported as saying, 'distrusted their slaves. Yet slaves were then born on the same estates, in the same houses, as their masters, who had treated them kindly from birth. But nowadays our huge households are international. They include every alien religion – or none at all. The only way to keep down this scum is by intimidation. Innocent people will die, you say. Yes, and when in a defeated army every tenth man is flogged to death, the brave have to draw lots with the others. Exemplary punishment always contains an element of injustice. But individual wrongs are outweighed by the advantage of the community.'[10] Cassius Longinus, echoing the fears and anxieties of many Romans, had his way, and the dead man's slaves, men, women and children alike, were taken off for execution. But in view of the outcry among the rest of the population (so many of whom were descended from slaves), Nero had to line the whole route, along which they were taken, with troops.

So the slaves prompted fear, but also prompted sympathy; and one can trace two main elements in current thinking in many contemporary and later writers, who did not go into the matter as deeply as Seneca, but nevertheless made interesting passing remarks. The elder Pliny describes slave field-workers in Italy as 'men without hope', and does not believe that they work as well as free men.[11] Columella, on the other hand, for practical reasons, recommends favourable treatment for slavewomen who produced children. By producing four, they had repaid their purchase price.

And he had similar practical considerations to apply to the treatment of slave-overseers:

My advice at the start is not to appoint a [farm] overseer from that sort of slaves who are physically attractive, and certainly not from that class which has busied itself with the voluptuous occupations of the city. This lazy and sleepy-headed class of servants, accustomed to idling, to the Campus Martius (Field of Mars), the Circus and the theatres, to gambling, to cookshops, to bawdy-houses, never ceases to dream of these follies; and when they carry them over into their farming, the master suffers not so much loss in the slave himself as in his whole estate . . .

But be the overseer what he may, he should be given a woman companion to keep him within bounds and yet in certain matters to be a help to him. And this same overseer should be warned not to become intimate with a member of the household, and much less with an outsider . . .

Soothsayers and witches, two sets of people who incite ignorant minds through false superstition to spending and then to shameful practices, he must not admit to the place.[12]

As far as possible, it was thought desirable to give slaves an education. The younger Pliny wrote a letter about the murder of the senator Larcius Macedo by his slaves (108), a repetition of the Pedanius case. Macedo (himself the son of a slave) was evidently a nasty man, yet Pliny concludes: 'no master can feel safe [even] because he is kind and considerate'; and he advises that, for security's sake, one's slaves should be of different nationalities, and speaking different languages.[13]

Dio Chrysostom delivered two speeches *On Slavery and Freedom*, in which, after investigating the whole institution, he concluded, by implication, that barbarians were naturally slaves, so that they got what they deserved.[14] The physician Galen was aware that what they got was sometimes cruel treatment. The Latin novelist Apuleius gives us our only real portrait of a slave-woman, Photis, which is not unattractive. But he paints the degradation of flour-mill slaves in gloomy colours:

> Ye gods, what miserable human beings were there! Their skins were seamed all over with the marks of old floggings, as you could easily see through the holes in their ragged shirts that shaded rather than covered their scarred backs: but some wore only loin-cloths. They had letters branded on their foreheads, and half-shaved heads, and irons on their legs. Their complexions were frightfully yellow, their eyelids caked with the smoke of the baking ovens, their eyes so bleary and inflamed that they could hardly see out of them, and they were powdered like athletes in the arena, but with dirty flour, not sand.[15]

Apuleius's Greek counterpart, Achilles Tatius, shows some of the various domestic employments, of a less oppressive character, that were entrusted to slaves.

But meanwhile attention was being directed towards slaves' personal contributions to culture. Two second-century authors devoted themselves to this theme. Gellius gave a list of philosophers who had been slaves. And Hermippus of Berytus wrote *On Slaves Famous in the Cultural Domain*. According to antique tradition the role of the slave had been that of the *paedagogus*, who looked after the children and took them to school. But ever since Republican days they had also provided teachers. There were also slave doctors, and doctors' assistants, and nurses. Doctors for the Romans, slaves and freedmen, had been imported from Greece since the second century BC, and free-born doctors employed slave doctors to help them. Greek physicians were not always well regarded, and one reason why the medical profession stood in low repute was because it recruited slaves (of an advanced age). In the time of Nero a Greek claimed to be able to turn an unskilled slave into a doctor within six months. Be that as it may, the slaves, collected as they were from all parts – and particularly from Greek lands – represented a varied collection of talents.

Nevertheless, in spite (or because) of the partial recognition of this by

Romans as a whole, there is evidence that a substantial number of slaves remained disaffected. When there was an uprising in Gaul under Commodus, for example, free men and slaves exceptionally cooperated. And when Bulla Felix – whether he himself was a slave is uncertain – led a gang of marauders round Italy in the time of Septimus Severus, he said to an imperial official: 'tell your masters that if they would put a stop to brigandage, they must feed their slaves.'[16] That, then, was why slaves, like others, joined his cause: because they did not get enough to eat. But Bulla's movement, such as it was, did not aim to free slaves in general, or abolish slavery.

After about AD 200 there was a decline in the number of slaves in the Roman empire, though it came about slowly, and was perhaps not as large as was formerly thought. The slave population, in the long run, did not reproduce itself: and the 'colonate', involving the reduction of many men to serfdom (Chapter 5), meant that the same quantity of slaves was no longer necessary, or profitable. Or at least not everywhere: because in the fourth century, according to Synesius (as we saw), every wealthy home was still full of Gothic or Scythian slaves. Symmachus assumes slaves were a standard part of the Italian scene, and Augustine writes of a nocturnal raid by Galatian slave-dealers;[17] while Melania the younger (c.383–439) owned 24,000 slaves.

And people still felt they had to be on guard against them. An Edict of Diocletian (284–305) had shown awareness of this. In the time of Constantine I the Great (306–337), an appeal was made to their feelings by a law that the murder of a slave and a free man were equally serious crimes, with the same penalties. Constantine also thought it reasonable that slave families should not be divided:

> When . . . estates in Sardinia were recently distributed among the various present proprietors, the division of holdings ought to have been made in such a way that a whole family of slaves would remain with one individual land-holder. For who could tolerate that children should be separated from parents, sisters from brothers, and wives from husbands?[18]

Nevertheless, discontent among slaves continued, and although it did not bring about the fall of the western empire, as some Marxists have suggested (Appendix 2), it did nothing to prevent the process. For the various 'peasant' revolts of the time, which helped to undermine the imperial régime, attracted slave supporters: a wealthy landowner in the hands of the rebel Bagaudae in Gaul became the slave of his own slaves. Moreover, slaves were attracted to the causes of invading barbarians. Out of the 40,000 people who escaped from Rome to the Visigoth Alaric's camp in 408–409 a large number were people of slave status. And in 417 we learn that a town in Gaul was handed over to the barbarians by what was described as a slave faction (*factio servilis*).

When the empire had become Christian under Constantine, despite the humanitarian legislation of the time (which was not specifically Christian), the event made little impact on slavery as a practical phenomenon. Jesus, in his parables, had seen the slave's subjection as a symbol of the relation between man and God. And Paul did not harbour the runaway slave Onesimus, but instead tried to persuade him to return to his Christian master Philemon.[19] When he says that 'there is no such thing as . . . slave and free-man', he is talking in a spiritual sense, and pointing out that they are equal in the sight of God. But, in earthly terms, he exhorts them to be obedient, and obey their masters: he is anxious that Christianity should present no scandal to the eyes of the authorities.

True, slaves, like women, figured largely in early Christian society – and they were comforted by the insidious theory, which had originated so many centuries earlier, that the good and wise person was never 'really' a slave. St Jerome, it is true, was critical of the institution in one, moral respect – seeing domestic slavery as a peril to household virtue. And Augustine recognised that the system was evil in principle. Yet he saw no alternative to accepting it. Indeed he and Ambrose felt that slavery could actually be good for the slave, who would earn a special reward, in the afterlife, for the disadvantages he had suffered and overcome on earth.

8

Freedmen and Freedwomen

In ancient Greece and Rome, as in other communities of the ancient world, a considerable proportion of the population were slaves, without any rights at all, the property of their masters. And in Greece and Rome, as we have seen, this proportion became very large indeed, so that, in spite of reservations, it has seemed possible to describe them as 'slave societies'. But what is noteworthy is that there were means, abundant means, by which slaves could escape the iron grip of this institution, and become free men. The fact that this was so, and that the rigorous hierarchical nature of the system could be, and was, transformed into upward mobility, is one of the most remarkable features of the social history of Greece and Rome.

Aristotle, in his *Politics*, observes: 'how slaves should be employed, and why it is advantageous that all slaves should have their freedom set before them as a reward, we will say later'.[1] Regrettably he does not do so, but he has said enough already to show that he is in favour of manumission. Another unfortunate thing is that we really have no knowledge of how frequent in the Greek world it was. Opinions differ widely between those who think it was a common phenomenon, and those who believe that it was rare. The trouble is that we have not enough information. It would, I think, be safe to conclude that it occurred fairly frequently, and started at quite an early date – we are told that Cleisthenes, at Athens, extended citizenship to certain slaves,[2] and we have evidence for the same practice in *c*.500 at Chios.

It is also clear that there was more than one way of bringing it about. The Athenians offered freedom to their slaves who fought at Arginusae (406), but the most famous Greek freedman was Pasion (d.370 BC), the wealthiest banker and manufacturer of his time at Athens (where banking and moneylending were generally held in disrepute). He began his career as a slave with a banking firm, becoming a freedman and later an Athenian citizen. He derived a large income from his bank and shield-workshop, enjoyed credit at all Greek commercial centres, and left extensive real estate and capital. We know of him from speeches of Demosthenes and from the *Trapeziticus* of Isocrates.

But Pasion must have had many obstacles to overcome, because when the Greeks did manumit a slave he was subjected to numerous legal disabilities. He was still regarded as a 'natural slave', could not buy land (of which there was a shortage), and had to be represented at law by a citizen patron, who was, normally, his former master, to whom he continued to owe extensive obligations: indeed, manumission was regarded as a free gift which could be revoked, and was therefore precarious. Moreover, it was exceptional that Pasion became a citizen of Athens. Generally, a manumitted Athenian slave acquired the status of a foreigner or metic (see Appendix 1; in certain other Greek states citizen status *could* subsequently be acquired, though it was never automatic).

To sum up, it could be said that the Greeks did manumit some of their slaves, thus creating a significant precedent, but that owing to their preoccupation with their own rights and privileges they only did so somewhat grudgingly, and without shedding their nervous inhibitions.

Alexander the Great was not keen on manumission, but subsequently, in the Hellenistic world, it increased considerably. This was largely because of impoverishment, which meant that people could not afford to keep many slaves; and when they freed someone they expected him to help support his former master. Our most important source of information on the subject is a mass of 1,200 inscriptions from Delphi, describing the manumissions that took place there between 200 BC and AD 200. As the Hellenistic period developed, it seems that the conditions attached to the process had become more onerous, involving, sometimes, a postponement of the emancipation until the master's death, and that the beneficiary had to pay him, or his heir, a considerable sum of money:

Critodamus son of Damocles, of Physcus [Locris], sold to Pythian Apollo a male slave whose name is Maiphatas, of Galatian origin, and a female slave whose name is Ammia, of Illyrian origin, for the

113

price of seven *minai* of silver. Maiphatas and Ammia shall remain with Critodamus for as long as Critodamus lives, doing for Critodamus what they are told to. If they do not remain and do what they are told to, the sale shall be null and void. When Critodamus dies, Maiphatas and Ammia shall be free, and the sale shall remain with the god, on condition that they are free and not to be claimed as slaves by anyone for their whole life, doing whatever they wish and going wherever they wish.[3]

There are also some statistics from Thessaly, and many of the eunuchs who served the Ptolemaic court (see below, on the later Roman empire) had formerly been slaves. At Pergamum, freedmen did not rank highly.

In Rome the situation was fundamentally different, because there – from a very early date – manumission made a new freedman *a Roman citizen*. Provided, that is to say, that his former master was a Roman citizen, that is what he, too, would become; he would become a citizen with full civil rights (except that he was limited to one of the four city tribes). In other words, he was entitled to inherit part or all of his former master's estate. True, he was ineligible for the senate or knighthood (*ordo equestris*) or municipal magistracies and priesthoods, and the top echelons of the army. But none of those exclusions applied to his sons – who became citizens in the fullest sense of the word, and were admitted by Appius Claudius Caecus (censor in 312) to the senate. All that was a big step forward, and amounted to a major breakthrough in respect of the rigid hierarchies that governed the ancient world. It was made possible, in part – and its limitations, too, were imposed – by the Roman cliental system, in which the citizen world was divided between patrons and their clients, who owed each other mutual obligations. These obligations, naturally, were powerfully evident when a citizen manumitted his slave. That slave remained his client, and continued to owe him obligations (*obsequia, officia, operae*), which were sacred, unavoidable, reciprocal, and clearly formulated, like the obligations of a son to his father. Nevertheless, their existence encouraged the slave-owners to a programme of manumissions which the Greeks would have found wildly liberal.

The Romans traced manumissions back to the semi-legendary age of King Servius Tullius. The Twelve Tables (457–450 BC) allowed the freeing of slaves by will – with the remarkable result that any citizen could confer citizenship on another. The first tax on manumissions was ascribed to 357 BC. There were three sorts of informal manumission (to escape the tax) and three of a formal kind; testamentary manumission was much the most frequent (and childless couples often freed and adopted their favourite slave). The process was not, indeed, universal or even normal for agricultural slaves – and most slaves never achieved freedom at all. But none the less, manumission was much commoner among the Romans than among the Greeks.

In 214 BC this was pointed out by King Philip V of Macedonia in a historic letter to the chief magistrates and city of Larissa in Thessaly. Objecting to Larissa's restrictive policy regarding its own citizenship, he wrote:

> It is best by far when, with as many as possible sharing in the citizenship, the city is strong and the countryside is not, as now, being shamefully deserted. This I think not even any of you could deny; and it is possible to observe others who similarly enrol citizens, among whom are also the Romans, who admit to citizenship even slaves when they manumit them, and grant them a share in the offices of state.[6]

Philip was exaggerating somewhat, since not the Roman freedmen themselves, but their descendants, were entitled to hold office, but his main point – that the Romans were more liberal than the Greeks in their manumissions of slaves – is clear and accurate. For there was a Roman feeling, not so much about the conduct of agriculture to which Philip referred, but that a loyal domestic servant should be automatically freed in due course, in order to show generosity and reward service and obedience. And, indeed, this happened quite often, as soon as slaves had reached the age of thirty. Yet even if that early target was not achieved, many slaves, *most* domestic slaves, could expect emancipation if they lived long enough.

There were, of course, conditions; the peculiar Roman relationship of client to patron has already been mentioned, and applied particularly to the continued dependence of the freedman upon his master. For what was essential, and the essential difference of Rome from Greece, was the Roman slave's ability to save up money, as his *peculium* (cf. last chapter). This meant that he could purchase his freedom, and what remained of the sum gave him relative independence thereafter. Yet the former master had also done well. He had made money, and gained a free supporter, and the prestige that this conferred. Thus it was a form of social manipulation or exploitation that worked out to his advantage. But the important thing was that it happened at all, far more frequently than in Greece, and with incalculably large social consequences.

Emergencies accelerated the process. In the Second Punic War, for example, the Romans enlisted two legions of slaves after the disaster at Cannae, and freed them. Then, after the war was over, manumissions, mostly of urban slaves, increased, to make up for casualties, and restrictions were of little avail. The playwright Terence was probably an ex-slave. Roman history had become a tale of the continuous extension of citizen rights, and Philip V of Macedonia was correct, and seized on a fact of overriding importance, when he commented, as we saw, on Rome's distinctive willingness to admit new citizens. The result was, during the late Republic, that former slaves far outnumbered the freeborn. Tomb inscriptions show three freedmen to every man of free birth, and they dominated the upper urban plebs. Probably 80 per cent of the urban population came to be descended from slaves. Dionysius of Halicarnassus knew this, and painted a hostile picture of the evils of indiscriminate manumission, unchecked by law.[7]

The new freedmen not only, as we have seen, benefited their former masters, but fulfilled useful roles in the state. They were not averse, very often, to manual labour (and so fuelled the Roman prejudice against it). And they provided teachers, as well as the occasional literary man, such as Publilius Syrus, the first author of mimes, from Antioch. Many of his maxims advocate self-regarding behaviour. That was not surprising, and it was equally unsurprising that manumission was exploited by aspirants to political power. For example, it lay behind much of the agitation about the free distribution of grain. Freedmen, by becoming citizens, became entitled to this, so that a politician might well feel eager to manumit more and more people, who would then feel under an obligation to him if he could claim to have given them more free grain.[8] Thus the increase in grain-dole recipients from 62 BC was largely due to manumissions, and out of 280,000 recipients in 56 nearly half were recently emancipated freedmen. Gangs of thugs whom politicians such as Clodius gathered around themselves included a considerable number of freedmen who had received this type of benefit.

The Civil Wars provided further opportunities for freedmen, whose ranks were swelled by manumissions from all the contestants (while other slaves, too, just liberated themselves during the turmoil). Both Pompey and Caesar gave freedmen big jobs, and Caesar's were very rich. He was particularly lavish with manumissions, and quite a lot of freedmen's sons were admitted to the senate, which had long been the entitlement even of their fathers but had not often happened. Octavian (the future Augustus) pressed 20,000 freed slaves into service against Sextus Pompeius, and employed many of them, and gave them his prinicipal naval commands. Indeed, that was a feature of the periods, since leading commanders on Sextus's and Antony's sides, too, were of freedman status. Lower down the scale there were also a lot of freedmen to be seen. They served in the fleets, and, during crises, in the army as well. Horace, the son of a freedman, became a military tribune. One freedman, Gaius Caecilius Isidorus, lost heavily in the Civil Wars, but left huge sums all the same, perhaps by purchasing the lands of the proscribed.[9]

When Octavian imposed unpopular taxes before the battle of Actium, freedmen were blamed for the rioting and incendiarism that followed.[10] There was obviously a strong feeling that this increased element in the state had got out of hand, and when Octavian became Augustus, and controlled the entire Roman state, he took a series of steps to restrict manumission, and bring the whole process back into order, while hoping at the same time to restrict the influx of foreign blood (Appendix 1). In the first place, the practice of informal liberation needed regularising, and in 17 BC a Lex Junia Norbana (?) conceded the benefit of legal sanction to this custom, while nevertheless lowering the status of a man thus freed. He was not entitled to call himself a Roman citizen any longer, but belonged to an intermediary category (*Latini Juniani*). And this meant that on his death his property reverted to his former master. In 2 BC the Lex Fufia Caninia limited the number of slaves a master could liberate in his will. In AD 4 the Lex Aelia Sentia fixed the minimum age of 30 for a manumitted slave, and of 20 for his owner. Such was the legislation which attempted to regularise the situation, or set back the clock.

Yet, at the same time, Augustus did something to show his respect for freedmen by increasing and standardising their religious privileges. They formed the great majority, for example, of the *vicomagistri*, who superintended the worship of the Lares Augusti at crossroads, as well as performing (at first at least) certain other administrative tasks. This cult, remarked Hugh Last, 'the only Roman cult which belonged to the poor . . . offered the masses a regular occasion for simple ceremonial, which was at the same time a reminder of their obligation to the man who embodied the ideals of the new Italy.[11] The cult was given into the hands of freedmen. Moreover, in the municipal towns, although excluded from public office, they became (when rich enough to pay the entry fee) members of the Augustales, who helped to celebrate the worship of the emperor. Augustus also allowed them to serve in the fleets (which were still usually commanded by freedmen) and in the cohorts of the Vigiles, the city's fire brigade and police. And he showed generosity to individual freedmen, conferring equestrian rank, for example, upon his own doctor, Antonius Musa – and a freedman, Licinus, became a notorious financial administrator (procurator) in Gaul.

Augustus's aim had been to satisfy freedmen, and give them some privileges, without altogether breaking down the preexisting social barriers. But his new regulations proved hard to enforce. For example, the Lex Aelia Sentia was got round. And marriages between freedmen and free women, and between free men and freedwomen, continued, although Augustus had done his best to make them difficult. Rich freedmen found it easy to marry free women, and, conversely, men often found freedwomen more agreeable than their free counterparts, who nowadays made such a fuss about their rights.

That is to say, Augustus's tidy schemes did not prove entirely effective. One of the principal reasons for this was his own imperial household, the *familia Caesaris*, and the political influence of its growing bureaucracy. The men who worked there, even though excluded from the senate or traditional official careers, enjoyed special opportunities for power and wealth. To take a single example, the freedmen who found it easiest to marry free women were the members of the imperial household. And then, under Claudius, some of these freedmen – Polybius, Callistus, Narcissus, Pallas – became the most important men in the empire. Tacitus enlarges on this phenomenon at great length, and to some extent, no doubt, he exaggerates. But not entirely, especially in relation to Claudius's last years, when his powers were failing. Furthermore, the situation continued under Nero, when Polyclitus had a vast retinue, and Claudius Etruscus (to whom Statius dedicated a vast poem)[12] became financial secretary. After that, it is true, the phenomenon was brought under control, so that in *c.*AD 100 knights (*equites*) replaced freedmen in the imperial civil sevice. But many provincial financial agents (procurators) still remained freedmen.

Before then, however, the freedman had enjoyed a mighty role. The imperial household led the way, their freedmen, the *liberti Augusti*, being the most spectacular examples of social mobility in the empire. But freedmen were successful at other upper levels as well. Five out of sixteen of the richest men known in the early empire belonged to this category; or, according to another calculation, four out of ten. The iron hierarchy of the Roman class structure had been thoroughly broken down and interpenetrated by this small minority, through their exploitation of trade, banking, crafts and land. And so the sons and grandsons of freedmen made their way into town councils, even if the freedmen themselves had not been able to do so themselves.

The wealthy freedman was encapsulated and pilloried for all time by Trimalchio, the creation of the novelist Petronius. Of course, his vulgarity, augmented by the social taint of his freedman status, is enhanced and caricatured, but he bears witness to a type which no doubt existed: a certain Calvisius Sabinus, described by the younger Seneca,[13] could be described as his counterpart in real life. Furthermore, we know of other such men too, particularly from the inscriptions that celebrate them as benefactors (in which, indeed, they are statistically over-represented, on surviving monuments, owing to their and their heirs' anxiety to display their grandeur). A large monument was erected to Aulus Kapreilius Timotheus, a former slave who became a slave dealer. And Gaius Fundilius Doctus made statues of his patroness and himself.

The result was a good deal of savage criticism. Horace's fourth *Epode* is a malevolent attack on a freedman who had become wealthy.

> As falls by fate between wolves and lambs,
> So is the strife betwixt me and you,
> Whose flanks are calloused from Spanish bonds
> And shanks from hard shackles.
> Although you stroll puffed up with wealth,
> Fortune does not change your kind.[14]

And the satirist Juvenal expressed similar sentiments, at greater length. When the patron's staff are distributing hand-outs of food,

> The crier has his orders:
> Each man to answer his name, nobility included.
> Oh, yes, our Upper Ten are scrounging with the rest.
> 'The praetor first, then the tribune – '. But a freedman blocks
> Their way. '*I* got here first,' he says, 'why shouldn't I keep
> My place? I don't give *that* for you. Oh, I know I'm foreign:
> Look here, at my pierced ears, no use denying it – born
> Out East, on the Euphrates. But my five shops bring in
> Four hundred thousand, see? So I qualify for the gentry.'[15]

And Juvenal goes on to say that it was only yesterday that the man's feet were white with the chalk of the slave-market. Some of these freedmen were, no doubt, tiresome and pretentious, but all the same the snobbery of Horace and Petronius and Juvenal is narrow-minded and misguided, since the upward social mobility to which the two writers bear witness was in fact something new, and one of the outstanding features of ancient social history.

Indeed, while those poets were writing, new manumission cases still kept coming up – in a variety of different forms. Servius Sulpicius Galba, when he was provincial governor of Nearer Spain, presided over some of them. Moreover, Acte, the mistress of Nero – whom Galba superseded as emperor shortly afterwards – was a freedwoman, and the ballet-dancer Mnester, executed under the previous emperor Claudius, had been of the same status.

Freedmen's sons, too, could rise not only to municipal office, but to high Roman rank. Larcius Macedo, an ex-praetor murdered by his slaves in *c.*AD 100, was the son of a freedman, and so was Marcus Gavius Maximus, one of the most prominent of Antoninus Pius's officials. The process reached its climax when another son of a freedman, Pertinax, actually became emperor of Rome in AD 193. Indeed, the historian Tacitus observed that a large proportion of the Roman nobility was descended from freedmen, and even if he was exaggerating there was something in what he said. It was even rumoured, by his enemies, that the great-grandfather of Augustus himself had been of that rank, and another emperor Vitellius, it was said, came of a family which a freedman had founded.

Freedmen also made their mark in the literary and artistic professions. The most famous writer of this origin is Phaedrus (*c.*15 BC–AD 50), a Thracian freedman of Augustus, who made the fable an independent Latin genre, in the manner of Aesop, and earned the displeasure of Tiberius's minister Sejanus by satirising contemporary social customs. Suetonius also made a list of other freedmen who were prominent in culture and literature – some of them manumitted because of these literary talents. Among them was Staberius Eros, the first grammarian. But the most famous of all was the Phrygian freedman Epictetus (c. AD 55–c.135), a Stoic who had something to say about the sufferings of the humbler members of his class, in contrast to slaves. Moreover, out of some 400 artists that we have heard of, nearly half were of freedman status. Freedman doctors, too, had existed for a long time, and continued to do so.

Lawyers sought to explain and justify this widespread practice of manumission by harking back to the Greek doctrine that slavery was unnatural and had only been introduced by convention – so that another convention had subsequently been established which reversed the process, and set slaves free:

> Manumission took its rise from the law of nations. For by the law of nature all men were born free; and manumission was not heard of, as slavery was unknown. But when slavery came in by the law of nations, the boon of manumission followed. And whereas we all were denominated by the one natural name of 'men', the law of nations introduced a division into three kinds of men, namely free men, and in opposition to them, slaves; and thirdly, freedmen who had ceased to be slaves.[16]

Within the second century AD, however, the great age of Roman freedmen was over. Symbolic was the fact that the emperor Hadrian (117–138) no longer gave them the cabinet posts that they had held before, but only left them secondary jobs. Henceforward they do not seem to have fared particularly well. The rebel gangster Bulla Felix, under Septimius Severus (205–208), was joined by imperial freedmen, discontented with their pay. But there were still freedmen at the courts of the emperors, since in 212, when Caracalla killed his brother Geta, he also murdered Geta's freedmen and slaves. Then, in the later empire, the complexities regarding different types of manumission were abolished:

> Freedmen were formerly divided into three classes . . . [But] we have made all freedmen whatsoever Roman citizens, without any distinc-

tion as to the age of the slave, or the interest of the manumitter, or the mode of manumission.[17]

Melania the younger (383–439), who was said to have owned 24,000 slaves (see Chapter 7), allegedly manumitted 8,000 of them on a single day.

At a higher level, too, in her time, freedmen were enjoying a curious and somewhat specialised come-back. For the eunuchs at the fourth- and fifth-century courts of Ravenna and Constantinople were slaves or freedmen, holding the posts of *cubicularii* or chamberlains. Eunuchs had played a large part at oriental courts from time immemorial, owing to the belief that their marginal condition would make them impervious to disloyal entanglements and ambitions. In the later Roman empire castration was illegal, so that in theory all the eunuch *cubicularii* were imported barbarians, although this was not always so, since slave-dealers illegally undertook castrations. Some court eunuchs were barbarians from outside the empire, and others no doubt came from its various provinces. The historian Ammianus Marcellinus attacked them, and the senate scorned them, and the men who sold them were despised. But the eunuchs were powerful, the most powerful of the emperor's servants, and thus at the very centre of the vortex. The chief eunuch outranked almost everyone, except the prefects and the very highest generals. The eastern emperor Leo I (457–474) thought it ridiculous that any people of such importance should be slaves, and ordered that all eunuchs should be freed on admission to the imperial household (*c*.473).[18]

Foreigners

The Greeks and Romans, like most people, today or at any other time, were pretty heavily xenophobe; and it was a familiar rhetorical point that even people who travel abroad, or live away from home, are not entirely reputable.

This xenophobia was, historically speaking, somewhat ironical, since the Greeks and Romans alike owed an enormous part of their civilisation to foreigners. As to the Greeks, their culture would have been inconceivable without the contributions of the Egyptians, Babylonians, Syrians and Phoenicians, even if we do not have to go the whole way with Martin Bernal (*Black Athena*, 1987, 1991) and describe the whole of Greek civilisation as originally Afro-Asiatic.

However, by way of contrast, the Greeks soon came to realise that they were, or had become, extremely different from foreigners – from whom, therefore, they showed great anxiety to differentiate themselves. Their tendency in that direction was accentuated by the mythology of the Trojan War, and then by the actual experience of the Persian Wars. Moreover, the Greeks being fragmented into many city-states, the people of one city-state were often hostile to the people of another. But, leaving such internal Greek differences aside, there was a general, popular tendency to regard the Greeks as good, and non-Greeks as barbarians, beyond the pale. The point, however, was restated and readjusted in the fourth century BC by the Athenian Isocrates, who asserted that whether one was Greek or not was a matter of culture, not of race.[1]

In Greek states there were commonly four groups of foreigners: permanent residents, known as metics (*metoikoi*), more or less permanent residents who had not yet been recognised as metics, temporary visitors, and numerous slaves (Chapter 5). Metics were to be found in many Greek states, but those in Athens are much the best known. There every metic had to have a citizen as patron (*prostates*), had to be registered in the district (*deme*) in which he resided, and to pay an annual poll tax, as well as contributing to other taxation. Metics were not permitted to contract marriages with citizens, and could not own houses or land except by special dispensation.

In return, they enjoyed some protection from the courts. They served in the army, in separate units, and were employed as oarsmen in the fleet. Although, obviously, they were at a serious disadvantage vis-à-vis citizens, and were not infrequently denounced for xenophobic reasons, they were important in commerce and industry (which some philosophically-minded Greeks despised) – even if it is an exaggeration to say that these activities were largely in metics' hands.

Before Hellenistic times Athens contained the largest number of metics, and gave them the most favourable treatment. Both Solon and Cleisthenes encouraged them, and the Panathenaic festival, founded in the sixth century BC, seems to have recognised the contribution of non-citizen groups, among which the metics were so prominent, to Athenian life. There were also certain well-known metics in classical Athens. Protagoras of Abdera settled there, and so did many other important sophists, philosophers and doctors, finding the city agreeably free of small-town prejudices, despite the grudging aspects of its attitudes to immigrants. Protagoras became Pericles's friend, and it was Pericles, too, who persuaded Cephalus of Syracuse to settle at Athens. Cephalus's son Lysias owned a successful shield factory at the Piraeus. The labour force in the Acropolis included metics as well as citizens. Many sculptors, vase-painters and potters were also metics, although it is not always certain whether they were metics or slaves. But one particularly successful metic was the fifth-century painter Polygnotus of Thasos, who subsequently became an Athenian citizen and achieved an unprecedented social position.

The Old Oligarch noted that metics had achieved *isegoria* – freedom of speech – which can perhaps be regarded as the equivalent of 'social equality':

> We have effected social equality . . . for resident aliens in relation of citizens, since the city needs resident aliens, owing to the abundance of crafts and the fleet. Therefore we have quite reasonably given social equality to resident aliens . . .[2]

He adds that this process was facilitated by the Athenians' increased knowledge of foreigners, owing to the city's maritime contacts.

> By virtue of domination of the sea they [the Athenians] have in the first place discovered all sorts of good cheer through mingling with various foreigners . . . And by hearing every way of speaking, they have picked out this expression from one, that from another. The Greeks tend to have distinctive dialects, ways of life, and fashions of dress; but the Athenians employ mixed modes, taken from all the Greeks and the barbarians.[3]

Metics, unusually, took part in the democratic restoration at Athens in 403 BC, and the fourth century witnessed an easing of their legal position, because their work was seen to be so valuable, and their numbers had increased. Xenophon's thoughts on the subject, in *Ways and Means*, are partly bold, but also, in other respects, restrictively and traditionally conventional. As Moses Finley writes,

> Xenophon's scheme opens with six suggestions for increasing the number of metics in Athens:
> (1) release them from the burdensome obligation of service in the infantry; (2) admit them to the cavalry, now an honorific service; (3) permit 'worthy' metics to buy building-lots in the city on which to construct houses for themselves; (4) offer prizes to market officials for just and speedy settlement of disputes; (5) give reserved seats in the theatre and other forms of hospitality to deserving foreign merchants; (6) build more lodging houses and hotels in the Piraeus and increase the number of market places . . .
> Xenophon's ideas, bold in some respects, never really broke through the

conventional limits. It was bold to propose a breach in the land-citizen tie to the extent of allowing metics to own house property (for their own use). But it is significant that he went no further than that.

Nor did he touch the head-tax, the *metoikion*, a drachma a month for males, half a drachma for females, imposed on every non-citizen who resided in the city beyond a very short period, perhaps no more than a month . . . any form of direct tax on citizens was condemned as tyrannical (except in war emergencies), and the *metoikion*, a poll tax, the direct tax *par excellence*, was thus the degrading mark of the outsider.[4]

Xenophon's attitude to foreigners outside the Greek world is also interesting. His *Anabasis* describes the withdrawal of his Greek force from Mesopotamia, where it had been supporting Cyrus (who was killed) against his brother King Artaxerxes II Mnemon of Persia. Xenophon understood the Persian empire better than most Greeks, and his attitude towards it is complex and not unbalanced. Plato gave thanks that he was not born a woman *or a foreigner*, and defined what he thought should be the position of resident aliens,[5] though he displayed a grudging attitude to foreign traders:

One category of foreign visitor turns up every year without fail, usually in summer, with the regularity of migrating birds.

Most of them are on business trips in search of profit, and throughout the summer they wing their way like so many birds across the sea to foreign parts. They must be received at trading posts and harbours and in public buildings outside but not far from the state by officials appointed for the purpose, who should

(a) take good care that none of this category of visitor introduces any novel custom,

(b) handle with proper impartiality the lawsuits that affect them, and

(c) keep intercourse with them down to the unavoidable minimum.[6]

Yet it was in this fourth century, too, that Isocrates, as we have seen, asserted that whether one was Greek or not was not a matter of race at all, but of culture. He went on, however, to urge Philip II of Macedonia to 'force the barbarians to become the Helots of the Greeks'.[7] The barbarians were the Persians, and the old view that they were utterly foreign still figured prominently in Isocrates's mind.

A much discussed issue was whether 'barbarians are slaves by nature', so that it was right to enslave them (a view encouraged by the large number of Greek slaves who were of foreign origin: Chapter 6). Plato and Aristotle thought so, but others disagreed (seeing no basic difference between Greeks and barbarians). But even if that was how they felt, some of them also believed that another war against the Persians might be profitable: as Alexander soon showed that it was.

What Alexander thought of all the foreigners he conquered was a mystery. He was credited with broad-minded, cosmopolitan views:

Alexander did not follow the advice of Aristotle and treat the Greeks as a leader would but the barbarians as a master, nor did he show much care for the Greeks as friends and kinsmen. Rather . . . he brought men together from all over the world, mixing together, as it were, in a loving cup their lives, customs, marriages and ways of living . . . The difference between Greeks and barbarians was not a matter of cloak or shield, or of a scimitar of Median dress. What distinguished Greekness was excellence, while wickedness was the mark of the barbarian.[8]

It is not altogether likely, however, that Alexander went much further than sponsoring the idea that there should be some sort of partnership, within his empire, between Greeks and Persians.

The relationships of the Greeks with peoples other than the Persians were, at all times, varied and complex. Herodotus has a good deal to say about these relationships. They fall, roughly, into two parts: those with foreign peoples in more or less far-off lands, and those with peoples adjacent or subject to the Greeks themselves – a theme which was naturally of concern to the settlers in Greek colonies, notably in south Russia, north Africa, south Italy and Sicily. Sometimes these colonists got on well with these neighbours, and sometimes they did not. It is a topic that deserves profounder study than it has so far received.

In Hellenistic times the vast areas occupied by the Greeks, since the conquests of Alexander, meant that the whole subject had to be re-explored. In the Seleucid kingdom, in particular, a relatively small number of Greeks lived among huge numbers of foreigners, most of whom did not speak the Greek language, or intend to. On the whole, the Hellenistic Greeks did not absorb a great deal from these foreign cultures, though there are Indian motifs on the coins of the Greeks who ruled on the Indus; and as time went on there were assimilations in Ptolemaic Egypt.

The Seleucid monarch Antiochus IV Epiphanes proved unable to tolerate the obvious detachment of the Jews from Hellenic culture.

> The king then issued a proclamation to the whole of his kingdom that they should all form one people and that they should each give up their own customs . . . The king also sent letters by messenger to Jerusalem and the cities of Judaea that they should follow customs alien to their land . . . and profane the sabbaths and festivals, defile the sanctuary and the holy men.[9]

The result was the great Jewish revolt that led to the establishment of the Maccabean Jewish kingdom (167–152 BC).

As for the Stoic philosophers, they scorned aliens as much as they scorned others not privileged to possess a Greek education.

With regard to blacks, Xenophanes, in the sixth century BC, had noted their differences from whites, but without adding pejorative comments. He had been arguing that the Greek gods are only shown in the particular guise in which we find them because it was Greeks who were describing them; and he makes the relativistic, unchauvinistic point that the Thracians, by the same token, see their gods as red-haired and blue-eyed, and the Ethiopians envisage them as snub-nosed and black.[10]

The Greeks did not feel any particular colour prejudice, and Hellenistic poets wrote appreciatively of their black girl friends. Here, for example, are the tributes of Philodemus and Asclepiades:

A small thing and moreover black is she,
But kinkier than parsley is Philainion's hair,
And sleeker than dawn is her complexion . . .
May I settle for Philainion as is, until,
Oh golden Cypris, I find a more developed one.[11]

Didyme waved a branch at me.
I melt as wax before her beauty.
If she is black, so's coal that glows,
When it's alight, more than the rose.[12]

Nevertheless, as Philodemus hinted, there were derogatory stereotypes lurking in the Greeks' attitudes to blacks. For black was a colour which stood for darkness and the underworld, and many slaves and prisoners of war were black. So they sometimes figure as grotesques in art, and are often represented as entertainers − as marginal characters.

The Romans were also a xenophobe people, but even before they had acquired a vast multinational empire they learnt to handle foreigners better than the Greeks ever had.

Their first problem, which continued for centuries, was how to deal with the numerous other Italian peoples against whom they had to fight before securing the unification of their own peninsula of Italy. They did this by patiently building up a mass of bilateral treaties, and by establishing friendly social relationships with the leaders of the other Italian peoples − a number of whom, indeed, were welcomed to Rome as immigrants. On the whole, Rome found it advisable to keep its bargains with its allies, displaying a calculated self-restraint, and indeed generosity, which the world had not seen before, and which proved successful for generation after generation.

But then Rome became involved with the Greek states, first in south Italy and Sicily, and subsequently, during and particularly after the traumatic Second Punic (Carthaginian) War, in the wider eastern world beyond. The last two centuries BC witnessed Rome's conquest of the Greek east. And it also witnessed an influx of foreign blood to Rome, mainly by the freeing of slaves (Chapter 8), so that Scipio Aemilianus could address the people with the words, 'Silence, ye to whom Italy is but a stepmother',[13] although Philip V of Macedonia, as has been seen (Chapter 8), thought it clever of the Romans to extend their citizenship so widely.

The Romans' attitudes to the Greeks posed a historic dilemma. On the one hand, they were well aware that the Greeks were their cultural superiors, and indeed, that it was to the Greeks that they themselves owed their own entire culture. On the other hand, they felt almost unmitigated contempt and dislike for contemporary Greeks (except for a few devoted and obedient secretaries). Nevertheless, in the convulsions of the civil wars, the freedmen who were given the commands of the contestants' fleets were mostly Greek.

When Augustus took over, after conquering the last accessible Hellenistic state (Cleopatra's Egypt), he converted this schizophrenic attitude into a formula. The Romans were to rule, while admiring Greek culture. The formula was neatly summed up by Virgil (in words ascribed to Aeneas's father Anchises in the underworld):

> There are others, assuredly I believe,
> Shall work in bronze, more sensitively moulding
> Breathing images, or carving from the marble
> More lifelike features; some shall plead more
> > eloquently,
> Or gauging with instruments the sky's motion
> Forecast the rising of the constellations:
> But yours, my Roman, is the gift of government.
> That is your bent – to impose upon the nation
> The code of peace: to be clement to the conquered,
> But utterly to crush the intransigent.[14]

So the Greeks duly provided a great deal of the art, architecture, medicine and teaching that the Romans wanted. But meanwhile Augustus took steps to check the further inflow of Greek blood into Rome, by his legislation restricting the manumission of slaves. For it was partly towards the slowing down of foreign, that is to say mainly Greek, infiltration, that the laws, according to Suetonius, were directed.[15]

But there were powerful foreigners, of Greek culture, at Rome among the freedmen of the emperor Claudius. Narcissus, Pallas, and the others who ruled the empire for him were Greeks, or from Greek lands, and Statius (as we saw) produced an elaborate encomium for another such functionary, Claudius Etruscus, who came from Smyrna – though the poet glosses over his ancestry.[16]

But what a lot of hatred, at a lower level too, such men must have aroused among Romans. One of the most malevolent, resentful pieces of writing in all Latin literature is Juvenal's attack on the Greeks at Rome.

> Now let me turn to that race which goes down so
> > well
> With our millionaires, but remains *my* special pet
> > aversion,
> And not mince my words. I cannot, citizens,
> > stomach
> A Greek-struck Rome . . .
> > Here's one from Sicyon,
> Another from Macedonia, two from Aegean islands –
> Andros, say, or Samos – two more from Caria,
> All of them lighting out for the city's classiest
> > districts
> And burrowing into great houses, with a long-term
> > plan
> For taking them over. Quick wit, unlimited nerve,
> > a gift
> Of the gab that outsmarts a professional public
> > speaker –
> These are their characteristics. What do you take
> That fellow's profession to be? He has brought a

<pre>
                              whole bundle
Of personalities with him – schoolmaster,
                                rhetorician,
Surveyor, artist, masseur, diviner, tightrope-walker,
Magician or quack, your versatile hungry Greekling
Is all by turns. Tell him to fly – he's airborne . . .
                  What's more, their talent
For flattery is unmatched . . .
                      Greece is a nation
Of actors. Laugh, and they split their sides. At
                        the sight
Of a friend's tears, they weep too – though quite
                          unmoved . . .
Besides, he holds nothing sacred, not a soul is
                          safe
From his randy urges . . .[17]
</pre>

Nor was Juvenal by any means the only writer who vilified the Greeks; Petronius and others did as well. And yet all Greek things were fashionable! It was an ambivalent, love-hate relationship; and it lay at the heart of Roman social life and history.

Juvenal was well aware, however, that a lot of these so-called Greeks were not Greeks at all, but easterners (like so many slaves – see Chapter 7).

<pre>
          What fraction of these sweepings
Derives, in fact, from Greece? For years now
                        Syrian
Orontes has poured its sewerage into our native
                        Tiber –
Its lingo and manners, its flutes, its outlandish
                        harps
With their transverse strings, its native
                        tambourines,
And the whores who hang out round the race-course.
            (That's where to go
If you fancy a foreign piece in one of those saucy
                    toques).[18]
</pre>

There is no doubt a certain amount of rhetorical exaggeration here, but it was true that quite a number of the 'Greeks' who arrived in Rome – including many who were originally slaves, bought or acquired by war or piracy – had in fact originated some way to the east. Demetrius, a rich freedman and envoy of Pompey, came from Gadara. The inventor of the Roman mime, the ex-slave Publilius Syrus, was from Antioch. Many others imported eastern skills to Rome. What proportion of eastern or Greek blood they possessed in their veins it is impossible to tell.

As regards other parts of the world, Caesar's henchman Lucius Cornelius Balbus was a portent. He came from Gades, from an entirely non-Roman (Semitic) family, and gained power and wealth at Rome, being defended, on one occasion, by a famous speech from Cicero. According to Pliny the elder, he was the first foreigner (*primus externorum*) to become consul (40 BC).[19] Caesar also made Gauls senators, and there were jokes about their outlandish appearance. There were two consuls from Narbonese Gaul under Caligula (AD 37–41), and Claudius, as censor in 48, added further Gallic notables, from the northern and central parts of the country, to the senate. He also took the opportunity to offer the senators a justification of this policy, no doubt in the face of opposition. A considerable fragment of his speech has survived on an inscription (rewritten by Tacitus):

> By a new policy, both my great-uncle, the deified Augustus, and my uncle Tiberius, wished all the cream of the colonies and municipalities everywhere, that is good worthy men, to be members of this house. What then? Is not an Italian senator better than a provincial one? I will show you, now that I am beginning to justify this part of my censorship, what I think on the matter. I believe that not even provincials can be rejected, if only they can adorn the senate house.[20]

Nero's principal advisers, in the earlier years of his reign, were both western provincials: Seneca came from Corduba, and Burrus from Vasio. When, after Nero's death, Gaul and the Rhineland revolted, Tacitus reproduced, or invented, a notable oration by the Roman commander Quintus Petillius Cerialis defending Rome's imperial domination of such foreigners:

> Throughout the whole of Gaul there were always despots and wars until you passed under our control. We ourselves, despite many provocations, imposed upon you by right of conquest only such additional burdens as were necessary for preserving peace.
>
> Stability between nations cannot be maintained without armies, nor armies without pay, nor pay without taxation. Everything else is shared equally between us. You often command our legions in person, and in person govern these and other provinces. There is no question of segregation or exclusion.
>
> Again, those emperors who are well spoken of benefit you as much as they do us, though you live far away, whereas tyrants wreak their will upon such as are nearest to them. You adopt an attitude of resignation towards natural disasters like bad harvests or excessive rainfall. In the same way you must put up with spending and avarice on the part of your masters. There will be faults as long as there are men.
>
> But the picture is not one of uninterrupted gloom. From time to time there are intervals of relief by way of compensation . . . If the Romans are expelled – which Heaven forbid! – what else will result but world-wide war in which each nation's hand will be turned against its neighbour?[21]

Owing to the demise of senatorial families, local élites replaced them, especially from outside Italy, constituting one-quarter of the senate by Flavian times. Snobbish attitudes towards foreigners continued but lost their dominant influence, and the first consul from Africa appeared in *c.*AD 80, followed ten years later by one from Asia. In the ethnic melting-pot of Antonine Rome, provincials for the first time formed a majority of the consular élite. Emperors, too, had now begun to come from foreign parts. The first was Trajan (AD 98–117), from Italica in Spain – descended from Roman settlers; his mother was a Spaniard, and his wife Plotina originated from Nemausus in Gaul. So did the family of Antoninus Pius

(138–161). It was not surprising that this was the epoch in which the ex-slave Epictetus, from Hierapolis in Phrygia, taught the common brotherhood of man.

Septimius Severus (193–211) was descended from an equestrian family, with senatorial but also perhaps Punic connections, of Lepcis Magna in north Africa; by this time more than half of the senators were provincials, among whom one third were north African like the emperor. His powerful wife Julia Domna was Syrian, and she was the great-aunt of Elagabalus, the first Syrian emperor (218–222). Most of the third-century emperors came from somewhere on the periphery of the empire, and were brought to the throne by the army in which they had served. Maximinus I (235–238) was a Danubian ex-ranker, and Philip I (244–249) the son of an Arab sheikh from Trachonitis. His successor Trajanus Decius (249–251) was a Pannonian from Budalia, Aurelian (270–275) came of a poor family from Lower Moesia, Diocletian (284–305) was of humble Dalmatian origin, and his colleague Maximian originated from a peasant family from Sirmium in Lower Pannonia.

And so it went on. Constantine's father Constantius I (305–306) was of Illyrian stock, and his co-emperor Galerius belonged to a family of farm-workers at Serdica. Magnentius (350–353) had a British father and a Frankish mother. Valentinian I (364–375), a Pannonian, was sneered at as a barbarian. So, by the poet Claudian, were two upstart rulers of the decades that followed, Magnus Maximus and Eugenius:

> Two tyrants burst upon the western climes,
> Their savage bosoms stored with various crimes.
> Fierce Britain was to one the native earth:
> The other owed to Germany his birth,
> A banished, servile wretch: both soiled with guilt:
> Alike their hands a master's blood had spilt.[22]

Many or most of the powerful eunuch *cubicularii* (chamberlains) of these late rulers (Chapter 8) were likewise of foreign origin.

Nevertheless, there was still a good deal of xenophobic feeling about. The historian Ammianus Marcellinus, himself from Syria, was disgusted when in AD 353 a shortage of food caused the governing class to throw foreigners (including himself) out of Rome:

> At last we have reached such a baseness that not so very long ago, when there was fear of a scarcity of food, foreigners were driven neck and crop from the city . . . There is no doubt that when, once upon a time, Rome was the abode of all the virtues, many of the nobles detained here foreigners of free birth by various kind attentions . . . But now the vain arrogance of some men regards everything born outside the limits of our city as worthless, except the childless and unwedded.[23]

As for the German invaders who contributed so largely to the downfall of the western empire, they had been preceded by a wide variety of German groups which had been settled in the empire at different periods from the time of Julius Caesar onwards, by the initiative of Roman leaders and emperors. The invaders felt rather like the people of Third World countries today. What they wanted, initially, was not to destroy the Roman empire, but to gain a share of its material advantages. It was only when that policy had visibly failed that they became hostile and destructive. I have written elsewhere, in *The Fall of the Roman Empire*, about the failure of the Roman authorities, or Roman public or literary opinion, to achieve any kind of sympathetic symbiosis with the Germans, which contributed largely to the downfall of the western empire, although so many of Rome's own principal generals were German.

As for one set of foreign invaders with whom Rome had to cope, the Huns, Ammianus Marcellinus really lets himself go about their foreignness:

> The Huns . . . are quite abnormally savage . . . They have squat bodies, strong limbs, and thick necks, and are so prodigiously ugly and bent that they might be two-legged animals, or the figures crudely carved from stumps which are seen on the parapets of bridges. Still, their shape, however disagreeable, is human.
>
> But their way of life is so rough that they have no use for fire or seasoned food, but live on the roots of wild plants and the half-raw flesh of any sort of animal, which they warm a little by placing it between their thighs and the backs of their horses . . .
>
> Once they have put their necks into some dingy shirt they never take it off or change it till it rots and falls to pieces from incessant wear . . . They remain glued to their horses, hardy but ugly beasts, on which they sometimes sit like women to perform their everyday business.[24]

But while the Romans were giving voice to such derogatory views about foreigners, they were also oppressing their own, Roman or Romanised, subjects so severely, by taxation and conscription, that many of the latter fled and decamped to the foreign invaders. In the end, the Romans' talent for handling foreigners, exhibited so often during the previous centuries, had deserted them, with terminal, fatal results.

Karl Marx

It is difficult to say anything useful or to 'take sides' about the attitudes of Karl Marx to ancient history, because such a lot has been said about them already, much of it contradictory. This is because his own observations on the subject were fragmentary, and he never gave it systematic attention, looking on the history of the ancient world, rather, as a selective lever to be employed for the promotion of his views about the present and future. It is also hard to distinguish the views of Marx himself from those of his successors, and particularly Friedrich Engels (with whom his relations have been so much discussed) and Lenin (supposed by many to have deviated from Marx), and neo-Marxists (who have indulged in obscurantist excesses of their own).

Nevertheless, something can, and should, still be said, at least tentatively. In the first place, communism, the creation of Marx, has failed in practice, as its abandonment in so many countries, and the convulsive chaos in the former Soviet Union, has made clear. Indeed, when one thinks of the coercions, miseries and murders communism has caused, and its inability or refusal to create a tolerable way of life for the people under its control, this is one of the most abject and spectacular failures in history. There are, however, two ways of looking at this. First, one can say that the failure is directly due to the flaws and inadequacies of Marxist doctrine, which is therefore squarely to blame for the collapse – with special censure attached to the appalling cruelties that its application has involved. Secondly, one can argue that Marxist doctrine, as such, is not to be blamed at all, but that it has been misapplied.

This second attitude, however, is of dubious validity, since it would be a strange coincidence, indeed, if Marxism had been misapplied *everywhere* (except in the very few dinosaur states where it still persists). One remains, therefore, with the suspicion that Marxist doctrine has not been misapplied, but that the societies which have applied it have proved hopelessly unsuccessful, and have given it up.

However, to proclaim such a conclusion in positive terms is beyond the scope of this book. Here we are concerned with ancient history, ancient social history, and – without altogether forgetting what has happened today – it is our duty to see if Karl Marx has contributed anything to our task.

Two things can immediately be said, one for and one against. In favour of Marx and Marxism it must be said that they have greatly helped to put economic and (interrelated) social factors on the historical map. Nor would it be fair to say that all other aspects of history have been neglected in the process, or at least not in the hands of Marx himself, and the best practitioners of his theories. Against the Marxist view of history, on the other hand, it must be pointed out that its portrait of inevitability, in the future as well as the present and past, is nonsense. For example, the collapse of capitalism and of the market economy, which according to this doctrine is one of the inescapable preliminaries to the inevitable Utopianism of the future, is just not happening, and there is no sign of it happening in the future: no serious social theorist, it has rightly been observed, can now speak in such terms.

The apocalyptic optimism of Marx was a bit of mid-Victorian confidence, influenced by the 'predictions' of the natural sciences, which is outdated and can no longer be taken seriously in our time: to which it does not belong. He constantly and invariably regarded the historical process from the point of view of the future liberation of humankind, and, as a historian, he had no justification for doing so. It may occur, or it may not (leaving aside the question of what such 'liberation' means), and it is misleading and misguided just to see the past as a series of incidents on the way to this supposedly ineluctable conclusion.

It was observed above that Marx's attention to ancient times was patchy, and selectively related to his view of the future. He possessed no coherent or important ideas about Greek and Roman history or social history, of which his treatment is not only schematic and deterministic, but sketchy, superficial, inconsistent, disorganised and uneven, in keeping with an ignorance about ancient (pre-capitalist) societies in general, about which his anachronisms (based on what he saw in the contemporary world of his own day) abounded. Indeed, he never devoted a great deal of attention to the interpretation of the ancient world, since he was not a historian at all, but a political activist.

It was therefore ridiculous of Kovalov to describe him as 'the greatest of original historians'[1], which he was not. Because he was not, Soviet ancient historians have had a hard time. Although Lenin liberally sprinkled his speeches with classical quotations, there was a lack of interest in the subject in the 1920s, and its 'revival' in 1934 got off to a handicapped start. No modern doctrine, it has become customary to say, has been refuted, and continues to be refuted, as often as Marxism.

In view of all this, it may well be asked why, in this attempt at a social history of Greece and Rome, a whole Appendix needs to be devoted to these nineteenth-century views of Karl Marx about ancient history. Is it worth the effort? Yes it is, because those views have had too much influence on ancient historians, and particularly on those concerned with social history, during the present century. First, there have been older historians who, although too sensible to agree with what Marx said, have derived a large part of their interpretations from his analytical method and terminology, which is illogical and unnecessary, since they are, as has been said, out of date, having been devised at and for a different epoch (the 'class struggle' is an example: see below, on Chapter 4). And, secondly, there are many younger historians who still, often unconsciously, purvey obsolete Marxist views to their students (e.g. about 'individualism': see below, on Chapter 3).

But let us now look at Marx's observations about the ancient world in relation to the themes considered in successive chapters of the present book.

PART I: WOMEN

Chapters 1 (Greek Women) and 2 (Roman Women)

Marxism has, on the whole, ignored the separate importance of women's history, because Karl Marx could not get away from Victorian values. He and Engels never seriously considered the 'class' status of ancient women, but Engels was prepared to consider them an exploited and oppressed 'class' in the Marxist sense.[2] Others, however, including a number of Marxists, have refused to accept this interpretation, since, quite apart from the uncertainties attached to the term 'class' (see below on Chapter 4), some women were exploited and oppressed (almost, as Marx and Engels believed, to the point of being slaves or slave-like), but others, emphatically, were not.

The whole Marxist approach to the origins of Greco-Roman womanhood is invalidated by Engels's conviction that Greek patriarchy was preceded by an aboriginal Bronze Age matriarchy, as supposed by Bachofen von Echt (1815–1887). But this theory is unprovable, dubious, and likely to be wrong, or at the very least irrelevant.

PART II: MEN

Chapter 3 (The Rich)

Marx's Greek 'merchant class' is a misleading myth. As to the much bandied-about term 'capitalism', it need not be discussed here, since it is inapplicable to the Greek and Roman world, as Marx himself realised, pronouncing ancient times to be 'pre-capitalist'.[3]

On a different point, he much too easily accepted Athens as the main, and typical, Greek phenomenon.

His doctrine also allowed too small a role to powerful individuals. This is largely due to Engels's disastrous remark that 'Napoleon did not come by chance, and if he had not come another man would have taken his place'.[4] This has caused many Marxists to belittle decisive men, who, according to them, merely identified themselves with conditions independent of them. Not all, however, have made this mistake (nor, without quaiifications, did Marx himself). And the supposition of these supra-individual tendencies and developments, at the expense of an interest in individuals, created an embarrassing dilemma when it became necessary to glorify the individual personality of the 'great leader' Stalin.

The truth rather is, as suggested in Chapter 3, that history is, indeed, directed by only a few men, good or bad, although these, of course, have their being and development within the framework of their community. Engels's belittlement of the individual, however, has proved popular, first among those who supported the communist point of view, and secondly among people who were disgusted by the atrocities of potent individuals of recent date such as Hitler (and Stalin), and thirdly among sociologists who are concerned less with individuals than with social groups. As a result, therefore, this doctrine has been overrated by teachers about the ancient world. In its naked state, however, it is absurd. For clearly history would not have taken quite the turn it did if the peculiar personal characteristics of Napoleon, or Augustus, had not influenced what happened. Things would have turned out differently, in a variety of ways. It is permissible to suppose that after the Treaty of Versailles some sort of Hitler was bound to emerge in Germany. But to suppose that, if it had not been Hitler, someone else with precisely the same kind of ideas would have 'taken his place' is a gratuitous assumption, and wholly improbable.

Karl Marx was worried, however, by the operations of Chance, and offered several explanations of the force that it obviously plays in history, which theoretically it ought not to do, under his systematised plan of progress. Another vital factor in the ancient world, religion, Marx saw as a buttress of the established order, designed to control the oppressed ('the opium of the masses') – which has some truth in it, but underestimates many other roles that religion, ancient and modern, has played.

Chapter 4 (The Poor)

Marx upsets his supporters and apologists by never managing to define the word 'class', which he uses in a variety of different senses. Certainly, it is useful that he identifies the poor with the people who carry out production for the benefit of the rich. But his concepts of class as a collective social expression, though of central importance to him (too important, some say), are left distressingly vague, and, as far as they go, ignore the varying nuances of the ancient (or modern) social scene. The result has been endless and not very fertile discussions about whether, and when, one should use the word 'class' at all in speaking of the ancient world – seeing that it was a product of the British Industrial Revolution – or whether one ought to use instead some other term such as (social or economic) group or status or even order. Or, alternatively, if the term 'class' *has* to be used, what section of the population does it comprise?

In simple, practical terms it can be concluded that Marx intended to say, rightly, that there were two main classes, the exploiting rich and the exploited poor. But it has been suggested that these can, and should, only be described as 'classes' when waging a collective struggle, one against the other. Here, however, a leading problem about Marxism arises. The central concept of the thought of Karl Marx, the great motive power of history according to him, was the class struggle, and G. E. M. de Sainte Croix has called an important book *The Class Struggle in the Ancient Greek World* (1981). He is, or was, a Marxist, but although not lacking in reverence for that cause shows a profound consciousness of the criticisms that can be launched against its theory. Nevertheless, that is what he calls his book. It is about a vast number of matters, handled with great skill and learning. But the book's title is misleading. Despite the 1848 Communist Manifesto's declaration, at its outset, that *all* past history was the history of class struggles, the greater part of the history of Greece and Rome witnessed no overt class struggle at all, and Marx's attempts to locate a permanent struggle were, and could only be, fluctuating and erratic.

For one thing, the oppressed 'class' – if one can employ that term – was not sufficiently organised or unified or class-conscious to undertake such a struggle.

136

True, there were, at intervals, antagonisms and conflicts in which certain oppressed people rose against their oppressors. But these conflicts scarcely ever turn out to be 'class struggles', in any meaningful sense of the word. In almost every case, peculiar, localised, special aims were in mind, which did not involve the interests or participation of the oppressed 'class' as a universal whole. De Sainte Croix is well aware of the arguments that these circumstances marshal against his title, and of the theme that it involves (arguing, for example, that 'overtness' is irrelevant, and that 'veiled hostility' is enough to justify the label). But he persists with his theme all the same. It is generally held, however, that he is wrong to do so. Perhaps there *ought*, morally speaking, to have been a class struggle persisting throughout the history of the ancient world, but there was not. Karl Marx's 'class struggle' is more a hypothesis about what the world might be than what it was (or is). The idea of a constant, perpetual class struggle is not accurate, particularly in regard to Greece and Rome.

Karl Marx believed that the Roman conflict between debtors and creditors caused the ruin of the former, which was, up to a point, not untrue, although it underestimates or ignores the subsequent efforts by Julius Caesar, among others, to rectify the situation. But what is more curious, or hard-hearted, is that Marx, devoted as he was to the class struggle, called the dispossessed peasants of the late Roman Republic a 'mob of do-nothings'.[5] For he and Engels could not help comparing them to the 'poor whites' in the southern slave states of the USA before 1861.

Marxists also believed that the class struggle is the principal explanation for the ultimate downfall of the western Roman empire, in which the productive forces, they say, declined and the division of labour collapsed. There is an element of truth in this, because the alienation of the poor from the state caused them to show all too little enthusiasm for its defence against the invaders. But when Marxists add the explanation that the state was the main extractor of a surplus in the later Roman empire, and that this was why economic collapse occurred, their argument is too intricate and beside the point. And, in any case, there were other reasons for the collapse as well, as I tried to point out in my book *The Fall of the Roman Empire* (1976, 1990). External menaces were as powerful as internal, though Stalin (deviating from the standard Marxist view, quoted above) oversimplified when he remarked that the non-Romans united against the common enemy and overthrew Rome with a loud crash, an almighty bang.

PART III: THE UNFREE AND THE FREED

Chapter 5 (Serfs)

Marx did not appreciate the various grades of Greek and Roman society intermediate between the free and the slaves. Or rather, he knew that they existed, but did not attach enough importance to them – except as forerunners of a new, medieval mode of production.

Chapters 6 (Greek Slaves) and 7 (Roman Slaves)

Here Marxism deserves notice, to a unique degree, because its exponents are the only writers who have attempted a really systematic and integral approach to slavery, treating it as the principal form of the exploitation of society, and the creator of wealth that made leisure activity possible for the free. This is salutary. Sometimes, however, these arguments go too far. True, when Engels declared that, without ancient slavery, degrading and backward though it was, modern socialism would never have existed, he may have had a point – not surprisingly, since without what happened in the ancient world many features of the modern world would not have been what they are today. But, in the Leninist and Stalinist eras, such assertions became greatly exaggerated, when efforts were made to show that slavery lay at the root of every conceivable ancient material and cultural phenomenon.

Furthermore, a grave dilemma was posed by the role of the slaves in the so-called class struggle in the ancient world: first, because any 'class struggle' which, on limited occasions, can be legitimately identified, was between the free rich and the free poor, with the slaves left outside – as some Marxists have appreciated – and, secondly, because if one extends the 'class struggle' to cover the relationship between slave-owners and slaves, it remains difficult to locate a 'class' of slaves, since they were so extremely mixed, and never formed a single, recognisable, conscious class.

Moreover, the Marxist interpretations of the three Slave Revolts against Rome as manifestations of the 'class struggle' prove unsatisfactory, since, as stated earlier in this book, they displayed no signs of a unified 'class struggle' at all, but were manifestations of particular grievances, with limited, pragmatic aims. The Marxist elevation of the revolt of Spartacus is especially overdone and fatuous. He was a brave and able man, but surely Marx should not have called him 'the most splendid fellow in the whole world of ancient history'.[6] In the 1920s, Spartacus was the only hero of antiquity that Soviet schoolchildren ever heard of.

However, Karl Marx does not seem to have been unaware of the problems involved in this overestimation of slavery (by people who claimed to echo his views), since he remarks that 'perhaps slaves formed only the pedestal on which the ancient class conflicts took place'.[7] Some have declared that this was only a momentary aberration on Marx's part, but it is a judicious remark. However, when Marx talks of the 'slave mode of production', he does not use the term consistently, and it is often difficult to know exactly what he means. And traditional Marxists have overestimated the proportion of chattel-slaves in the population.

Finally, too, the Marxist belief that both Greece and the Roman Republic and then the western Roman empire collapsed because of slavery is untenable. It was not, for example, because of a class conflict between slave-owners and slaves that Athenian democracy declined.[8] There were many reasons why it declined (including military pressures from outside), but that was not one of them. Nor was it because of Spartacus's slave revolt that the Roman Republic fell, nor, very emphatically, did the western Roman empire collapse because it was a slave society. The lower classes in general, as we have seen, had become alienated during the later empire, but slaves, in these final phases, had been partially replaced by other dependent elements, as Marx knew. And once again, there were external pressures, as, indeed, Marxists cannot fail to have realised.

To sum up, Marxism made great contributions owing to the detailed care it devoted to ancient slavery. But Marxist handling of the theme has been flawed, in a number of respects. One trouble, it may be repeated, was that Karl Marx was a child of his times. That is to say, although well aware of the difference between ancient slavery and modern wage labour, he did base a lot of his views on the contemporary slave situation in the United States of America. That, partly, is why his treatment of the subject is unsatisfactory.

Chapter 8 (Freedmen and Freedwomen)

I do not believe that Karl Marx sufficiently recognised the enormous contribution of manumission to upward mobility in the ancient world, which was by this means, to a considerable extent, emancipated from the iron social constraints of which Marxists are so well aware.

Appendix 1 (Foreigners)

Marx was notably Europocentric, which was not perhaps so astonishing as it seems when one thinks of the attitudes of his times. One conspicuous example is his insistence on the stagnant 'Oriental/Asiatic mode of production', a static system based on a despot's arbitrary whim, in contrast to western dynamism.[9]

There is no need to comment on this theory in detail here, since it was based on historical and anthropological ignorance, and has been shot down by many writers, including some with impeccable Marxist credentials. Naturally the Chinese (not to speak of a lot of Russians) do not care for such an attitude, but the strongest indication of its falsity is offered by the present powerful position of Japan – and the future that evidently lies ahead of that country. Curiously enough, however, leaving Japan (and possibly one or two other countries) aside, this viewpoint begins to strike a chord again today, when an antithesis seems to be building up again between developed Europe and the undeveloped and increasingly resentful Third World.

Marx had very little to say about Greek metics.

References

Introduction

1 G. M. Trevelyan, *The Use of History*, 1946, p. 69.

PART I: WOMEN

Chapter 1. Greek Women

1 Sophocles, *Ajax*, 293.
2 Thucydides, II, 44 (tr. R. Warner).
3 Demosthenes, *Against Simon*, 96, 6f. (tr. W. R. M. Lamb).
4 Aristophanes, *Lysistrata*, 15–19 (tr. J. Ferguson and K. Chisholm).
5 Ibid., 641ff. (tr. M. Hadas).
6 Homer, *Iliad*, VI, 429–32 (tr. R. Fagles).
7 Ibid., 440–450, 454–63 (tr. R. Fagles).
8 Homer, *Odyssey*, XXIII, 232ff. (tr. E. Rees).
9 *Iliad*, IX, 120ff. (tr. R. Fagles).
10 Ibid., VI, 490ff. (tr. R. Fagles).
11 Hesiod, *Works and Days*, 57ff. (tr. D. Wender).
12 Semonides (tr. H. Lloyd Jones), *Females of the Species: Semonides on Women*, pp. 36, 40, 42, 43, 46, 48, 50, 52, 54.
13 Sappho, *Oxyrhynchus Papyri*, 1231, 50–54 (J. M. Edmonds, *Lyra Graeca*, I, p. 216, no 46, tr. P. Roche).
14 Sappho, *Berliner Klassikertexte*, p. 9722.2 (Edmonds, *op cit*, p. 240, no 83, tr. M. Barnard).
15 Aeschylus, *Eumenides*, 657ff. (tr. R. Fagles).
16 Sophocles, *Antigone*, 44ff. (tr. R. Fagles).
17 Euripides, *Children of Heracles*, 474ff. (tr. R. Gladstone).
18 Euripides, *Medea*, 231ff. (tr. R. Warner).
19 Xenophon, *Oeconomicus*, VII, 35ff. (tr. *The World of Athens*, J.A.C.T., 1984, p. 168).
20 Lactantius, *Divine Institutions*, III, 19.
21 Plato, *Timaeus*, XLIX, 91 (tr. H. D. P. Lee).
22 Diogenes Laertius, VI, 12.
23 Demosthenes, *Against Neaera*, 59, 118–22.
24 Pliny the elder, *Natural History*, XXXV, 133.
25 M. Grant, *The Visible Past* (1990), pp. 44f.
26 Hyperides, *For Euxenippus*, 36.
27 Plutarch, *Alexander*, 68, 3.
28 S. B. Pomeroy, *Women in Hellenistic Egypt* (1990), p. 15.

29 Theocritus, *Idylls*, XV.
30 Ibid, II, 37ff. (tr. A. Holden).
31 Apollonius Rhodius, *Argonautica*, III, 1013ff. (tr. G. Allen).
32 Meleager, *Greek Anthology* (ed. P. Jay), 5, 24, 8 (tr. P. Whigham).
33 Diogenes Laertius, VI, 97.
34 *Palatine Anthology*, VII, 718.
35 Tebtunis Papyri, 104 (tr. A. S. Hunt and C. C. Edgar).
36 Plutarch, *Agis*, 7, 5ff. (tr. M. M. Austin).
37 Diodorus Siculus, I, 27, 2.

Chapter 2. Roman Women

1 Cicero, *For Murena*, 12, 27.
2 Dessau, *Inscriptiones Latinae Selectae*, 8403 (tr. R. Lattimore).
3 Plutarch, *Tiberius Gracchus*, 1 (tr. I. Scott-Kilvert).
4 Nepos, preface, 6.
5 Livy, II, 40.
6 Cato the elder; Livy, XXXIV, 2ff.
7 Livy, XXXIX, 8.
8 Cicero, *For Caelius*, 49ff. (tr. M. Grant).
9 Sallust, *Jugurtha*, 24f. (tr. I. Scott-Kilvert).
10 Cicero, *Letters to Atticus*, IV, 11, 18; *Letters to Brutus*, I, 18, 1f., etc.
11 *Laudatio Turiae* (tr. E. Wistrand).
12 Appian, *Civil Wars*, IV, 32ff.
13 Gaius, *Institutes*, I, 145.
14 Propertius, IV, 11.
15 Suetonius, *Caligula*, 23.
16 Suetonius, *Augustus*, 19, 1.
17 Tacitus, *Annals*, XII, 7, 10.
18 Dessau, *Inscriptiones Latinae Selectae*, 3785.
19 Seneca, *On Consolation*, 16 (tr. J. W. Basore).
20 Pliny the younger, *Letters*, VII, 5 (tr. B. Radice).
21 Plutarch, *Moral Essays*, 138a (*Advice on Marriage*, 19) (tr. R. Warner).
22 Plutarch, *Moral Essays*, 242.
23 Juvenal, *Satires*, VI, 28–31, 42–6 (tr. P. Green).
24 Maccius, *Greek Anthology* (ed. P. Jay), 5, 114 (tr. W. G. Shepherd).
25 Anonymus, *Selections from the Greek Anthology* (tr. A. Sinclair).
26 *Oxyrhynchus Papyri*, 1380, 214–16.
27 Dio Cassius, LXXVIII, 18 (tr. E. Cary).
28 *Scriptores Historiae Augustae, Severus Alexander*, XIV, 7 (tr. D. Magie).
29 Ammianus Marcellinus, XIV, 6, 19, XXVIII, 4, 34 (tr. W. Hamilton).

PART II: MEN

Chapter 3. The Rich

1 Karl Marx, *The German Ideology* (tr. T. B. Bottomore), in P. G. Gardiner, *Theories of History* (1959), p. 129.

2 Homer, *Iliad*, XII, 310ff. (tr. R. Fagles).
3 Ibid., II, 255ff. (tr. R. Fagles).
4 Homer, *Odyssey*, VIII, 159ff. (tr. E. Rees).
5 *Iliad*, IX, 602ff. (tr. R. Fagles).
6 Theognis, 183–92W (tr. A. W. H. Adkins).
7 Plutarch, *Solon*, 22.
8 Pindar, *Olympian Odes*, XIII, 13.
9 Ibid., X, 20.
10 Pindar, *Nemean Odes*, III, 41 (tr. C. M. Bowra).
11 Aristotle, *Politics*, III, vii, 7ff.
12 Demosthenes, *Against Eubulides*, 30–6.
13 Aristotle, *Politics*, IV, ix, 6ff. (tr. H. Rackham).
14 M. Grant, *The Classical Greeks*, p. 263.
15 Homer, *Iliad*, XI, 784f. (R. Fagles).
16 Demosthenes (*Erotic Essay*), LXI, 52.
17 G. M. Trevelyan, *British History in the Nineteenth Century*, p. vii.
18 Velleius Paterculus, II, 126.
19 R. Syme, *The Roman Revolution*, p. 7.
20 Augustine, *The City of God*, IV, 27.
21 Sallust, *Jugurthine War*, 41f. (tr. I. Scott-Kilvert).
22 Symmachus, *Letters*, I, 52; *Panegyrici Latini*, IV, 352.
23 Synesius, *On Kingship* (AD 399).
24 Ammianus Marcellinus, XXVIII, 4, 5 (W. Hamilton).
25 Salvian, *On the Governance of God*, III, 50.
26 *Codex Theodosianus*, XII, 1, 11; XVI, 2, 3.

Chapter 4. The Poor

1 Theognis, 173–8 (tr. T. F. Higham); cf. 1117.
2 Alcaeus, fragment 18 (J. M. Edmonds).
3 Amphis, fragment 17.2f. (T. Kock).
4 Homer, *Iliad*, II, 216ff.
5 Homer, *Odyssey*, XI, 480 ff. (tr. R. Lattimore).
6 Herodotus, VII, 102, 1.
7 Pseudo-Xenophon (Old Oligarch), *Constitution of Athens* (tr. C. M. Gray) (A. W. H. Adkins and P. White [eds], *Readings in Western Civilization*, I, *The Greek Polis*, p. 48).
8 Aristotle, *Constitution of Athens*, 243, e.
9 Thucydides, III, 83.
10 E.g., Xenophon, *Hellenica*, III, 311.
11 Aristotle, *Politics*, III, 1297b 6ff.
12 Aristotle, *Rhetoric*, 1367a.
13 Aeneas Tacticus, *Poliorcetica*, XIV, 1.
14 Diodorus Siculus, XIX, 9 (tr. M. M. Austin).
15 Diodorus Siculus, III, 12, 1ff.
16 Plutarch, *Tiberius Gracchus* (tr. I. Scott-Kilvert).
17 Ibid., 9 (tr. I. Scott-Kilvert).
18 Plutarch, *Gaius Gracchus*, 3 (tr. I. Scott-Kilvert).

19 Sallust, *Jugurthine War*, 86.
20 Sallust, *Catiline*, 14 (tr. I. Scott-Kilvert).
21 Appian, *Civil War*, V, ii, 12f. (tr. H. White).
22 Tacitus, *Annals*, I, 2.
23 Juvenal, *Satires*, X, 81.
24 Tacitus, *Annals*, I, 1.
25 Velleius Paterculus, II, 126.
26 Pliny the younger, *Letters*, IX, 5.
27 Dessau, *Inscriptiones Latinae Selectae*, 7457.
28 Juvenal, *Satires*, XVI.
29 *Oxyrhynchus Papyri*, 1490, 1469, 1477.
30 *Panegyrici Latini*, V, 5–14 (tr. N. Lewis and M. Reinhold).
31 Cf. M. Grant, *The Fall of the Roman Empire* (1990 ed.), p. 56.
32 Salvian, *On the Governance of God*, V, 28, 34–36 (tr. E. Sanford).
33 Ammianus Marcellinus XIV, 6, 25; XXVIII, 4, 28 (tr. W. Hamilton).
34 *Codex Theodosianus*, I, 29, 1 (tr. C. Pharr).

PART III: THE UNFREE AND THE FREED

Chapter 5. Serfs

1 Pollux, *Onomasticon*, III, 83.
2 Strabo, VIII, 5, 4.
3 Athenaeus, XIV, 74, 657cd (tr. C. W. Fornara).
4 Thucydides, IV, 84 (tr. R. Warner).
5 Solon, fragments 5, 34.
6 E.g., Pliny the younger, *Letters*, III, 19, 6.
7 *Codex Theodosianus*, V, 17, 1.
8 Salvian, *On the Governance of God*, V, 21, 24–7 (tr. E. Sanford).

Chapter 6. Greek Slaves

1 Plato, *Republic*, IX.
2 Aristotle, *Politics*, I, 1253b.
3 Pseudo-Aristotle, *Oeconomica*, 1344a, 22.
4 Dioscorides, *Palatine Anthology*, VII, 178 (tr. R. A. Furness).
5 Homer, *Odyssey*, XVII, 323.
6 Thucydides, VII, 27.
7 Euripides, *Helen*, 726ff. (tr. J. Ferguson and K. Chisholm).
8 Pseudo-Xenophon (Old Oligarch), *Constitution of Athens* (tr. C. M. Gray) (A. W. H. Adkins and P. White [eds], *Readings in Western Civilization*, I, *The Greek Polis*, p. 50).
9 Xenophon, *Hieron*, 4, 3.
10 Antisthenes in Y. Garlan, *Slavery in Ancient Greece* (1988), p. 15.
11 Aristotle, *Politics*, 1255a, 5ff.; 1253b, 20ff. (tr. H. Rackham).
12 Ibid., 1255a, 31f.; 1255b, 8ff.
13 Pseudo-Aristotle, *Oeconomica*, 5 (tr. E. S. Foster).
14 Menander, *The Sicyonian* (tr. P. Vellacott).
15 Diogenes Laertius, VI, 121.

Chapter 7. Roman Slaves

1 Ulpian, *Digest*, 5.1.122.
2 Cato the elder, *On Agriculture*, II, 4, 7.
3 Plutarch, *Cato*, 21 (tr. B. Perrin).
4 Diodorus Siculus, XXXIV, 25ff. (N. Lewis and M. Reinhold).
5 Appian, *Civil War*, IV, 13.
6 Publilius Syrus, fragment 596.
7 Augustus, *Res Gestae*, 25.
8 Seneca, *Epistulae Morales*, 47 (tr. R. M. Gummere).
9 Dessau, *Inscriptiones Latinae Selectae*, 1514.
10 Tacitus, *Annals*, XIV, 43f.
11 Pliny the elder, *Natural History*, XVIII, 36 and 4.
12 Columella, *On Farming*, 8 (tr. H. B. Ash).
13 Pliny the younger, *Letters*, III, 14.
14 Dio Chrysostom, *On Slavery and Freedom*, 16.
15 Apuleius, *Metamorphoses*, IX, 12f. (tr. R. Graves).
16 Dio Cassius, LXXVII, 10, 2.
17 Augustine, *Letters*, 10.
18 *Codex Theodosianus*, II, 25, 1 (tr. N. Lewis and M. Reinhold).
19 Paul, Letter to Philemon, 12.

Chapter 8. Freedmen and Freedwomen

1 Aristotle, *Politics*, VII, 1330a, 32f.
2 Ibid., III, 1275b, 37.
3 H. Collitz and F. Bechtel (eds), *Sammlungen der griechischen Dialekt-Inschriften*, II, 1854.
4 *Digest*, 40, 4 (cf. Ulpian, *Disputationes*, 6).
5 Dessau, *Inscriptiones Latinae Selectae*, 8763 (letter from Philip V of Macedonia to Larissa).
6 *Inscriptiones Graecae*, IX, 517, W. Dittenberger, *Sylloge Inscriptionum Graecarum*, 3rd ed., 543 (tr. N. Lewis and M. Reinhold).
7 Dionysius of Halicarnassus, IV, 23.
8 Ibid., IV, 24, 5.
9 Pliny the elder, *Natural History*, XXXIII, 47, 135.
10 Dio Cassius, L, 10, 4.
11 H. M. Last, *Cambridge Ancient History*, X, 461, 479f.
12 Statius, *Silvae*, III, 3.
13 Seneca the younger, *Letters*, 27, 5.
14 Horace, *Epodes*, 4, 1–6 (tr. W. G. Shepherd).
15 Juvenal, I, 95ff. (tr. P. Green).
16 Justinian, *Institutes*, 5 (tr. T. C. Sandars).
17 Ibid.

Appendix 1. Foreigners

1 Isocrates, *Panegyricus*, IV, 50.
2 Pseudo-Xenophon (Old Oligarch), *Constitution of Athens* (tr. C. M. Gray)

REFERENCES

(A. W. H. Adkins and P. White [eds], *Readings in Western Civilization*, I, *The Greek Polis*, p. 50).
3 Ibid., p. 52.
4 M. I. Finley, *The Ancient Economy*, p. 163.
5 Plato, *Laws*, VIII, 850.
6 Ibid., XII, 952f. (tr. T. J. Saunders).
7 Isocrates, *Letter to Philip*, III, 5.
8 Plutarch, *On the Bravery and Virtue of Alexander the Great*, 328c–329d (tr. M. M. Austin).
9 I Maccabees 1: 10ff.
10 Xenophanes, fragment 16.
11 Philodemus, *Greek Anthology* (P. Jay ed.), 5, 121, (tr. W. Moebius).
12 Asclepiades, *Selections from the Greek Anthology* (tr. A. Sinclair).
13 Valerius Maximus, VI, 2, 3.
14 Virgil, *Aeneid*, VI, 847ff. (tr. Patric Dickinson).
15 Suetonius, *Augustus*, 40, 3.
16 Statius, *Silvae*, III, 3.
17 Juvenal, III, 59ff. (tr. P. Green).
18 Ibid., 62ff.
19 Pliny the elder, *Natural History*, VII, 43.
20 Dessau, *Inscriptiones Latinae Selectae*, 212 (embroidered by Tacitus, *Annals*, XI, 23).
21 Tacitus, *Histories*, IV, 74 (tr. K. Wellesley).
22 Claudian, *De Quarto Consulatu Honorii*, 73ff.
23 Ammianus Marcellinus, XIV, 6, 19 (tr. W. Hamilton).
24 Ammianus Marcellinus, XXXI, 2 (tr. W. Hamilton).

Appendix 2. Karl Marx

1 Quoted by W. Z. Rubinsohn, *Spartacus's Uprising and Soviet Historical Writing*, p. 11.
2 F. Engels, in Marx-Engels, *Selected Works*, pp. 494f.
3 K. Marx: see P. Lekas, *Marx on Classical Antiquity*, index, s.v. Precapitalism.
4 F. Engels: quoted by R. N. Carew-Hunt, *The Theory and Practice of Communism*, p. 72.
5 K. Marx to *Otechestvenniye Zapiski*, p. 294.
6 K. Marx: letter to Engels 27/2/1861, Marx-Engels, *Selected Works*, pp. 151f.
7 K. Marx, Preface to second edition of *The Eighteenth Brumaire of Louis Bonaparte*, p. 145.
8 As F. Engels, *Anti-Dühring* (preparatory notes), English translation, pp. 413f.
9 About Marx's complex ('best forgotten') variations on this theme, see G. E. M. de Sainte Croix, *The Class Struggle in the Ancient World*, pp. 29, 544 n. 15.

145

Notes

Introduction

Social History. G. M. Trevelyan's definition is commented on by H. J. Perkin in H. P. R. Finberg (ed.), *Approaches to History: A Symposium* (1962, 1963), pp. 51ff. But on the problems of completely divorcing social from political history see H. R. Trevor-Roper, *The Gentry 1540–1640* (1953), p. 44. Perkin attempts a more positive definition of the former in *History: An Introduction for the Intending Student* (1970), pp. 86ff.

PART I: WOMEN

Chapter 1. Greek Women

Matrilinear succession was retained, unusually, at Locri Epizephyrii. In Lycia men were known by their mother's rather than their father's name.

Greek goddesses. Hera, whose great shrines were at Argos (where the priestesses were eponymous) and on the island of Samos, was surely the earth-mother, although some question this. Artemis, whose most important temple was at Ephesus, was the Great Goddess of Asia Minor, the Mistress of Animals (Homer, *Iliad*, XXI, 470). The Greeks tamed her and made her a virgin goddess. Aphrodite, who likewise had dual roles, possessed cults at Paphos and Corinth (where her worship was associated with prostitution). Athena was a blend of the warrior daughter of Zeus and the pre-Hellenic goddess of Athens. She was the goddess of both wisdom and weaving. Demeter, whose solemn Mysteries were celebrated at Eleusis, was a fusion between a pre-Hellenic underworld deity and a Mesopotamian grain-goddess, and stood for the revival of the earth's fertility. The Homeric *Hymns to Demeter and Aphrodite* reflect terror as well as beneficence. The *Hymn to Apollo* presents the female as beneficent when subjected to the male. Gaia, the goddess of the Earth (one of the primal couple in Hesiod's *Theogony*), has her own *Hymn*. Even in patriarchal Olympus the goddesses were more intimately involved than the gods in the lives of human beings.

Argus was a monster with three, four or many eyes, killed by Hermes.

Sappho saw Helen as an active director of her own life, choosing and desiring; she celebrates Helen and does not judge her. Stesichorus's *Palinode* denied the traditional stories against Helen (probably so as not to offend those who worshipped her).

Subordination of Athenian women. They were thought of as wild things (almost like domestic animals) who must be tamed by marriage, were excluded from inheriting land in their own name, and had to be represented at law by male

146

guardians. But strict segregation could not be afforded by the poor, who also allowed their women various work outside the home. Male superiority was largely based on the great importance attached to soldiering. Women were less numerous than men – partly because female infanticide by exposure was commoner than male.

Festivals. The absence of men from the Thesmophoria gave the festival a secretive, uncanny quality, suggesting the dissolution of the patriarchal family and criticism of male arrogance and insufficiency. The Skira and Adonia festivals (in which the women broke out into passionate lamentation) aroused the suspicion of men who could not, however, impede these sacred occasions. The Panathenaic festival (probably inaugurated in the sixth century BC) recognised the contributions of non-citizen groups, including women. Segregated and politically excluded women participated in religion as compensation for lack of access to other aspects of public life, and tended to turn to orgiastic ecstasy.

Education of Greek women. The circle of Sappho was clearly well-educated and the Pythagorean circle included women. Athenian girls, although principally instructed in domestic arts, were often taught to read and write, but few received higher education, except *hetairai* (women shown reading on vase paintings may often be of this status). In extant tragedy, only Euripides's Phaedra reads, but later literature is full of women who can read and write; though there was no widespread educational reform which dealt with their requirements.

Pericles's citizen law of 451–450, which was based on the view that the number of citizens had increased too greatly, stressed the family as the source of new citizens and of property inheritance.

Sparta. The whole system was a reaction against the household (*oikos*) tradition: family values were repressed (except as a focus for the supervision of the agriculturally dependent economy) and the sole aim was to produce soldiers.

Freedom, women's. The Gortyna Code shows a degree of freedom closer to Sparta than to Athens. Women were also freer in western colonies, such as Acragas (colonists often did not take their women with them).

Thargelia. There may have been two (M. Grant, *The Classical Greeks* [1989], p.310).

Macedonia. Eurydice I learnt to read and write when she already had two mature sons. Cleopatra, the sister of Alexander I (*c*.495–450), had been sought in marriage by army generals. Cynane, the daughter of Philip II and Audata-Eurydice (an Illyrian), hired a mercenary force with her own funds and was killed in battle.

Hellenistic queens. On their coins, the Ptolemaic Cleopatras wear the diadem (*tainia*) of kings. Arsinoe II, Berenice II and Phila were patrons of literature, and Artemisia II of Halicarnassus promoted a literary competition. Towards the end of the fourth century, Cratesipolis ruled Sicyon for seven years, and Amastris, the niece of Darius III, was tyrant of Heraclea in Bithynia. Agathocleia Theotropos was associated with the Indo-Greek Strato I (*c*.130–75) in her own right. In Sparta, Agesistrata and Archidamia were not queens, but their wealth was essential to their son and grandson Agis IV (*c*.262–241).

Chapter 2. Roman women

Tanaquil (Tancvil) of Etruscan Tarquinii was said to have possessed a knowledge of divination and medicine, and to have spurred on her husband Tarquinius Priscus to the kingship of Rome in the seventh century BC.

The Vestal Virgins, priestesses of Vesta (whose temple was in the Roman Forum), normally six in historical times, were entitled to numerous privileges.

Marriage. Average age fourteen. 95 per cent of the women on north African gravestones are married.

Servilia took the lead at two meetings, on 8 June and 25 July 44 BC.

Augustus's laws were aimed at keeping women married and bearing children, and limiting the power exercised by the daughters of great houses. Before him, there had been no law forbidding adultery (which had been treated as a family matter), but Augustus punished adultery of women with freedmen and slaves. He also forbade senators and their descendants to marry freedwomen, and penalised childless widows who did not marry, though he permitted a freeborn woman with three children to dispense with a guardian.

Dedications by Eumachia to Concordia Augusta (imperial harmony) and Pietas (devotion to gods, country and family).

Early third century AD. According to Ulpian (*Digest*, V, 1, 12, 2), only custom exlcuded women (and slaves) from public life.

Saints Jerome and Augustine. It has recently been argued, somewhat dubiously, that St Jerome was not as anti-feminist as had been supposed, and that Augustine deserves to be described as the first Christian feminist. Christian heroines go back to Perpetua and Felicitas, the former of whom described their martyrdom in AD 202–203.

PART II: MEN

Chapter 3. The Rich

Sarpedon and Glaucus. The commander and second-in-command of Priam's Lycian allies at Troy.

Gifts. Greek ethical thought was much concerned with mutual gift-giving and obligations to friends.

Hetaireiai were not only political but military (the poorest class was not in the armies).

Solon on rich. Wealth was the basis of his hierarchy: M. Grant, *The Rise of the Greeks* (1987), p. 52.

Commerce was sneered at by philosophers, etc., but not universally. Herodotus (II, 167) remarked that the Corinthians despised trade least.

Agriculture. Land was the fountain-head of all good, material and moral. The ruling class at Syracuse were the *gamoroi*, 'those who divide the land'.

Solon catalogued the ways of making money, noting that the richest 'have twice the eagerness that others have'.

Fifth-century Athens continued to draw most of its leaders from the rich, among whom Cimon (died *c*.450) was notable. The demagogues were rich, but not of the old nobility; later generations did not share Aristophanes's and Thucydides's low opinion of Cleon. The rich helped to preserve their own ascendancy by lavishness, and the *demos* never attacked their fortunes and honours. By the end of the century 20–25 per cent of Athenians possessed no land.

Upper-class terrorism at Athens. E.g. the murder of Ephialtes (462), and oligarchic coups of 411 and 404.

Fourth century. Xenophon still maintained that agriculture was the only work suitable for an Athenian citizen, because it promoted the qualities needed by the state; Aristotle, however, rejected agriculture in common with trade. He also felt that the new rich create more annoyance than the old rich (*Rhetoric*, II, 1387a). Demosthenes complained that politicians made money out of offices of state.

Middle-class bias is apparent in Greek moralising, which condemns both rich and poor. For the term, see G. E. M. de Sainte Croix, *The Class-Struggle in the Ancient Greek World*, p. 548.

Individualism. The principle was introduced (into the modern world) by the Protestant Reformation, and reinforced in 1789. Alexis de Tocqueville (1805–1889) seems to have coined the term. For the obstacles it encountered from Marxism, see Appendix 2. It maintains that the individual is an end in himself and of supreme value, society being only a means to individual ends, and the role of the liberal state being to maximise individual freedom and opportunity. But the individual's inextricable link with his social background was understood by F. D. Roosevelt: 'favour comes [to man] because, for a brief moment in the great space of human change and progress, some general purpose finds in him a satisfactory embodiment' (speech at Poughkeepsie on 7 November 1932).

The city-state seemed to the Greeks to give men the chance to be themselves – to release all the potential of their human nature.

Individualism of Greek lyric poets. Much of their so-called 'emergent individualism' is an effort to define the role of the poet, or experiment in the depiction of types – though the picture they present of themselves is often a theoretical, literary construction.

Cato the elder believed that the best way to make money was by cattle-raising. The larger estates (often under absentee ownership) were aggregates of small and medium-sized farms. Cato, like Appius Claudius Caecus and Scipio Aemilianus, was an example of the new individualism, which became such a prominent feature of the Roman Republic.

Cicero stressed the obligation upon individual members of the aristocracy to live up to their mission, in which, he said, they had failed. He also developed the familiar antithesis between individual (desiring selfish acquisition) and community (requiring national solidarity): man could only realise himself fully as a social creature, and Cicero, in *On the State*, accepts Stoic views on the possibility of reconciling individual rights with the needs of society.

Imperial dynasticism was encouraged by the Roman army, which saw its continuity as of prime importance.

Christianity encouraged individualism against collectivism, e.g. prompted generals such as St Martin of Tours to withhold allegiance to the empire ('I am Christ's soldier, therefore I cannot fight').

Later empire. The senate and knights were merged.

Chapter 4. The Poor

Athenian citizenship, acquired by birth and rarely granted to others (Chapter 7), was a tangible benefit which seemed to make poverty more tolerable.

Achilles and the *thes*. The Homeric poor lived on the borders of starvation.

Hesiod is anti-heroic, and looks at the aristocratic world from outside, rather sourly.

Control over one's own labour. The philosophers despised a man who worked for someone else. And so did others, but how widely this view was held is disputed: and so is the question of whether poor owner-occupiers, small free peasants, were of early or relatively late appearance.

Agriculture. Aristotle, *Politics*, VI, 1319a, 19–38, maintained that the best democracy had a large rural hinterland and many farmers and herdsmen (who did not attend the Assembly).

Mobility. Greek upward mobility was scarce (and caused cries of outrage when it occurred), whereas downward mobility was always a not too distant threat. But such social mobility as occurred was generally lateral, involving changes of habitation or profession.

Effect of slavery on the poor. The free poor struggled to maintain the citizen-slave distinction; but it is disputed whether, or to what extent, slave competition worsened their lot or embittered them. Free and slave worked together on large estates, as on the Athenian Acropolis.

Roman patricians and plebeians. Tribunes of the people, officers of the *plebs*, were created in 500–450, to protect humble Romans from oppression. The most important event thereafter was the Twelve Tables (451–450), which published the law. At first only patricians could contract regular marriages, but in 445 the Lex Canuleia authorised intermarriage with plebeians. After 400, tensions heightened, because the landless were multiplied by population increases. In 367 the Lex Licinia Sextia opened the consulship to the plebs. The Lex Hortensia of 287 made *plebiscita* binding on the whole community, and as valid as the laws of the *comitia centuriata*. According to one view, however, the Conflict of the Orders could be regarded as continuing until *c.*217/216. Dionysius of Halicarnassus stressed the un-Greek moderation of this long, legally fought, struggle (though its early stages may be fictitious: like the idea that the earlier king, Servius Tullius, was a democratic reformer). Yet it did not achieve a great deal, since, in fact, the governing class prevailed.

Population of Rome. In the mid-fourth century BC the population of the city of Rome was 50–60,000, rising to an uncertain figure – very much larger – under the principate. Even by the later first century probably only 15 per cent of the Roman citizen body (including women) lived in the city. The urban lower classes were not merely beggars and pensioners but craftsmen, shopkeepers, etc.

Numantia. The last stronghold of the Celtiberian resistance to Rome, captured by Scipio Aemilianus in 133 BC.

Late Republic. There were proverbial opportunities for advancement under Sulla (Sallust, *Catiline*, 37, 6 – despite the predicaments of his ex-soldiers, see text) and Pompey. Military service, in particular, could bring a family to the order of knights and the senate within two or three generations, but (although evidence is defective) this did not happen very often until later on. Ex-soldiers became prominent in the smaller cities of recent foundation.

Outside the army, extremes of wealth and poverty, in the late Republic, made social mobility hard, though many administrators were needed. Something like one-fifth of the free population of Italy emigrated, and were replaced by imported slaves. Many of those who remained were distressed and ready to respond to the Gracchi and Catiline and Clodius, and politicians found that they could exploit these underprivileged citizens for their own violent purposes – and saw that, bypassing the senate, they could appeal to the Assembly for land or grain for the poor, and relief of debtors.

The army under the principate received good pay and retirement remuneration, and ex-centurions became civil servants and gained equestrian rank and jobs (e.g., procuratorships), achieving – though not very often – spectacular social mobility. In the third century, the military reached elevated social positions as a privileged class: Septimius Severus advised his sons Caracalla and Geta to give absolute priority to the army's requirements (Dio, LXXVI, 15.2).

Aedui, a Gallic tribe which occupied most of modern Burgundy.

Catulus (who introduced awnings in theatres): Quintus Lutatius Catulus, consul 78 BC.

In the later empire, despite its harsh caste system, the opportunities of the soldiery remained great. The eastern usurper Procopius (365) also appealed to the civilian poor, offering redistribution of land and abolition of debts; his cause was joined by considerable numbers of them.

PART III: THE UNFREE AND THE FREED

Chapter 5. Serfs

Definition of serfs. The ancient writers often leave it uncertain whether the people they are writing about were of serf-like status or slaves.

Sparta, during the Peloponnesian War, lost the Messenian fortress of Pylos to the Athenians in 425. The Peace of Nicias (421), which briefly suspended the War, provided that Athens would help Sparta against Helot risings. Another category of the Laconian population comprised the *perioikoi*, 'dwellers around', who were not serfs but lacked political rights: their principal activities were the procurement of metals and manufacture of arms.

Hektemoroi were liable to be sold into slavery in case of default. According to an alternative view, they only had to pay over one-sixth of their produce.

The Roman colonate. By the end of the third century AD the whole agricultural population of the Greco-Roman world had virtually become serfs, tied to the land by hereditary bonds. In about 395 Theodosius I defined them as being 'of free status', though they 'must be regarded as slaves of the very land to which they were born'.

Chapter 6. Greek Slaves

Slaves in mines. The number employed in the silver-mines in Laurium is un-

151

certain; perhaps there were about 11,000 (*pace* Thucydides, VII, 27, who estimated the number of slave deserters at more than 20,000). Nicias had 1,000 slaves in the mines.

Slaves in armed services. More often in the fleet than in the army; rowers had lower prestige than hoplites.

Employment. Doctors had slave assistants (Plato, *Laws*, IV, 720). It is uncertain whether there were independent Greek slave doctors.

Aristophanes. In the *Knights*, Demos is in the power of a loud-mouthed and brutal slave-steward (alias Cleon).

Stoics. Posidonius felt a Stoic sympathy for the plight of the Sicilian slaves (Chapter 7).

Chapter 7. Roman Slaves

Religion. Bacchic rites (repressed in 186 BC, Chapter 4) were popular among slaves (as well as free poor and women). The temple of Fors Fortuna across the Tiber was one of the few that slaves could attend.

Slave-revolts. It is uncertain if Aristonicus's revolt in western Asia Minor (133–130) was chiefly supported by free poor or by slaves and serfs. The extent to which slaves were involved in Andriscus's uprising in the north-west of the same peninsula (*c.*150–148) is also uncertain.

First century BC. By the end of the Republic slave *contubernia* (nearly marriage) and family life were encouraged. This did a little to help slave women, who had become victims because their menfolk lacked the power to protect them.

First and second centuries AD. Some argue (though others disagree) that slavery in Italian agriculture diminished in the first century AD, because free tenants were available. There seems to have been a certain decrease in foreign supply. Evidence is patchy, but slaves became less numerous in Noricum and Dalmatia from the middle of the second century AD.

Decree of Claudius. Marriages between free-born and slaves were particularly frequent in the *familia Caesaris* (in which the differences between personal names, in the two categories, broke down during the second century AD). Concubinage, however, was socially acceptable, though it weakened the marriage bond.

Chapter 8. Freedmen and Freedwomen

Peloponnesian War. The Spartans, too, owing to manpower shortages, enrolled Helots among their hoplites; they were known as *Neodamodeis*.

Hellenistic age. The 'slaves freed' by Nabis of Sparta (207–192) were probably Helots.

Delphi manumissions. A *mna* (*mina*) constituted 100 Attic drachmas.

Early first century BC. The history of the corn-dole after Sulla's dictatorship (81) suggests a marked interest in manumissions.

Roman freedmen included doctors and teachers (first imported from Greece in the second century BC) and in the first century BC (as mentioned in the text) Publilius Syrus of Antioch, the first author of mimes. But rhetoric teachers tended to be free-born from the time of Augustus, though freedmen (and slaves) continued to work as, or for, doctors.

Second Triumvirate. Freedman commanders included Menas, Menecrates, Demetrius, Helenus and Machaerus.

Augustan manumissions. The tax (*vicesima libertatis*), dated to AD 6 by Dio Cassius, LV, 25, 5–6, had also existed earlier (T. Frank, *American Journal of Philology*, LIII, 1932, p. 360). Perhaps the Lex Junia Norbana (?) dates from AD 19, not 17 BC.

Freedmen at Rome. Inscriptions suggest that the plebeian population of Rome, from the time of Augustus at least, consisted largely of freedmen (and slaves).

Freedmen in later empire. John Chrysostom (354–407) suggested that slaves enjoyed a more privileged status than freedmen. The three grades of freedmen unified by the Theodosian Code (under Theodosius II, AD 408–450) comprised citizens, *Latini Juniani* (those informally manumitted by the Lex Junia Norbana (?), see above), and *dediticii*, slaves of ill-repute given incomplete liberty. The view of A. M. Duff (1928) that population mixture with freedmen and slaves was one of the causes of the fall of the western empire must be regarded with suspicion.

Eunuchs had appeared at the court of Ptolemaic Egypt.

Appendix 1. Foreigners

Blacks. The influence of middle-eastern peoples on early Greek art is undoubted, but M. Bernal, *Black Athena*, I (1987), was too reluctant to reject the theory that the ancient Egyptians could be described as black. For non-acceptance of his views see J. Griffin, *New York Review*, 15/6/89, and *Arethusa* (fall, 1989, 'The Challenge of Black Athena', M. Levine [ed.]).

Cicero's attitude to foreigners fluctuates according to his brief (see *For Flaccus*, *For Balbus*): but his admiration for natural law (*ius gentium*) inclined him to take a favourable view of them.

Foreigners' feelings. G. E. M. de Sainte Croix, *The Class Struggle in the Ancient World* (1981), p. 443: 'three remarkable documents in Latin . . . reveal some recognition by members of the Roman governing class of the mentality of Rome's victims – it would be going much too far to speak of genuine sympathy'. He refers to Sallust, *Histories*, IV, 69; Tacitus, *Agricola*, 30–32; and Tacitus, *Annals*, I, 17.

Jewish revolts. Due to total mutual incomprehensions and unusual Roman mishandling, M. Grant, *The Jews in the Roman World* (1973), pp. 171–260.

Later empire. The best Latin poet and historian of the epoch were both Greek-speaking foreigners, Claudian and Ammianus Marcellinus.

Appendix 2. Karl Marx

Initial difficulty. Marxism, it has been said, will provide almost any suitable text in the hands of a believing interpreter.

Failure of Marxism in practice. 'The Soviet Union', remarks Bernard Levin in the *Sunday Telegraph*, 'endured for some three-quarters of a century. It was supposed to free all people from bondage and imposed a slavery more terrible and complete than any seen until then; it was heralded as the bringer of equality, and created a ladder of hierarchies steeper than those of the most cruel of ancient emperors; it was defined as a system that would make all mankind one, and turned a mighty nation into 270 million informers, spies and *agents provocateurs*; it was proclaimed as the provider of bounty that would make its citizens uniquely prosperous and comfortable, and scores of millions of families still know no better home than a corner of a crowded room, and scores of millions have grown to maturity without ever setting eyes on meat; it was followed as the light of the world, and turned into the blackest and longest night in the universe. And now, at last, the foul thing is dying, and with it the lie on which it stood. Yet Marxism absurdly justifies itself by its claim to improve the human condition.' 'Marxism-Leninism's ghastly achievement was the almost complete destruction of the human decencies without which true society can hardly exist' (D. Pryce-Jones, *Financial Times*, 28/4/90). But V. Kiernan, *History Today*, July 1991, p. 42, somehow sees a role for Marxism, 'revived by remedying of past shortcomings', in the next century.

Outdated teaching of Marxism. 'Many shallow left primers of the 1970s, still being reprinted, continue to be lazily imposed on our students in university politics and social science departments; in the more inert faculties, the very Marxology which Eastern Europe has cast out remains undisturbed on the academic agenda as if nothing untoward had happened' (D. Selbourne, *Times Literary Supplement*, 10/5/91, p. 7). 'At many western universities the best categories within which social historians and sociologists operate are still his [Marx's]. He did not invent them . . . Marx took existing words and cannibalized them for his own purposes' (D. Johnson, ibid., 26/4/91, p. 10).

Marx's recognition that history is not entirely economic. 'Marx, *like the other thinkers I have mentioned* (my italics: Bloch, Pirenne, Weber, Veblen are among them), put an end to any idea that the study of history is an autonomous activity and to the corollary that the various aspects of human behaviour – economic, political, intellectual, religious – can be seriously treated in isolation' (M. I. Finley, quoted by editors of his *Economy and Society in Ancient Greece*, 1981 ed., p. xi).

Marxist claims to superiority. The Great Soviet Encyclopaedia ridiculously claimed that historiography is 'the study of the history of the victory of Marxist-Leninist science over bourgeois pseudo-science'.

Utopian future. Exemplified by the assertion that government will eventually wither away. (When Marx spoke of the intermediate 'dictatorship of the proletariat', he seems to have had the Roman dictatorship – initially limited in duration – in mind.)

Greek women (Chapter 1). Marx tried to think through the relationship between production and reproduction.

Engels liked Bachofen von Echt's **matriarchal theory** (unduly) because it supported the idea that the earliest (i.e. natural) form of human existence had been communal. For this controversy see S. B. Pomeroy, *Goddesses, Whores, Wives and Slaves* (1975), pp. 13ff.

The Rich (Chapter 3). For the mythical nature of the 'merchant class' at Aegina and Corinth see G. E. M. de Sainte Croix, *The Class Struggle in the Ancient Greek World*, p. 41.

Marxist belittlement of the individual (R. N. Carew-Hunt, *The Theory and Practice of Communism*, 1950, pp. 72–3) did not do justice to Marx himself, who commented that 'men make their own history, but they do not make it just as they please . . . but under circumstances directly encountered, given and transmitted from the past'. For his 'ambiguous legacy' in this respect see S. H. Rigby, *Marxism and History* (1987), p. 10. Marxists accused Sigmund Freud of overestimating the individual; see E. H. Carr, *What is History?* (1961), pp. 138ff.

Collectivism had emerged in the eighteenth century as a reaction against individualism, emphasising the priority of the community and its rights. Pity the poor Soviet writers whose denunciations of 'great men' came to the attention of Stalin. Ten years after his death the Soviet scholar G. G. Diligensky attacked the cult of personality in ancient history (1963). For Marx's comments on Chance (Marx and Engels, *Works* [Russian ed.], XXVI, p. 108), see E. H. Carr, *What is History?*, pp. 101ff.

The Poor (Chapter 4). Marx's central emphasis on 'modes of production' was excessive, and (while understandably identifying human labour as the basis of the whole edifice) he oversimplified by treating 'antiquity' as embodying a single, universal mode.

Slaves (Chapter 6). Marx was wrong to see Aristotle as a proto-Marxist. For one thing, Aristotle had paid no attention to the slaves' part in production.

The slave revolts against Rome were sometimes presented by Soviet text-books as 'tactical failures' but great moral victories all the same. Preobrazensky was put to death for his critical review of Mišulin's book glorifying Spartacus's uprising, but V. V. Vinogradoff understood that the rebellion did not impede the slave-owners' growth. Staerman argued that the revolt played a decisive part by showing that henceforward only a military dictatorship (or principate) could guarantee the interests of the slave-owners. Utcenko, however, after taking the opposite view, finally denied that Spartacus played a decisive part in the transition to imperial rule. (As regards earlier revolts, it is by no means certain that the uprisings of Andriscus, *c.*150–148, and Aristonicus, 133–130, were slave-rebellions at all; cf. note on Chapter 7). The general theme of the relation between slave-owners and slaves was discussed in *Vestnik Drevnej Istorii*, 1953/5 and 1961 (4), pp. 30–1.

Foreigners (Chapter 7). Marx only made a brief reference to metics in *Grundrisse* (Penguin ed., 1973, pp. 501f.). Engels attacked backward races as 'ethnic trash' and demanded that they should be killed (*Neue Rheinische Zeitung*, January – February 1849). He was abusive about South Slavs and Pan-Slavs.

Tables of Dates

(1) The Greeks

Greek Lands	Others
	1300 Departure of Joseph for Egypt
1250 BC Supposed capture of Troy by the Greeks	
	1200-200 Early Horizon period of Andean South America, dominated by Chavin culture
late 13th and early 12th cent. Destruction of Mycenaean civilisation (and others)	13th cent. Moses founds religious community in Israel
	1200/800–400/300 Olmec culture (Early-Middle Formative period) based on Gulf coast of Mexico
11th cent. Early Iron Age	1030–771 Early (western) Chou Dynasty in China (capital Shensi)
1075–1000 Dorian invasions and immigrations	
1050–900 Migrations of Ionians, Aeolians and Dorians to W. Asia Minor and islands	1000 Rise of Phoenician city-states
	1000–965 King David of Israel (Solomon 965–927)
	1000–300 Adena culture in Ohio, Kentucky, Indiana, Pennsylvania and West Virginia
900–750 Creation of Greek city-states. Replacement of monarchic by aristocratic governments	926–722 Kingdoms of Israel (north) and Judah (south)
	814 Traditional foundation date of Carthage (colony of Tyre)
776 Traditional date of first Olympic Games	771–249 Later (eastern) Chou Dynasty in China (capital Loyang)
750–700 *Iliad* and *Odyssey* of Homer; Hesiod	745–727 Tiglath Pileser III in Assyria
8th-7th cent. Colonisation	

8th–7th cent. Orientalising art
750 Adoption of alphabet
740/30–720/10 Sparta's First Messenian War
late 8th cent. Hoplite revolution
700–675 First Doric temples

early 7th cent. First surviving lyric poems
7th cent (?) Sparta's socio-political system (*agoge*) developed

7th or 6th cent. Triremes
675–600 Age of 'tyrants' (dictators; often replaced by oligarchies)
7th cent. First lawgivers
650–620 Sparta's Second Messenian War
late 7th cent. First Greek coinages
from late 7th cent. Black-figure pottery

586/5 or 582/1 Pythian Games at Delphi
6th cent. Solon, Pisistratus and Cleisthenes at Athens

by mid-6th cent. Peloponnesian League under Sparta

534 First Attic tragedy of Thespis
530 Red-figure pottery

510 Destruction of Sybaris by Croton

493 Themistocles archon at Athens
490, 480–79, 469/8 Persian Wars against Darius I and Xerxes
480 Invasion of Sicily by Carthaginians repelled by Syracuse and Acragas
478–463 Athens's Delian League becomes empire
474 Hiero I of Syracuse defeats Etruscans off Cumae

742 Isaiah begins to prophesy
738–696 Midas in Phrygia
722 Fall of Israel to Shalmaneser V of Assyria

689 Fall of Babylon to Sennacherib of Assyria
687 Kingdom of Lydia founded by Gyges

600 Mexico. Destruction of La Venta, Olmec cultural capital

671 Fall of Egypt to Esarhaddon of Assyria
664–526 26th (Saite) Dynasty in Egypt (Greek mercenaries and settlements)

629–539 New Babylonian empire
625–585 King Cyaxares of Media
612 Fall of Assyrian Nineveh to Medes and Persians
600 Jeremiah begins to prophesy
600 BC–AD 200 Epic period of Indian philosophy and religion
560–480 BC Gautama Buddha
560/59–530 Cyrus II the Great founds Achaemenid Persian empire
551–479 Confucius
546–539 Conquest of Media, Lydia (Croesus), Ionia and Babylonia by Cyrus II the Great of Persia

525 Conquest of Egypt by Cambyses of Persia
513–512 Expedition of Darius I of Persia to Thrace and Scythia

500 Earliest Zapotec temple at Monte Alban, Oaxaca, Mexico
See 'Greek Lands' for Persian Wars and invasion of Sicily

474 For Etruscan defeat by Hiero I of Syracuse see 'Greek Lands'

470–57 Temple of Zeus at Olympia
465/4–461/0 Helots' revolt against
Spartans in Messenia
462/1 Ephialtes's reform of Athenian
Areopagus (assassinated 461)
460–445 'First Peloponnesian War'
(Corinth Athens's principal enemy)
460–454 Athenian expedition to Egypt
ends in disaster
458 Aeschylus's *Oresteia*
454–429 Pericles's generalships at   454 Athenians ejected from Egypt
Athens
mid-5th cent. Protagoras of Abdera,
first Sophist, at Athens
*c.*450 the Riace bronzes and Myron's
Discobolus
449/8 Peace of Callias between Athens   449/8 Peace of Callias arranged by
and Persia   Artaxerxes I Macrocheir of Persia
447–432 The Parthenon at Athens
442/1 Sophocles's *Antigone*   440 Pissuthnes, Persian satrap of
Sardes, helps Samian revolt against
Athens

431–404 Peloponnesian War (temporary peace 421)
431 Euripides's *Medea*
425 Aristophanes's *Acharnians*
415–413 Disastrous Athenian expedi-   414/412 (or earlier?) Athens aids
tion to Sicily   Persian dissident Amorges in Caria
411 Oligarchic governments of Four   408/7 Cyrus the younger in Asia
Hundred and Five Thousand at   Minor forms alliance with Lysander
Athens   of Sparta
406–367 Dionysius I, tyrant of
Syracuse, fights four Carthaginian
wars
405 Victory of Lysander at
Aegospotami causes capitulation of
Athens and rule of Thirty Tyrants
(404)
400–325 Diogenes, founder of Cynic
school
399 Trial and death of Socrates   396–4 Campaigns of King
Agesilaus II of Sparta against the
Persians
387/6 Peace of Antalcidas, or King's   387/6 Peace of Antalcidas imposed on
Peace   Greece by Persian king
Artaxerxes II Mnemon
380s/370s Plato's *Republic*
377 Second Athenian League
370s–300 Sculptor Lysippus of Sicyon

158

371 Thebans under Epaminondas defeat Spartans at Leuctra

365/360–275/270 Pyrrho (founder of Sceptic school)
362 Battle of Mantinea between Thebans and Spartans (Epaminondas killed)
359–336 Philip II of Macedonia
357–5 'Social War': revolt of Athens's subject allies
351–341 Demosthenes's speeches against Philip II
345–337 Timoleon at Syracuse
343/2 Aristotle succeeds Plato
338 Philip II defeats Athenians and Thebans at Chaeronea
336 Philip II succeeded by Alexander III the Great

323–283 Reign of Ptolemy I Soter of Egypt (defeats Demetrius I Poliorcetes at Gaza 312)
323–2 Antipater defeats Athens in Lamian War
322 Theophrastus succeeds Aristotle as head of Peripatetic school

late 4th cent. Pytheas of Massalia circumnavigates Britain

317–289 Agathocles at Syracuse
late 4th and early 3rd cent. Teaching of Epicurus and Zeno (founder of Stoicism) at Athens
295 Foundation of Museum and Library of Alexandria
early 3rd cent. Callimachus and Theocritus
281–261 Antiochus I Soter (Seleucid)

270–215 Hiero II of Syracuse
263 and 256/5 and 247 Eumenes of Pergamum, Diodotus I Soter,

371 Persians support abortive Greek treaty
367/6 Artaxerxes II Mnemon receives Greek envoys at Susa

336 Philip II's general Attalus launches expedition against the Persian empire
334–327 Alexander III conquers Persian empire; death of Persian king Darius III Codomannus (330)

321 Accession of Chandragupta, founder of Mauryan Dynasty (capital Pataliputra, Patna)

300 BC–AD 400 Hopewell culture in Ohio and Illinois

300 BC–AD 300 Later Pre- and Proto-Classic Maya culture in Yucatan, etc.

274/268–232/1 Mauryan emperor Asoka
273 Gauls (Galatians) defeated by Antiochus I Soter

256/5 Independence of Parthia (see Greek Lands)

governor of Bactria, and Arsaces I of Parthia, break away from Seleucid empire

241–197 Attalus I of Pergamum

221–179 Philip V of Macedonia
223–187 Antiochus III the Great (Seleucid)

230 Gauls (Galatians) defeated by Attalus I

206/2 BC–AD 221 Han Dynasty in China (first capital Ch'ang-an)
200 BC Large population at Monte Alban, Oaxaca, Mexico
197 Philip V defeated by Romans
191–190 Antiochus III defeated by Romans
185 Mauryan empire falls to Sung Dynasty

179–168 Perseus of Macedonia
175–163 Antiochus IV Epiphanes (Seleucid)
170–130 Expansion of Indo-Greek kingdom
146 Corinth sacked, Achaean League dissolved, Macedonia and Greece annexed, by Romans

168 Perseus defeated by Romans
167 Measures of Antiochus IV against Jews lead to Maccabean revolt
Indo-Greek kingdom: see 'Greek Lands'
146 Roman conquest of Greece: see 'Greek Lands'
141–87 Wu Ti enlarges Chinese empire: travels of explorer Chang Ch'ien (138–125), earliest historian Ssu-ma Ch'ien (100)

138–3 Attalus III of Pergamum

120–63 Mithridates VI Eupator of Pontus (three Roman wars end in annexation)
51–30 Cleopatra VII of Egypt
30 BC–AD 10 Strato II and III the last Indo-Greek monarchs

133 Attalus III leaves Pergamum to Rome

63 Romans annex Pontus
30 Romans annex Egypt
AD 10 Indo-Greek state fully incorporated in Kushan empire of Kadjula Kadphises I

(2) The Romans

Rome	Others*

*For the Near and Middle East, India, China and America in early times, see Part 1 of the Date Table

753 Traditional date of foundation of Rome and its monarchy
509 Traditional date of foundation of Roman Republic

750–700 Urbanisation and power of Etruscan city-states
late 6th cent. Lars Porsenna of Clusium

494–287 'Secessions' of plebeians from patricians

451–450 Decemvirates and Twelve Tables

396 Fall of Etruscan Veii

For Roman wars, see other column

387 Gauls defeat Romans on River Allia and capture Rome

383–290 Wars against Samnites

340–338 Wars against Latins and Campanians

264–241, 218–201, 149–6 Punic Wars

200–196, 171–168 Macedonian Wars

192–189 War against Seleucid Antiochus III the Great

139–132, 104–100, 73–71 Slave revolts

133 Numantia captured by Scipio Aemilianus

133, 123–2 Tribunates of Tiberius and Gaius Sempronius Gracchus

133–129 Pergamum bequeathed to Rome and annexed as province of Asia

121 Annexation of Gallia Narbonensis (southern Transalpine Gaul)

112–105 War against Jugurtha of Numidia

102–101 Teutones and Cimbri defeated by Marius

91–87 Social (Marsian) War

81 Dictatorship of Sulla

88–63 Wars against Mithridates VI of Pontus

81–72 Revolt of Sertorius in Spain

70 Consulships of Pompey and Crassus

66–63 Suppression of pirates and annexation of Syria by Pompey

63 'Conspiracy' of Catiline. Cicero's *Catilinarian Orations*

60 First Triumvirate of Pompey, Crassus and Caesar, followed by first consulship of Caesar (59)

58–51 Caesar's Gallic War

49–45 Caesar victorious over Pompey and Pompeians in Civil War

48–47 Caesar's Alexandrian War and defeat of Pharnaces II of the (Cimmerian) Bosphorus at Zela (47)

43 Second Triumvirate of Antony, Octavian (the future Augustus) and Lepidus. Death of Cicero.

42 Death of Brutus and Cassius, defeated at Philippi

36 Octavian's admiral Agrippa defeats Sextus Pompeius at Naulochus

37–4 Herod the Great in Judaea

161

31 Octavian and Agrippa defeat
Antony and Cleopatra VII at
Actium
19, 8 Deaths of Virgil and Horace

AD 14–88 Julio-Claudian Dynasty
(Tiberius, Gaius [Caligula], Claudius, Nero)

65 Deaths of Seneca and Petronius

68–69 Civil Wars (Galba, Otho, Vitellius)
69–96 Flavian Dynasty (Vespasian,
Titus, Domitian)
79 Destruction of Pompeii,
Herculaneum, Stabiae and Oplontis
by eruption of Mount Vesuvius
80 Dedication of Colosseum
98–180 'Adoptive' emperors: Trajan,
Hadrian, Antoninus Pius, Marcus
Aurelius

104–after 127 Deaths of Martial,
Tacitus, Plutarch, Juvenal

122, 142 Walls of Hadrian and
Antoninus Pius in Britain

30 Death of Cleopatra VII and
Roman annexation of Egypt

20 Temporary settlement with
Phraates IV of Parthia over Armen-
ian question
AD 1–600 Moche culture on northern
Peruvian coast
AD 6–41, 44– Judaea a Roman province (30 or 33 crucifixion of Jesus)
9 Cheruscan (German) Arminius
defeats and kills Varus in Teutoburg
Forest
early 1st cent. AD Capital of Latter or
Eastern Han at Lo-Yang
1st cent. AD Major urbanisation at
Teotihuacan, Mexico
36 Settlement with Artabanus III of
Parthia
43–46 Annexation of Britain (revolt of
Boudicca 61)
58–63 Wars of Corbulo against Vologeses I of Parthia
66–73 First Jewish Revolt (Roman
War): fall of Jerusalem (70) and
Masada (73)
69–70 Gallo–German Revolt

100 (?) Accession of Kushan king
Kanishka (capital Purushapura
[Peshawar])
100 Moche tomb of 'Old Lord of
Sipán' in Peru
113–117 Trajan's failed attempt to
annex Mesopotamia. Revolt of Jewish Dispersion
132–135 Second Jewish Revolt
(Roman War)
162–176 War against Vologeses III of
Parthia
166–172, 177–180 Wars against
Marcomanni and Sarmatians

2nd cent. Novelist Apuleius

193–197 Rival emperors after murder of Commodus

193–235 'Military Monarchy' (Septimius Severus, Caracalla; then Elagabalus, Severus Alexander)

212 *Constitutio Antoniniana* conferring general citizenship

235–268 'Military Anarchy': many rulers

235–238, 249–251, 257, 303–311 Persecutions of Christians

268–283 Military Recovery (Claudius Gothicus, Aurelian, Tacitus, Probus, Carus)

284–337 Reorganisation of empire by Diocletian (d.305) and Constantine I the Great (d.337)

313 Edict of Mediolanum in favour of the Christians

324–330 Foundation of Constantinople on site of Byzantium

361–363 Julian the Apostate briefly restores paganism

364 Division of empire between Valentinian I (W., Mediolanum) and Valens (E., Constantinople)

373–397 St Ambrose bishop of Mediolanum

378–395 Theodosius I the Great

395–408 Stilicho commander-in-chief in west

395–430 St Augustine bishop of Hippo Regius

404 Western capital moved from Mediolanum to Ravenna

197–199 War of Septimius Severus against Vologeses IV of Parthia

200 The Six Systems of Indian philosophy

221–589 The Six Dynasties in China, split into several states

241–272 Shapur (Sapor) I king of Sassonian Persia

251 Goths defeat and kill Trajanus Decius at Abrittus

260 Persians defeat and capture Valerian

267–273 Zenobia, queen of Palmyra, independent

297–298 War of Galerius against Narses of Persia

300–900 Classic period of Maya culture

300 Moche tomb of 'Lord of Sipán' in Peru

319–320 Accession of Chandra Gupta I in north India (capital Pataliputra [Patna])

338–350 Wars of Constantius II against Sapor II of Persia

363 Jovian negotiates unfavourable peace with the Persians

378 Goths defeat and kill Valens at Hadrianopolis

387 Armenia divided between the eastern Roman and Persian empires

410 Capture of Rome by Alaric I the Visigoth

439, 455 Capture of Carthage and
Rome by Gaiseric the Vandal

432–454 Aetius commander-in-chief
in west

438 Theodosian Code (of Theodosius II in the eastern empire)

451 Attila the Hun defeated by Aetius
and Visigoths on Catalaunian Plains

456–472 Ricimer commander-in-chief
in west

476 Abdication of Romulus
Augustulus, last western emperor

476 Odoacer the Herulian (German)
becomes king of Italy

Bibliography

I. Ancient Writers

A. GREEK

ACHILLES TATIUS, 2nd century AD. Novelist; Leucippe and Cleitophon.

AENEAS TACTICUS, 4th century BC. Writer on military subjects.

AESCHYLUS, of Eleusis, 525/4–456 BC. Athenian tragic dramatist.

AESOP, 6th century BC. Slave of a Thracian. Composer of fables about animals.

AMPHIS, 4th century BC. Athenian tragic dramatist.

ANTISTHENES, born *c*.440 BC. Athenian founder or precursor of the Cynic school of philosophy.

APOLLONIUS RHODIUS, of Egypt, *c*.295–*c*.215 BC. Epic poet.

APPIAN, of Alexandria, 2nd century AD. Historian.

ARCHILOCHUS, of Paros, *c*.710–after 648 BC (?). Poet.

ARISTODAMA, of Smyrna, 3rd century BC. Poet.

ARISTOPHANES, of Athens, 457/445–before 385 BC. Dramatist (Old Comedy).

ARISTOTLE, of Stagirus, 384–322 BC. Philosopher and scientist. See also Pseudo-Aristotle.

ASCLEPIADES, of Samos, early 3rd century BC. Epigrammatist.

ATHENAEUS, of Naucratis, *c*.AD 200. Encyclopaedic writer.

CORINNA, of Tanagra, *c*.200 BC (?). Woman lyric poet.

CRATES, of Thebes, *c*.365–285 BC. Cynic philosopher and poet.

DEMOSTHENES, of Athens, 384–322 BC. Orator and statesman.

DIO CASSIUS, of Nicaea, *c*.AD 155–235. Historian of Rome.

DIO CHRYSOSTOM, of Prusa, 1st and early 2nd centuries AD. Philosopher and orator.

DIODORUS SICULUS, *c*.40 BC. Universal historian.

DIONYSIUS OF HALICARNASSUS, *c*.25 BC. Literary critic and historian.

EPICTETUS, of Hierapolis (Phrygia), *c*.AD 55–*c*.135. Stoic philosopher.

EPICURUS, of Samos, 341–270 BC. Founder of Epicurean school of philosophy.

ERINNA, of Telos, *c*.300 BC. Woman poet.

GALEN, of Pergamum, *c*.AD 129–199. Physician and medical writer.

ISOCRATES, of Athens, 436–338 BC. Rhetorician, educationalist and political theorist.

LIBANIUS, of Antioch, *c*.AD 314–393. Rhetorician.

LYSIAS, of Syracuse (metic at Athens), later 5th century BC. Orator.

MACCIUS (or Maecius), Quintus, 1st century BC–AD. Epigrammatic poet.

MELEAGER, of Gadara, *c*.100 BC. Elegiac poet and epigrammatist.

MENANDER, of Athens, *c*.342/1–293/89 BC. Dramatist (New Comedy).

165

MYRON, of Priene, 3rd century BC (?). Historian.

NOSSIS, of Locri Epizephyrii, early 3rd century BC. Poet.

OLD OLIGARCH, see Pseudo-Xenophon.

PAUL, St, of Tarsus, died c.AD 62/64. Christian theologian and missionary.

PHILODEMUS, of Gadara, c.110–c.40/35 BC. Epicurean philosopher.

PINDAR, of Cynoscephalae, c.518–c.438 BC. Lyric poet.

PLATO, of Athens, c.429–347 BC. Philosopher.

PLUTARCH, of Chaeronea, before AD 50–after 120. Philosopher and biographer.

PRAXILLA, of Sicyon, mid-5th century BC. Poet.

PSEUDO-ARISTOTLE. Unidentified writer of *Oeconomica*.

PSEUDO-XENOPHON. Unidentified writer of *Constitution of Athens* (later 5th century BC).

PYTHAGORAS, of Samos (settled at Croton), born c.580 BC. Philosopher.

SAPPHO, of Eresus (Lesbos), born c.612 BC. Lyric poet.

SEMONIDES, of Samos (lived on Amorgos), 7th or 6th century BC. Iambic and elegiac poet.

SIMONIDES, of Iulis (Ceos), c.556–468 BC. Lyric and elegiac poet and epigrammatist.

SOLON, of Athens, early 6th century BC. Statesman and poet.

SOPHOCLES, of Colonus, c.496–406 BC. Athenian tragic dramatist.

STRABO, of Amasia, c.63 BC–at least AD 21. Geographer and historian.

SYNESIUS, of Cyrene, c.AD 370–413. Neoplatonist and then Christian; writer of letters and hymns.

TATIUS, ACHILLES, see Achilles Tatius.

TELESILLA, of Argos, 5th century BC. Poet.

THEOCRITUS, of Syracuse (lived at Cos and Alexandria), c.300–260 BC (?). Bucolic (pastoral) poet and writer of mimes.

THEOGNIS, of Megara, second half of 6th century BC. Elegiac poet.

THEOPHRASTUS, of Eresus (Lesbos) (lived at Athens), c.370–288/5 BC. Peripatetic (Aristotelian) philosopher and scientist.

THEOPOMPUS, of Chios, 4th century BC. Historian.

THUCYDIDES, of Athens, c.460/455–c.400 BC. Historian.

XENOPHANES, of Colophon, 6th–5th centuries BC. Philosophical poet.

XENOPHON, of Erchia (Attica) (lived at Scillus), c.428–c.354 BC. Soldier, man of letters, historian.

B. LATIN

AMBROSE, St, of Treviri (bishop of Mediolanum), c.AD 339–397. Theologian and letter-writer.

AMMIANUS MARCELLINUS, of Antioch, c.AD 330–395. Historian.

Antoniniana, Constitutio, see *Constitutio Antoniniana*.

APULEIUS, of Madaurus, 2nd century AD. Novelist.

AUGUSTINE, St, of Thagaste (bishop of Hippo Regius). AD 354–430. Theologian.

AUGUSTUS, first *princeps* or emperor (31 BC–AD 14). Left autobiographical *Res Gestae Divi Augusti*.

CAESAR, Gaius Julius, 100–44 BC. Dictator, writer of *Commentaries* (*Gallic War*,

Civil War).

CARACALLA, see *Constitutio Antoniniana*.

CATO THE ELDER (the Censor), Marcus Porcius, of Tusculum, 234–149 BC. Statesman, writer on agriculture.

CICERO, Marcus Tullius, of Arpinum, 103–43 BC. Orator, writer on oratory and philosophy, letter-writer, statesman.

CLAUDIAN, of Alexandria (lived at Rome), *c.*AD 400. Pagan poet.

Codex Justinianus, law-code of the Byzantine emperor Justinian I (AD 527–565).

Codex Theodosianus, law-code of the eastern emperor Theodosius II (AD 408–450).

COLUMELLA, Lucius Junius Moderatus, of Gades, *c.*AD 65. Writer on agriculture.

Constitutio Antoniniana. Edict of Caracalla (AD 212) conferring widespread Roman citizenship.

GAIUS, 2nd century AD. Jurist.

Historia Augusta, see *Scriptores Historiae Augustae*.

HORACE (Quintus Horatius Flaccus), of Venusia, 65–8 BC. Poet.

JEROME, St, of Stridon, *c.*AD 348–420. Theologian.

JULIUS CAESAR, see Caesar.

JUSTINIAN, see *Codex Justinianus*.

JUVENAL (Decimus Junius Juvenalis), of Aquinum, early 2nd century AD. Satirical poet.

LACTANTIUS, of north Africa (professor at Nicomedia), born *c.*AD 250. Christian theologian.

Laudatio Turiae, inscription of Lucretius Vespillo (consul 19 BC) in honour of his wife Turia.

LIVY (Titus Livius), of Patavium, 64/59 BC–AD 12/17. Historian.

MAXIMUS, Valerius, see Valerius Maximus.

MUSONIUS RUFUS, Gaius, 1st century AD. Stoic philosopher, banished by Nero (AD 65–66).

NEPOS, Cornelius, of Ticinum (lived at Rome), *c.*100–*c.*25 BC. Biographer.

Panegyrici Latini. Collection of complimentary speeches by rhetoricians, late 3rd and 4th centuries AD.

PETRONIUS ARBITER (Titus Petronius Niger), consul AD 61. Novelist.

PHAEDRUS, Gaius Julius. Thracian slave in household of Augustus (31 BC–AD 14). Writer of fables.

PLAUTUS, Titus Maccius, of Sarsina, 3rd–2nd centuries BC. Comic dramatist.

PLINY THE ELDER (Gaius Plinius Secundus), of Comum, AD 23/24–79. Officer, administrator, historian, scientist.

PLINY THE YOUNGER (Gaius Plinius Caecilius Secundus), of Comum, AD 61/62–*c.*113. Literary letter-writer.

PROPERTIUS, Sextus, of Asisium, 54/47–before 2 BC. Elegiac love poet.

PUBLILIUS SYRUS, of Antioch (brought to Rome as a slave), 1st century BC. Writer of mimes.

SALLUST (Gaius Sallustius Crispus), of Amiternum, *c.*86–*c.*35 BC. Historian.

SALVIAN, of Treviri (presbyter at Massilia), *c.*AD 400–480. Theologian.

Scriptores Historiae Augustae. Authors (known under false names) of a collection of biographies of emperors (AD 117–284). Probably of the late 4th century AD.

SENECA THE YOUNGER (Lucius Annaeus Seneca), of Corduba, 4 BC–AD 65. Statesman, Stoic philosopher, tragic dramatist, literary letter-writer.

SIDONIUS APOLLINARIS (Gaius Sollius Apollinaris Modestus), of Lugdunum, AD 430–*c*.483. Christian bishop, poet, literary letter-writer.

STABERIUS EROS, freedman, 1st century BC. Teacher and grammarian.

SUETONIUS (Gaius Suetonius Tranquillus), of Hippo Regius, *c*.AD 69–after 121/ 122. Biographer.

SULPICIA, niece of Marcus Valerius Messalla Corvinus, patron of Tibullus (*c*.60– 19 BC), whose third book contains her love poems.

SYMMACHUS, Quintus Aurelius, BC 345–405. Prefect of Rome (384). Defender of paganism and literary letter-writer.

SYRUS, Publilius, see Publilius Syrus.

TACITUS, Publius Cornelius, of Gaul (German frontier?) or north Italy, *c*.AD 56–*c*.116 (?). Historian, biographer, ethnologist and writer on oratory.

TERENCE (Publius Terentius Afer), of Carthage (brought to Rome as a slave), *c*.190–159 BC. Comic dramatist.

Theodosian Code, see *Codex Theodosianus*.

Twelve Tables. Code of Roman law drawn up by a board of ten (*decemviri*), and published in 451–450 BC.

VALERIUS MAXIMUS, of the time of Tiberius (AD 14–37). Compiler of a collection of biographical anecdotes.

VARRO, Marcus Terentius, of Reate, 116–27 BC. Encyclopaedic writer. Work on agriculture has survived.

VELLEIUS PATERCULUS, Gaius. Officer of Augustus under the generalship of Tiberius (from AD 4). Historian.

VIRGIL (Publius Vergilius Maro), of Andes near Mantua, 70–19 BC. Poet (*Eclogues, Georgics, Aeneid*).

II. Modern Writers

GENERAL: SOCIAL HISTORY OF GREECE

ANDREWS, A., *The Greeks*, 1967

AUSTIN M. M., and VIDAL NACQUET, P., *Economic and Social History of Ancient Greece: An Introduction*, 1977

BERNAL, M., *Black Athena: The Afroasiatic Roots of Classical Civilization*, I, 1987; II, 1991

BEYE, C. R., *Ancient Greek Literature and Society*, 1975, 1987

BOARDMAN, J., GRIFFIN, J., and MURRAY, O. (eds), *The Oxford History of Greece and the Hellenistic World*, 1991

BOWRA, C. M., *Periclean Athens*, 1971

BOWRA, C. M., *The Greek Experience*, 1957

BURKERT, W., *Greek Religion*, 1985

CARTLEDGE, P., and HARVEY, F. D. (eds), *Crux: Essays in Greek History Presented to G. E. M. de Sainte Croix on his 75th Birthday*, 1985

CARTLEDGE, P., MILLETT, P., and TODD, S. (eds), *Nomos: Essays in Athenian Law, Politics and Society*, 1991

CARY, M., and HAARHOFF, T. J., *Life and Thought in the Greek and Roman World*, 1940

DOVER, K. J., *Greek Popular Morality in the Time of Plato and Aristotle*, 1974

DOVER, K. J., *The Greeks*, 1980, 1982

EASTERLING, P. E., and MUIR, J. V. (eds), *Greek Religion and Society*, 1985

EHRENBERG, V., *Society and Civilization in Greece and Rome*, 1964

FERGUSON, J., *Morals and Values in Ancient Greece*, 1991

FERGUSON, J., and CHISHOLM, K. (eds), *Political and Social Life in the Great Age of Athens*, 1978

FINLEY, M. I., *The Ancient Economy*, 1973, 1985

FINLEY, M. I. (ed.), *Studies in Ancient Society*, 1974

FISHER, N. R. E., *Social Values in Classical Athens*, 1976

FORNARA, C. W., *The Nature of History in Ancient Greece and Rome*, 1983

FORNARA, C. W., and SAMONS, L. J. *Athens from Cleisthenes to Pericles*, 1991

FROST, F. J., *Greek Society*, 1971

GALLANT, T. W., *Risk and Survival in Ancient Greece: Reconstructing the Rural Domestic Economy*, 1991

GARLAN, Y., *War in the Ancient World: A Social History*, 1975

GARLAND, R., *The Greek Way of Life: From Conception to Old Age*, 1990

GARNER, R., *Law and Society in Classical Athens*, 1987

GARNSEY, P. D. A. (etc., eds), *Trade in the Ancient Economy*, 1983

GRANT, F. C., *Hellenistic Religions: The Age of Syncretism*, 1953

GRANT, M., *From Alexander to Cleopatra: The Hellenistic World*, 1982, 1990

GRANT, M., *The Classical Greeks*, 1989

GRANT, M., *The Rise of the Greeks*, 1987

GRANT, M., and KITZINGER, R. (eds), *Civilization of the Ancient Mediterranean*, I–III, 1988

GREEN, P., *From Alexander to Actium*, 1990

GREEN, P., *The Shadow of the Parthenon*, 1972

GREENE, W. C., *The Achievement of Greece*, 1923

HOPPER, R. J., *Trade and Industry in Classical Greece*, 1979

HUMPHREYS, S. C., *Anthropology and the Greeks*, 1978

ISAGER, S., and SKYDSGAARD, J. E., *Ancient Greek Agriculture*, 1992

J.A.C.T., *The World of Athens: An Introduction to Classical Athenian Culture*, 1984

JENKINS, I., *Greek and Roman Life*, 1986

LITTMANN, R. J., *The Greek Experiment: Imperialism and Social Conflict 800–400 BC*, 1974

MAFFRE, J.-J., *La vie dans la Grèce classique*, 1988

MARROU, H. I., *A History of Education in Antiquity*, 1956

MARWICK, A., *The Nature of History*, 1970

MIKALSON, J. D., *Athenian Popular Religion*, 1983

MORETTI, L. (etc.), *La società ellenistica*, 1990

NICHOLS, R. and S., *Greek Everyday Life*, 1978

PERKIN, H. J., *Social History*, H. P. R. Finberg (ed.), *Approaches to History*, 1962, 1965, pp. 51–82

PRITCHETT, W. K., *The Greek State at War*, Parts I–V, 1974–91

QUENNELL, M. and C. H. B., *Everyday Things in Ancient Greece*, 1929/32, 1954

RICH, J., and WALLACE-HADRILL, A. (eds), *City and Country in the Ancient World*, 1992

RUNCIMAN, W. G., *Social Science and Political Theory*, 1963

SALLARES, R., *The Ecology of the Ancient Greek World*, 1991

169

STARR, C. G., *The Economic and Social Growth of Early Greece 800–500 BC*, 1977

STRAUSS, B. S., *Fathers and Sons in Athens: Ideology and Society in the Era of the Peloponnesian War*, 1992

TAPLIN, O., *Greek Fire*, 1989

VERNANT, J. P., *Myth and Society in Ancient Greece*, 1980, 1991

WEBER, M., *Economy and Society: An Outline of Interpretive Sociology*, 1968, 1978

WEBER, M., *General Economic History*, 1961

WEBER, M., *The Sociology of Religion*, 1963

WEBSTER, T. B. L., *Everyday Life in Classical Athens*, 1968

WHITLEY, J., *Style and Society in Dark Age Greece: The Changing Face of a Pre-Literate Society 1100–700 BC*, 1991

GENERAL: SOCIAL HISTORY OF ROME

ALFÖLDY, G., *Social History of Rome*, rev. ed., 1988

BALSDON, J. P. V. D., *Life and Leisure in Ancient Rome*, 1969

BETTINI, M., *Anthropology and Roman Culture*, 1991

BOARDMAN, J., GRIFFIN, J., and MURRAY, O. (eds), *The Oxford History of the Roman World*, 1991

BRAUND, S. H. (ed.), *Satire and Society in Ancient Rome*, 1989

BROWN, P., *The Body and Society*, 1988

BROWN, P., *The World of Late Antiquity*, 1971, 1989

CARCOPINO, J., *Daily Life in Ancient Rome*, 1941

CARY, M., and HAARHOFF, T. J., *Life and Thought in the Greek and Roman World*, 1940

COWELL, F. R., *Everyday Life in Ancient Rome*, 1961

CROOK, J. A., *Law and Life of Rome*, 1967

D'ARMS, J. H., *Commerce and Social Standing in Ancient Rome*, 1981

DILKE, O. A. W., *The Ancient Romans: How They Lived and Worked*, 1975

DILL, S., *Roman Society in the Last Century of the Western Empire*, 1898, 1958

DUDLEY, D. R., *Roman Society*, 1970, 1975

DUNCAN-JONES, R., *Structure and Scale in the Roman Economy*, 1990

DYSON, S. L., *Community and Society in Roman Italy*, 1991

EARL, D., *The Moral and Political Tradition of Rome*, 1967

EHRENBERG, V., *Society and Civilisation in Greece and Rome*, 1964

FERGUSON, J., *The Religions of the Roman Empire*, 1970

FINLEY, M. I., *Studies in Ancient Society*, 1974

FINLEY, M. I., *The Ancient Economy*, 1973, 1985

FORNARA, C. W., *The Nature of History in Ancient Greece and Rome*, 1983

FRANK, T., *Life and Literature in the Roman Republic*, 1957

GABBA, E., 'Riflessione sulla società romana fra III e II secolo a C.', *Athenaeum* LXI, 1986, pp. 472ff.

GAGÉ, J., *Les classes sociales dans l'empire romain*, 1964

GARDNER, J. F., and WIEDEMANN, T., *The Roman Household: A Sourcebook*, 1991

GARLAN, Y., *War in the Ancient World: A Social History*, 1975

GARNSEY, P. D. A., *Social Status and Legal Privilege in the Roman Empire*, 1970

GARNSEY, P. D. A., and SALLER, R., *The Roman Empire: Economy, Society and Culture*, 1987

GRANT, M., and KITZINGER, R. (eds), *Civilization of the Ancient Mediterranean*, 1988

JONES, A. H. M., *The Roman Economy* (ed. P. A. Brunt), 1974

LINTOTT, A. W., *Violence in Republican Rome*, 1968

MACMULLEN, R., *Changes in the Roman Empire: Essays in the Ordinary*, 1990

MACMULLEN, R., *Enemies of the Roman Order*, 1967

MACMULLEN, R., *Roman Social Relations 50 BC to AD 284*, 1974

MARROU, H. I., *A History of Education in Antiquity*, 1956

MARWICK, A., *The Nature of History*, 1970

MASSEY, M. (ed), *Society in Imperial Rome*, 1982

PAOLI, U. E., *Rome: Its People, Life and Customs*, 1940, 1990

PERKIN, H. J., 'Social History', H. P. R. Finberg (ed.), *Approaches to History*, 1962, 1965, pp. 51–82

SHELTON, J. -A., *As the Romans Did*, 1988

VEYNE, P., *A History of Private Life, I: From Pagan Rome to Byzantium*, 1987

WARDE FOWLER, W., *Social Life at Rome in the Age of Cicero*, 1928

WEBER, M., *Economy and Society: An Outline of Interpretive Sociology*, 1968, 1978

WEBER, M., *General Economic History*, 1971

WILKINSON, L. P., *The Roman Experience*, 1975

Part I: Women

CHAPTER 1. GREEK WOMEN

BLUESTONE, N. H., *Women and the Ideal Society*, 1987

CAMERON, A., and KUHRT, A. (eds), *Images of Women in Antiquity*, 1983

CANTARELLA, E., *Pandora's Daughters*, 1987

CLARK, G., *Women in the Ancient World* (Greece and Rome, New Surveys 21), 1989

DEJEAN, J., *Fictions of Sappho 1546–1937*, 1989

DES BOUVRIE, S., *Women in Greek Tragedy* (Symbolae Osloenses, Supplement 27), 1990

DOVER, K. J., *Greek Homosexuality*, 1980

DUBY, G., and PERROT, M. (eds), *Histoire des femmes en occident, I, L'antiquité*, 1991

FOLEY, H. P. (ed.), *Reflections of Women in Antiquity*, 1981

FOUCAULT, M., *The Care of the Self, III (History of Sexuality)*, 1988

GOETTNER ABENDROTH, H., *Die Matriarchat I: Geschichte seiner Erforschung*, 1988

HALPERIN, D. M., *One Hundred Years of Homosexuality*, 1990

HALPERIN, D. M., WINKLER, J. J., ZEITLIN, F. I. (eds), *Before Sexuality: The Construction of Erotic Experience in the Ancient Greek World*, 1990

HUMPHREYS, S. C., *The Family, Woman and Death*, 1983

JUST, R., *Women in Athenian Law and Life*, 1987

LACEY, W. K., *The Family in Classical Greece*, 1968

LAQUEUR, T., *Making Sex: Body and Gender from the Greeks to Freud*, 1990

LEFKOWITZ, M. R., *Heroines and Hysterics*, 1981

LEFKOWITZ, M. R., *Women in Greek Myth*, 1986, 1990

LEFKOWITZ, M. R., and FANT, M. B., *Women's Life in Greece and Rome*, 1982, 1992

LONGEGA, G., *Arsinoe II*, 1968

LORAUX, N., *Tragic Ways of Killing a Woman*, 1987

MACURDY, G. H., *Hellenistic Queens*, 1932

MACURDY, G. H., *Vassal Queens*, 1937

MASSEY, M., *Women in Ancient Greece and Rome*, 1988

PAGE, B. du, *Sowing the Body: Psychoanalysis and Ancient Representations of Women*, 1988

POMEROY, S. B., *Goddesses, Whores, Wives and Slaves*, 1975

POMEROY, S. B., *Women in Hellenistic Egypt*, 1984, 1990

POMEROY, S. B. (ed.) *Women's History and Ancient History*, 1992

POWELL, A. (ed.), *Euripides, Women and Sexuality*, 1990

REINSBERG, C., *Ehe, Hetärentum und Knabenliebe im antiken Griechenland*, 1989

ROUSSELLE, A., *Porneia*, 1988

SEALEY, R., *Women and Law in Classical Greece*, 1990

SERGENT, B., *Homosexuality in Greek Myth*, 1987

SISSA, G., *Greek Virginity*, 1990

SKINNER, M. (ed.), 'Rescuing Creusa', *Helios* NS XIII (2), 1986

SNYDER, J. MCI., *The Woman and the Lyre: Women Writers of Classical Greece and Rome*, 1989

SPRINGBORG, P., *Royal Persons: Patriarchal Monarchy and the Feminine Principle*, 1990

STURLA-THEODORIDOU, V., *Die Familie in der griechischen Kunst und Literatur des 8 bis 6 Jahrhundert vor Christus*, 1989

WALCOT, P., 'Greek Attitudes to Women', *Greece and Rome*, XXXI, 1984, pp.37–47.

WILKINSON, L. P., *Classical Attitudes to Modern Issues*, 1979

WINKLER, J. J., *The Constraints of Desire: The Anthropology of Sex and Gender in Ancient Greece*, 1990

CHAPTER 2. ROMAN WOMEN

BALSDON, J. P. V. D., *Roman Women*, 1962

BAUMAN, R. A., *Women and Politics in Ancient Rome*, 1992

BLUESTONE, N. H., *Women and the Ideal Society*, 1987

BRADLEY, K. R., *Discovering the Roman Family: Studies in Roman Social History*, 1990

BURCK, E., 'Die Frau im alten Rom', E. Olshausen (ed.), *Die Frau in der Gesellschaft, Vox Latina* XXIII, 1987, pp. 73–92

CAMERON, A., and KUHRT, A. (eds), *Images of Women in Antiquity*, 1983

CLARK, G., *Women in the Ancient World* (*Greece and Rome*, New Surveys 21), 1989

DIXON, S., *The Roman Family*, 1991 ed.

DIXON, S., *The Roman Mother*, 1988, 1990

DUBY, G., and PERROT, M. (eds), *Histoire des femmes en occident, I, L'antiquité*, 1991

EVANS, J. K., *War, Women and Children in Ancient Rome*, 1991

FAYER, C., *La famiglia romana*, 1989

FOLEY, H. P. (ed.), *Reflections of Women in Antiquity*, 1981

FOUCAULT, M., *History of Sexuality* (*The Care of the Self*, III), 1988

FRASER, A., *Boadicea's Chariot*, 1988

GARDNER, J. F., *Women in Roman Law and Society*, 1986

GRIMAL, P., *Love in Ancient Rome*, 1986

HALLETT, J. P., *Fathers and Daughters in Roman Society*, 1984

HODGE, P., *Roman Family Life*, 1974

HOLUM, K. G., *Theodosian Empresses: Women and Imperial Dominion in Late Antiquity*, 1989

HUMPHREYS, S. C., *The Family, Woman and Death*, 1983

JENKINS, I., *Greek and Roman Life*, 1986

KIEFER, O., *Sexual Life in Ancient Rome*, 1934

LAQUEUR, T., *Making Sex: Body and Gender from the Greeks to Freud*, 1991

MASSEY, M., *Women in Ancient Greece and Rome*, 1988

PEROWNE, S., *The Caesars' Wives*, 1974

RAWSON, B (ed.), *Marriage and Divorce in Ancient Rome*, 1991

RAWSON, B. (ed.), *The Family in Ancient Rome: New Perspectives*, 1986, 1992

SELTMAN, C., *Women in Antiquity*, 1956

SERVIEZ, J. R. DE, *The Roman Empresses*, 1899

SHIELS, W. J., and WOOD, D. (eds), *Women in the Church*, 1990

SNYDER, J. McI., *The Woman and the Lyre: Women Writers of Classical Greece and Rome*, 1989

THRAEDE, K., *Der Mündigen Zähmung, Frauen im Urchristentum*, 1987

TREGGIARI, S. M., *Roman Marriage*, 1991

WIEDEMANN, T., *Adults and Children in the Roman Empire*, 1990

WITHERINGTON, R., *Women and the Genesis of Christianity*, 1990

Part II: Men

CHAPTER 3. THE RICH (AND INDIVIDUALISM)

BENGTSON, H., *Griechische Staatsmänner*, 1983

CLOVER, F. M., and HUMPHREYS, R. S. (eds), *Tradition and Innovation in Late Antiquity*, 1989

CONNOR, W. R., *The New Politicians of Fifth Century Athens*, 1971

CURRIE, H. MACL. (ed.), *The Individual and the State*, 1973

D'ARMS, J. H., *Commerce and Social Standing in Ancient Rome*, 1981

DAVIES, J. K., *Wealth and the Power of Wealth in Classical Athens*, 1981

DEVANE, R. S., *The Failure of Individualism*, 1948

DEVIJVER, H., *The Equestrian Officers of the Roman Imperial Army*, 1989

DEWEY, J., *Individualism Old and New*, 1930

DUMONT, L., *Essai sur l'individualisme*, 1983

DYSON, S. L., *Community and Society in Roman Italy*, 1991

EISENSTADT, S. N., and RONIGER, L., *Patrons, Clients and Friends*, 1984

FINLEY, M. I. (ed.), *Studies in Roman Property*, 1976

GABBA, E., *Del buon uso della ricchezza*, 1988

GARDNER, J. F. (ed.), *Leadership and the Cult of Personality*, 1974

GELLNER, E., 'Holism versus Individualism in History and Sociology', P. Gardiner (ed.), *Theories of History*, 1959

HODKINS, S., 'Land Tenure and Inheritance in Classical Sparta', *Classical Quarterly*, XXXVI, 1986, pp. 378–406

MCKECHNIE, W. S., *The State and the Individual*, 1896

MANN, M., *The Sources of Social Power*, I, 1986

MITCHELL, R. E., *Patricians and Plebeians: The Origins of the Roman State*, 1990

MORRIS, I., *Burial and Ancient Society: The Rise of the Greek City State*, 1987, 1989

MURRAY, R. H., *Individualism and the State*, 1946

NORTH, J., 'Power and Aristocracy in Imperial Rome', *Abstracts of the American Philological Association* (1988), 1989

OBER, J., *Mass and Élite in Democratic Athens*, 1989, 1991

PELLING, C. B. R. (ed.), *Characterization and Individuality in Greek Literature*, 1990

RIESMAN, D., *Individualism Reconsidered*, 1955

ROMILLY, J. De, 'La notion des classes moyennes dans l'Athènes du V s. av. J.C.', *Revue des études grecques*, 1987, pp. 1–17

SALLARES, R., *The Ecology of the Ancient Greek World*, 1991

SALLER, R. P., *Personal Patronage under the Early Empire*, 1982

SHACKLETON BAILEY, D. R., 'Nobiles and Novi Reconsidered', *American Journal of Philology*, CVII, 1986, pp. 255–60

SYME, R., *The Augustan Aristocracy*, 1986

SYME, R., *The Roman Revolution*, 1939

WALLACE-HADRILL, A. (ed.), *Patronage in Ancient Society*, 1989

WISEMAN, T. P., *New Men in the Roman Senate 139 BC–AD 14*, 1971

CHAPTER 4. THE POOR

BRUNT, P. A., *Social Conflicts in the Roman Republic*, 1971

DAVIES, R. W., BREEZE, D., and MAXFIELD, V. (eds), *Service in the Roman Army*, 1989

DE NEEVE, P. W., *Peasants in Peril*, 1984

DE ROBERTS, F. M., 'Storia sociale di Roma: le classi inferiori', *Studia Historica* CXXVII, 1945, 1981

DE SAINTE CROIX, G. E. M., *The Class Struggle in the Ancient Greek World*, 1981, 1983

EISENSTADT, S. N., and RONIGER, L., *Patrons, Clients and Friends*, 1984

FUKS, A., 'Patterns and Types of 4th–2nd Century Economic Revolution in Greece', *Ancient Society*, V, 1974, pp. 51–81

GALLANT, T. W., *Risk and Survival in Ancient Greece: Reconstructing the Rural Domestic Economy*, 1991

GARNSEY, P. D. A., *Famine and Food Supply in The Greco-Roman World*, 1988, 1989

GARNSEY, P. D. A. (ed.), *Non-Slave Labour in the Greco-Roman World*, 1980

GLOTZ, G., *Ancient Greece at Work: An Economic History of Greece*, 1926

HANDS, A. R., *Charities and Social Aid in Greece and Rome*, 1968

KOHNS, H. P., *Hungersnot und Hungerbewältigung in der Antike*, 1988

LINTOTT, A., *Violence, Civil Strife and Revolution in the Classical City*, 1982

MITCHELL, R. E., *Patricians and Plebeians: The Origins of the Roman State*, 1990

MOSSE, C., *The Ancient World at Work*, 1969

NEESER, L., *Demiourgoi und Artifices: Studien zur Stellung freier Handwerker in antiken Städten*, 1989

NEWMAN, L. F. (ed.), *Hunger in History*, 1990

OBER, J., *Mass and Élite in Democratic Athens: Rhetoric, Ideology and the Power of the*

People, 1989

RAAFLAUB, K. A. (ed.), *Social Struggles in Archaic Rome*, 1986

SALLARES, R., *The Ecology of the Ancient Greek World*, 1991

SCOBIE, A., 'Slums, Sanitation and Mortality in the Roman World', *Klio* LXVIII, 1986, pp. 399–433

WALLACE-HADRILL, A. (ed.), *Patronage in Ancient Society*, 1989

WOOD, E. M., *Peasant-Citizen and Slave: The Foundations of Athenian Democracy*, 1988

WOOD, E. M. and N., *Class Ideology and Ancient Political Theory*, 1978

YAVETZ, Z., *Plebs and Princeps*, 1969

Part III: Free and Unfree

CHAPTERS 5–8. SERFS, GREEK SLAVES, ROMAN SLAVES, FREEDMEN, FREEDWOMEN

ALFÖLDY, G., *Antike Sklaverei*, 1988

ARCHER, L. J. (ed.), *Slavery and Other Forms of Unfree Labour*, 1988

BRADLEY, K. R., *Slavery and Rebellion in the Roman World 140 BC–70 BC*, 1989

BRADLEY, K. R., *Slaves and Masters in the Roman Empire*, 1987

CARANDINI, A., *Schiavi in Italia*, 1988

DAVIS, D. B., *Slavery and Human Progress*, 1984

DE SAINTE CROIX, G. E. M., *The Class Struggle in the Ancient Greek World*, 1981, 1983

DUFF, A. M., *Freedmen in the Early Roman Empire*, 1928, 1958

DUMONT, J. -C., *Servus: Rome et l'esclave sous la République*, 1987

FINLEY, M. I., *Ancient Slavery and Modern Ideology*, 1980

FINLEY, M. I., *Ancient Slavery and the Ideal of Man*, 1974

FINLEY, M. I. (ed.), *Classical Slavery*, 1987

GARLAN, Y., *Slavery in Ancient Greece*, 1988

GRANT, M., *The Fall of the Roman Empire*, 1976, 1990

GUENTHER, R., *Frauenarbeit, Frauenbindung: Untersuchungen zu unfreien und freigelassenen Frauen in den stadtrömischen Inschriften*, 1987

HOPKINS, K., *Conquerors and Slaves*, 1978

HOPKINS, K., 'Eunuchs in Politics in the Later Roman Empire', *Proceedings of the Cambridge Philological Society*, CLXXXIX, 1963, pp. 62ff.

HOPKINS, K., 'Slavery in Classical Antiquity', A. de Reuck and J. Knight (eds), *Caste and Race: Comparative Approaches*, 1967

KIECHLE, F., *Sklavenarbeit und technischer Fortschritt im römischen Reich*, 1969

KLEIN, R., 'Die frühe Kirche und die Sklaverei', *Römische Quartalschrift für christliche Altertunskunde*, LXXX, 1985, pp. 259–83

KLEIN, R., *Die Sklaverei in der Sicht der Bischöfe Ambrosius und Augustinus*, 1988

MARTIN, D. B., *Slavery as Salvation: The Metaphor of Slavery in Pauline Christianity*, 1990

PARISH, P. J., *Slavery: History and Historians*, 1990

PATTERSON, O., *Slavery and Social Death*, 1982

POMEROY, S. B., *Goddesses, Whores, Wives and Slaves*, 1975

SCHMIDT, J., *Vie et mort des esclaves dans la Rome antique*, 1973

SCHOLL, R., *Forschungen zur antiken Sklaverei, Beiheft I: Corpus der ptolemäischen*

Sklaventexte, 1990

SORDI, M., *Paolo e Filemone, o Della schiavitù*, 1987

STARR, C. G., 'An Overdose of Slavery', *Journal of Economic History*, VIII, 1959, pp. 17–32.

TREGGIARI, S., *Roman Freedmen during the Late Republic*, 1969

VOGT, J., *Ancient Slavery and the Ideal of Man*, 1974

WATSON, A., *Roman Slave Law*, 1988

WEAVER, P. R. C., *Familia Caesaris*, 1972

WEAVER, P. R. C., 'Liberti Augusti', *Classical Quarterly*, 1964, pp.315ff.

WELWEI, K. W., *Unfreie in antiken Kriegsdienst*, 1974, 1977

WESTERMANN, W. L., *The Slave Systems of Greek and Roman Antiquity*, 1955

WIEDEMANN, T. E. J., *Greek and Roman Slavery*, 1981

WIEDEMANN, T. E. J., *Slavery (Greece and Rome*, New Surveys 19), 1987

WOOD, E. M., *Peasant-Citizen and Slave: The Foundations of Athenian Democracy*, 1988

YAVETZ, Z., *Slaves and Slavery in Ancient Rome*, 1990

APPENDIX 1. FOREIGNERS

BALSDON, J. P. V. D., *Romans and Aliens*, 1979

BERNAL, M., *Black Athena: The Afroasiastic Roots of Classical Civilization*, I, 1987; II, 1991

COOK, J. M., *The Persian Empire*, 1983

CUNLIFFE, B., *Greeks, Romans and Barbarians: Spheres of Interaction*, 1988

CYRKIN, J. B., *Hellenism and the Peripheral Societies: The Black Sea Littoral* (in Russian), 1988

DAUGE, Y. A., *Le barbare*, 1981

DESCOENDRES, J. -P., *Greek Colonists and Native Populations*, 1990

DYSON, S. L., 'Native Revolts in the Roman Empire', *Historia*, XX, 1971, pp. 239–74

HALL, E., *Inventing the Barbarian: Greek Self-Definition through Tragedy*, 1989

HATT, H. J., 'L'opinion que les Grecs avaient des Celtes', *Ktema* IX, 1984, pp. 79–87

KAPLAN, M., *Greeks and the Imperial Court: From Tiberius to Nero*, 1990

L'étranger dans le monde grec (Actes du colloque organisé par l'Institut d'Études Anciennes, 1987), 1988

LEVINE, M. M., and PERADOTTO, J. (eds), *The Challenge of Black Athena*, 1989

LÉVY, E., 'Naissance du concept de barbare', *Ktema*, IX, 1984, pp. 5–14

LIEBESCHUETZ, J. H. W. G., *Barbarians and Bishops*, 1990

MCKECHNIE, P., *Outsiders in the Greek Cities in the fourth Century* BC, 1989

MACMULLEN, R., *Enemies of the Roman Order*, 1967

MOMIGLIANO, A., *Alien Wisdom: The Limits of Hellenization*, 1975

NEUWALD, B., *Germanen und Germanien in römischen Quellen*, 1991

PUCCI BEN ZEEN, M., 'Cosa pensavano i Romani degli Ebrei', *Athenaeum* LXV, 1987, pp. 335–9

SHERWIN-WHITE, A. N., *Racial Prejudice in Imperial Rome*, 1967

SNOWDEN, F. M.., *Before Color Prejudice: The Ancient View of Blacks*, 1991

THOMPSON, E. A., 'Barbarian Invaders and Roman Collaborators', *Florilegium*, II,

1980, pp. 71–88

THOMPSON, E. A., 'Peasant Revolts in Late Roman Gaul and Spain', *Past and Present*, I, 1952, pp. 1–23

THOMPSON, L. A., *Romans and Blacks*, 1989

THOMSON, J. A. K., *Greeks and Barbarians*, 1921

WHITEHEAD, D., *The Ideology of the Athenian Metic*, Cambridge Philological Society Supplement IV, 1977

APPENDIX 2. KARL MARX

BACKHAUS, W., *Marx, Engels und die Sklaverei*, 1974

BEBBINGTON, D. W., *Patterns in History*, 2nd ed., 1991

BERLIN, I., *Historical Inevitability*, 1954

BERLIN, I., *Karl Marx*, 1939, 1948

BOBER, M. M., *Karl Marx's Interpretation of History*, 1927

BURNS, E., *What is Marxism?*, 1939, 1947

CALLINICOS, A., *The Revenge of History: Marxism and the East European Revolution*, 1991

CANFORA, L., 'Antiquisants et Marxisme', *Dialogue d'Histoire Ancienne*, VII, 1981, pp. 329–436

CAPOGROSSI, L. (etc., eds), *Analisi marxista e società antiche* (*Nuova biblioteca di cultura*, 178: *Atti dell' Istituto Gramsci*)

CARVER, T., *A Marx Dictionary*, 1987

COHEN, G. A., *Karl Marx's Theory of History: A Defence*, 1978, 1979

COLE, G. D. H., *The Meaning of Marxism*, 1948

DE SAINTE CROIX, G. E. M., 'Karl Marx and the Interpretation of Ancient and Modern History', B. Chavance (ed.), *Actes du Colloque organisé par l'École des Hautes Études en Sciences Sociales*, 1985, pp. 159–87

DE SAINTE CROIX, G. E. M., *The Class Struggle in the Ancient Greek World*, 1981, 1983

ELSTER, J., *Making Sense of Marx*, 1985

FARRINGTON, B., 'Karl Marx: Scholar and Revolutionary', *Modern Quarterly*, VII, 1951–2, pp. 83–94

FEDELI, I., *Marx e il mondo antico*, 1973

FEDERN, K., *The Materialistic Conception of History*, 1939

FINLEY, M. I., *Ancient Slavery and Modern Ideology*, 1980

GRAHAM, H. F., 'The Significant Role of the Study of Ancient History in the Soviet Union', *Classical Weekly*, LXI, 3, 1967, pp. 85–97

HIRST, P. Q., *Marxism and Historical Writing*, 1985

HOBSBAWM, E. J., 'Class Consciousness in History', I. Mészaros (ed.), *Aspects of History and Class Consciousness*, 1971

HOBSBAWM, E. J., 'Karl Marx's Contribution to Historiography', R. Blackburn (ed.), *Ideology in Social Science*, 1972

HOBSBAWM, E. J., *Pre-Capitalist Economic Formations*, 1964

HOOK, S., *From Hegel to Marx*, 1936

LANZA D., and VEGETTI, M., 'Tra Marx e gli antichi', *Quaderni di Storia* V, 1977, pp. 75–87

LEKAS, P. *Marx on Classical Antiquity*, 1988

LOVE, J. R., *Antiquity and Capitalism: Max Weber and the Sociological Foundations of Roman Civilization*, 1991

LÖWITH, K., *Max Weber and Karl Marx*, 1982

LUKÁCS, G., *History and Class Consciousness*, 1971

MACINTYRE, A., *Marxism and Christianity*, 1968

MALEVANYI, A. M., ČIGLINCEV, J. A., and ŠOFMAN, A. S., *The Class Struggle in Antiquity* (in Russian), 1987

MAZZA, M., 'Marxismo e storia antica', *Studi storici* XVII, 1976, pp. 95–124

MOMIGLIANO, A., 'Marxising in Antiquity', *Times Literary Supplement*, 31/10/75

OLIVA, P., 'Classical Struggles in Classical Antiquity', *Eirene*, XI, 1984, pp. 59–74

PASCAL, R., *Karl Marx: Political Foundations*, 1943

RIGBY, S. H., *Marxism and History: A Critical Introduction*, 1987

RUBINSOHN, W. Z., *Spartacus's Uprising and Soviet Historical Writing*, 1990

RUNCIMAN, W. G., 'Capitalism without Classes', *British Journal of Sociology*, XXXIV, 1983, pp. 157–81

SULLIVAN, J. P., (ed), 'Marxism and the Classics', *Arethusa* VIII, 1, spring 1975, pp. 5–225

VITTINGHOFF, F., 'Die Theorien des historischen Materialisme über den antiken "Sklavenhalterstaat", Probleme der alten Geschichte bei den "Klassikern" des Marxismus und in der modernen sowjetischen Forschung', *Saeculum*, XI, 1960, pp. 89ff.

WOOD, E. M. and N., *Class Ideology and Ancient Political Theory*, 1978

ZHUKOV, Y. M., 'Marxism on Ancient Slaveholding', *Journal of World History*, II, 1954, p. 490

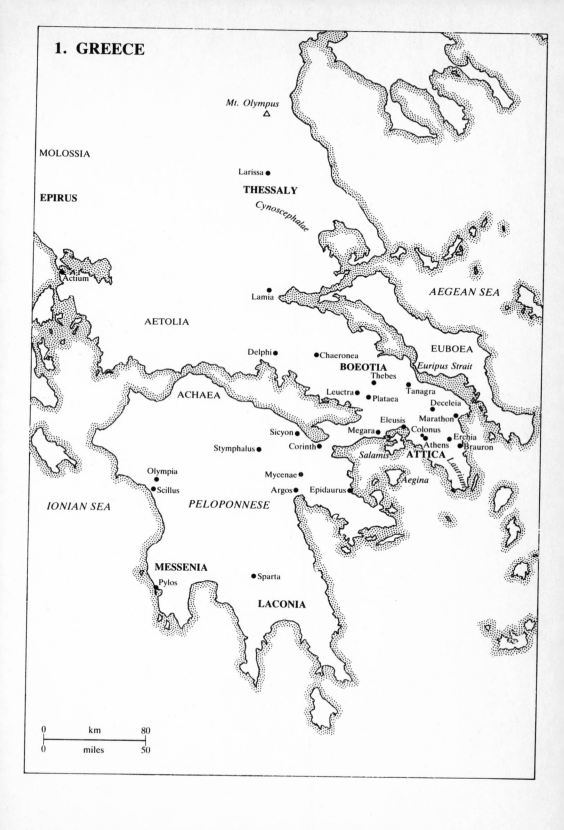

1. GREECE

Mt. Olympus △

MOLOSSIA

Larissa ●

THESSALY

Cynoscephalae

EPIRUS

● Actium

AEGEAN SEA

Lamia ●

AETOLIA

EUBOEA

Delphi ● ● Chaeronea

Euripus Strait

BOEOTIA

Thebes ●

ACHAEA

Leuctra ● ● Tanagra

● Plataea

Deceleia ●

Eleusis ● Marathon ●

Sicyon ● Megara ● Colonus

Stymphalus ● Corinth ● Athens ● Erchia ● Brauron

Salamis **ATTICA**

Aegina

Olympia ●

Mycenae ●

Laurium

● Scillus

Argos ● Epidaurus ●

IONIAN SEA

PELOPONNESE

MESSENIA

Pylos ● Sparta ●

LACONIA

| 0 | km | 80 |
| 0 | miles | 50 |

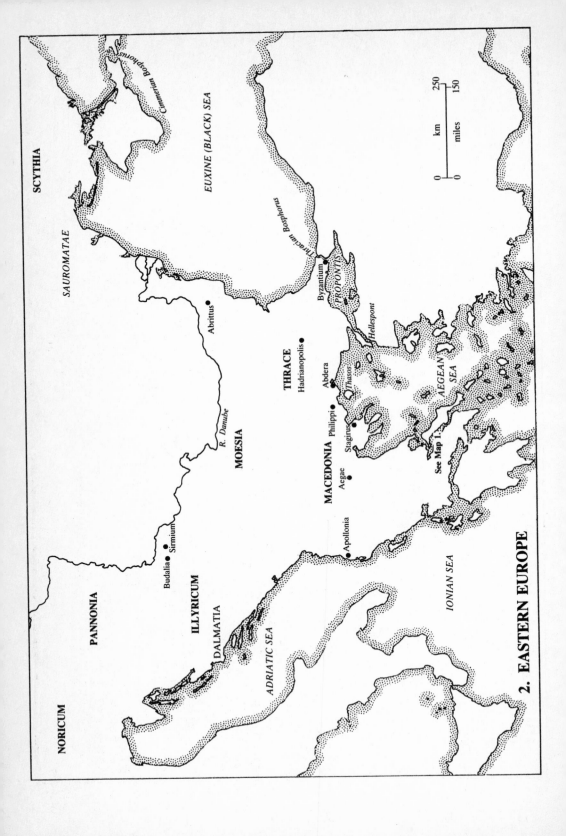

NORICUM

SCYTHIA

PANNONIA

SAUROMATAE

Cimmerian Bosphorus

EUXINE (BLACK) SEA

ILLYRICUM

Budalia● ●Sirmium

R. Danube

Abrittus●

MOESIA

DALMATIA

Thracian Bosphorus

Byzantium●

PROPONTIS

Hellespont

THRACE

Hadrianopolis●

Abdera●

Thasos

ADRIATIC SEA

Apollonia●

MACEDONIA

Philippi●

Stagirus●

AEGEAN SEA

See Map 1.1

Aegae●

IONIAN SEA

2. EASTERN EUROPE

250

150

km

miles

0

0

3. THE AEGEAN AND ASIA MINOR

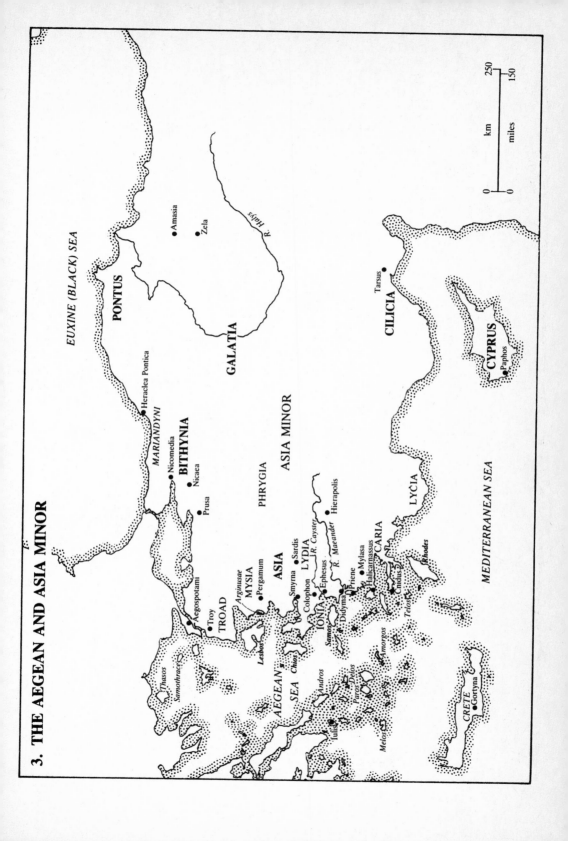

EUXINE (BLACK) SEA

PONTUS

GALATIA

Amasia
Zela
R. Halys

MARIANDYNI

Heraclea Pontica

BITHYNIA

Nicomedia
Nicaea

Prusa

PHRYGIA

ASIA MINOR

CILICIA

Tarsus

CYPRUS

Paphos

Troy
TROAD
Aegospotami
Arginusae
MYSIA
Pergamum
Lesbos
ASIA
Smyrna
Sardis
LYDIA
Colophon
IONIA
Ephesus
Samos
Didyma
Priene
Halicarnassus
Mylasa
CARIA
Cnidus
Teios
R. Cayster
R. Maeander
Hierapolis

LYCIA

Rhodes

Thasos
Samothrace

AEGEAN
SEA
Chios

Andros
Delos
Paros
Amorgos

Melos

CRETE
Gortyna

MEDITERRANEAN SEA

250
150

km
miles

0
0

4. ITALY

ALPS

CISALPINE GAUL

Comum

Mediolanum

Patavium

Mantua

R. Padus

Ravenna

Sarsina

ETRURIA

Clusium

Asisium

Volsinii

R. Tiber

Tarquinii

Amiternum

Veii

Reate

R. Allia

Rome

Tusculum

Arpinum

Aquinum

ADRIATIC SEA

SAMNIUM

Cannae

CAMPANIA

Venusia

Baiae

Herculaneum

Misenum

Oplontis

Stabiae

Neapolis

LUCANIA

CALABRIA

SARDINIA

Sybaris

TYRRHENIAN SEA

BRUTTII

Croton

Naulochus

Locri Epizephyrii

Himera

SICILY

IONIAN SEA

Acragas

Syracuse

0 ———— km ———— 200

0 ———— miles ———— 120

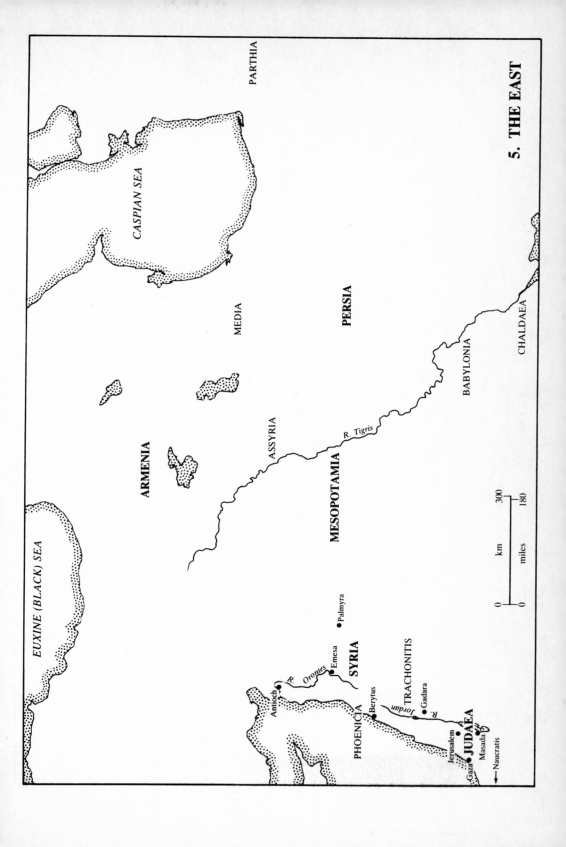

5. THE EAST

PARTHIA

CASPIAN SEA

EUXINE (BLACK) SEA

ARMENIA

MEDIA

PERSIA

ASSYRIA

R. Tigris

MESOPOTAMIA

BABYLONIA

CHALDAEA

Palmyra

Emesa

SYRIA

R. Orontes

Antioch

TRACHONITIS

PHOENICIA

Berytus

Gadara

R. Jordan

Jerusalem

JUDAEA

Gaza

Masada

Naucratis

km   0   300

miles 0   180

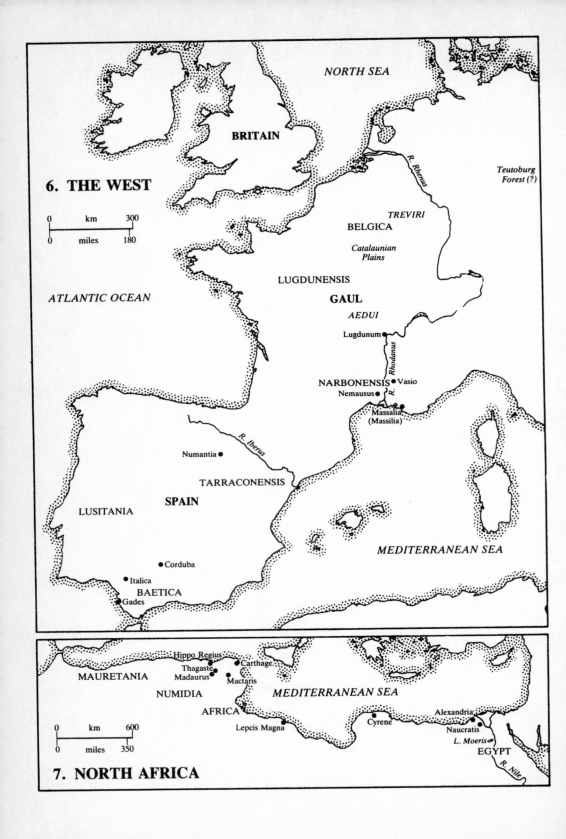

6. THE WEST

NORTH SEA

BRITAIN

R. Rhenus

Teutoburg Forest (?)

TREVIRI

BELGICA

Catalaunian Plains

LUGDUNENSIS

km 0 — 300

miles 0 — 180

GAUL

AEDUI

ATLANTIC OCEAN

Lugdunum

R. Rhodanus

NARBONENSIS ● Vasio

Nemausus ● *R.*

Massilia (Massilia)

R. Iberus

Numantia ●

TARRACONENSIS

SPAIN

LUSITANIA

MEDITERRANEAN SEA

● Corduba

● Italica
BAETICA
Gades ●

7. NORTH AFRICA

MAURETANIA

Hippo Regius ●

Thagaste ●
Madaurus ● ● Carthage
Mactaris ●

NUMIDIA

MEDITERRANEAN SEA

AFRICA

Lepcis Magna ●

● Cyrene

Alexandria ●
Naucratis ●
L. Moeris ●
EGYPT

R. Nile

km 0 — 600

miles 0 — 350

Index